My
Surface 2

Jim Cheshire

que®

My Surface 2

Copyright © 2014 by Pearson Education, Inc.

ISBN-13: 978-0-7897-5273-4
ISBN-10: 0-7897-5273-5

Library of Congress Control Number: 2012374279

Printed in the United States of America

First Printing: December 2013

Trademarks

All terms mentioned in this book that are known to be trademarks or service marks have been appropriately capitalized. Que Publishing cannot attest to the accuracy of this information. Use of a term in this book should not be regarded as affecting the validity of any trademark or service mark.

Warning and Disclaimer

Special Sales

For information about buying this title in bulk quantities, or for special sales opportunities (which may include electronic versions; custom cover designs; and content particular to your business, training goals, marketing focus, or branding interests), please contact our corporate sales department at corpsales@pearsoned.com or (800) 382-3419.

For government sales inquiries, please contact governmentsales@pearsoned.com.

For questions about sales outside the U.S., please contact international@pearsoned.com.

Editor-in-Chief
Greg Wiegand

Executive Editor
Loretta Yates

Development Editor
Todd Brakke

Managing Editor
Sandra Schroeder

Project Editor
Seth Kerney

Indexer
Ken Johnson

Proofreader
Kathy Ruiz

Publishing Coordinator
Kristin Watterson

Designer
Mark Shirar

Compositor
Tricia Bronkella

Contents at a Glance

Table of Contents

6   Backing Up Your Data   119

7   Searching and Browsing the Internet   133

22   Enhancing Windows with Apps   483

About the Author

Jim Cheshire is a technology expert with a passion for gadgets. He has written a dozen books and many online articles on technology and is the author of many best-selling technical guides. Jim works on the Azure Application Platform and Tools team at Microsoft and was an early adopter of Windows RT.

When Jim's not writing, he spends time with his family, plays keyboards with his band, and enjoys writing music.

You can contact Jim through his website at www.JimcoBooks.com.

Dedication

This book is dedicated to my wonderful mother. We will always miss you, but you left us with a brightly shining spirit that will endure forever in the lives of all who knew and loved you.

Acknowledgments

This book would not have been possible were it not for the small army of people at Que Publishing who work tirelessly to support me. I owe a great deal of gratitude to Loretta Yates, who always makes me feel like I'm the only author she has to deal with. Thanks also go to Todd Brakke, who did a great job of editing my work and offering creative ideas for additional content. Thanks also go to Seth Kerney and others who worked so hard to turn the hundreds of screenshots into the high-quality work you now hold in your hands.

We Want to Hear from You!

As the reader of this book, *you* are our most important critic and commentator. We value your opinion and want to know what we're doing right, what we could do better, what areas you'd like to see us publish in, and any other words of wisdom you're willing to pass our way.

We welcome your comments. You can email or write to let us know what you did or didn't like about this book—as well as what we can do to make our books better.

Please note that we cannot help you with technical problems related to the topic of this book.

When you write, please be sure to include this book's title and author as well as your name and email address. We will carefully review your comments and share them with the author and editors who worked on the book.

Email: feedback@quepublishing.com

Mail: Que Publishing
ATTN: Reader Feedback
800 East 96th Street
Indianapolis, IN 46240 USA

Reader Services

Visit our website and register this book at quepublishing.com/register for convenient access to any updates, downloads, or errata that might be available for this book.

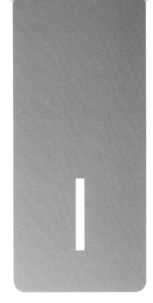

Introduction

Microsoft did something quite extraordinary with the release of the original Surface. Not only was it the first tablet computer Microsoft had ever developed, but the operating system (Windows RT) that ran on it was a significant departure from anything Microsoft had ever created.

Over the past year, Microsoft has had a chance to reflect on the original Surface. They've taken those things that made the Surface unique and expanded on them. For example, the kickstand that was such a standout feature of the original Surface now offers two positions so that the Surface 2 is easier to use in your lap. Microsoft has also significantly beefed up the hardware and made the tablet a much higher performer. The result is a unique tablet that's a pleasure to use.

Scratching the Surface

Your Surface 2 is made for work and play. Windows RT 8.1 includes Office 2013 RT, which includes Word, Excel, PowerPoint, OneNote, and Outlook. It also includes many other apps for information, entertainment, and productivity.

Here are just some of the things you can do with your Surface 2:

- Read news from major news outlets, sources for all your favorite topics, and even based on your own web searches.

- Get the latest weather, sports scores, travel ideas, stock quotes, and more.

- Listen to your music, discover new music, stream music, and buy music.

- Rent and purchase movies and TV shows from the Xbox Video Store.

- Access all your social networks, including pictures that are stored in the cloud, on Facebook, and SkyDrive.

- Open and edit Microsoft Office documents with full versions of Office applications.

- Watch video using Netflix, Hulu Plus, and more.

- Enhance your Surface 2 with apps from the Windows Store.

You can do all of this in a portable tablet; add a Touch Cover or a Type Cover, and you have a genuine laptop replacement in a lightweight package.

Why You'll Love *My Surface 2*

Surface 2 for Windows RT 8.1 is accessible to all kinds of users, and so is *My Surface 2*. If you're a nontechnical person, you'll find the step-by-step approach in *My Surface 2* to be refreshing and helpful. If you're a technical person new to Windows RT 8.1, you'll find plenty of tips and tricks to help you get the most out of your new tablet.

The book covers all the capabilities of your Surface 2 and is fully updated to reflect all the changes in Windows RT 8.1. I show you how to get the most out of each feature using a step-by-step approach, complete with figures that correspond to each step. You never have to wonder what or where to tap.

Each task shows you how to interact with your Surface using simple symbols that illustrate what you should do.

This icon means that you should tap and hold an object on the screen.

This icon means that you should drag an item on the screen.

This icon indicates that you should pinch on the screen.

This icon means that you should "reverse pinch."

This icon indicates that you need to swipe on the screen.

Along the way, I add plenty of tips that help you better understand a feature or task. I also warn you with It's Not All Good sidebars when you need to be careful with a particular task or when there are pitfalls that you need to know about. If you're the kind of person who likes to dig a little deeper, you'll enjoy the Go Further sidebars that provide a more in-depth look at particular topics.

Finally, for those of you with the paperback version of this book, you might notice that it isn't a big and bulky book. It's a handy size for taking with you when you go places with your Surface tablet. That way, you can always find the steps necessary to do what you want to do. Of course, if you prefer not to carry the book with you, you can always purchase the eBook version and read it on your Surface 2.

What You'll Find in the Book

Your Surface 2 is full of surprises. The major functions are easy to discover, but some of the neater features are hidden away. As you read through this book, you'll find yourself saying, "Wow, I didn't know I could do that!" This book is designed to invoke just that kind of reaction.

Here are the things covered in this book:

- Chapter 1, "An Introduction to Surface 2," provides an introduction to the Surface 2 hardware and gives you a primer on Windows RT 8.1.

- Chapter 2, "Connecting to Networks," shows you how to connect to wireless networks, how you can access shared resources on your network, and how you can log in remotely to other computers on your network using your Surface 2.

- Chapter 3, "Using and Customizing the Start Screen," walks you through using the new Windows Start screen, including details on how you can customize the Start screen and make it uniquely yours.

- Chapter 4, "Security and Windows RT 8.1," shows you how to use user accounts and secure your Surface 2.

- Chapter 5, "Using Family Safety," provides a thorough view of Family Safety, a feature that makes it easy to control what family members can do on your Surface 2, which apps they can use, and when they are able to use the device. You also learn how you can get reports on activity that kids and other family members are engaging in.

- Chapter 6, "Backing Up Your Data," shows you how to use the unique features in Windows RT 8.1 to back up your data and keep it safe from data loss.

- Chapter 7, "Searching and Browsing the Internet," covers the Bing app and Internet Explorer 11 on the Surface 2.

- Chapter 8, "Connecting with People," demonstrates how you can interact with friends and family on your social networks.

- Chapter 9, "Using Mail," covers the Mail app in Windows RT 8.1 and explains how to send and receive email.

- Chapter 10, "Using Calendar," walks you through using the Calendar app to keep track of your appointments.

- Chapter 11, "Keeping Up to Date with News," shows you how to read news and other information from sources all over the Web from within the News app.

- Chapter 12, "HomeGroups and SkyDrive," explains how you can share data with others on your network with HomeGroups and how to use Microsoft SkyDrive to store and share files in the cloud.

- Chapter 13, "Discovering and Playing Music," provides information on using the Music app to play your own music and to browse and play music from Xbox Music.

- Chapter 14, "Watching Video," covers the Video app and Xbox Video, a service for renting and buying movies and TV shows.

- Chapter 15, "Pictures," shows you how to use the Photos app to edit, view and manage pictures from your Surface 2 and from social networks and other computers.

- Chapter 16, "Using Maps," walks you through using Maps, an app that provides detailed maps as well as directions.

- Chapter 17, "Creating Documents with Microsoft Word 2013," covers using Microsoft Word to create and edit documents.

- Chapter 18, "Crunching Numbers with Microsoft Excel 2013," walks you through using Microsoft Excel to create workbooks, including how you can use formulas and functions to create complex sheets.

- Chapter 19, "Presenting with Microsoft PowerPoint 2013," walks you through using Microsoft PowerPoint to create compelling presentations.

- Chapter 20, "Organizing Notes with Microsoft OneNote 2013," shows you how to use Microsoft OneNote to organize notes, synchronize them across your devices, and access them from anywhere.

- Chapter 21, "Using Email and Staying Organized with Microsoft Outlook 2013," shows you how you can use Microsoft Outlook to send and receive email, keep track of calendar appointments, and organize daily tasks.

- Chapter 22, "Enhancing Windows with Apps," shows you how to enhance the operation of your Surface 2 using apps from the Windows Store, complete with some great app recommendations.

- Chapter 23, "Updating and Troubleshooting Windows RT 8.1," shows you how to update Windows RT 8.1 and how to troubleshoot and repair problems that you might encounter.

Go Beneath the Surface 2

Now that you know what's in store, it's time to start having fun digging deeper into the Surface 2. You're sure to learn new things and experience the thrill of what your Surface 2 can do, and you'll have fun doing it. Let's get started!

Learn how to use
Windows RT.

Learn about the
Surface hardware.

Master the basics
before diving in.

1

An Introduction to Surface 2

Congratulations on your purchase of the Microsoft Surface 2 for Windows RT 8.1! The Surface 2 for Windows RT 8.1 is a unique device running a version of Windows designed for ARM processors, the same processors that typically run in smartphones and some tablets. These ARM processors are specially designed for efficient power use, and because of that, you can expect to get many hours of use from your Surface 2 between charges.

The uniqueness of Surface 2 doesn't stop there. In fact, the Surface 2 offers several unique features, including a built-in Kickstand for convenient viewing and a revolutionary cover with a built-in keyboard.

The Surface 2 Device

The Surface 2 device's case is composed of magnesium, but it's made using a special method involving liquification of the magnesium and then *extremely* rapid cooling. The result is what Microsoft calls VaporMg (pronounced *vapor mag*), and it's extremely strong, light, and scratch-resistant.

The original Surface was also made from VaporMg, but it was painted a dark color. The Surface 2 is unpainted and is the actual color of the VaporMg material, a welcome change for those who may have experienced paint being scratched off of the original Surface device.

>>>Go Further

ON FIRE

For those of you who are science buffs, you might already know that when magnesium reaches a certain temperature, it ignites and burns at an intense temperature. Because of this, some naysayers of the Surface 2 claim that if the battery inside the Surface 2 were to ignite, it would cause the device to ignite and burn uncontrollably. In fact, a burning battery burns at just under 600 degrees Fahrenheit, and magnesium requires a temperature of approximately 1,022 degrees Fahrenheit to ignite. You can do the math yourself, but I think you're safe.

Ports and Controls

Along the right edge of the Surface 2, you'll find the right speaker, a micro-HDMI video port used for outputting video to an HD display, a full-sized USB 2.0 port, a microSDXC memory card port, and a proprietary port for the Surface 2's power adapter.

By inserting a microSDXC card into the microSDXC slot, you can increase the memory of your Surface 2 by up to 64GB. The microSDXC slot on the Surface 2 is hidden behind the right side of the Kickstand.

It's Not All Good

Using microSDXC Cards

Windows RT 8.1 does not enable you to easily use memory from a microSDXC card in specific ways. For example, you can't store movies that you download from Xbox Video or music that you get from Xbox Music to a memory card without taking some pretty complex steps.

For information on how you can get around this limitation, check out Paul Thurrott's tip on his WinSupersite website at www.winsupersite.com/article/windows8/surface-tip-microsd-content-libraries-metro-apps-144658.

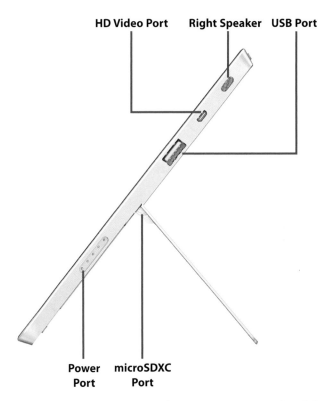

HD Video Port   Right Speaker   USB Port

Power   microSDXC
Port   Port

On the left edge of the Surface 2 is the left speaker, a 1/8-inch headphone jack, and the volume control. The bottom of the Surface 2 contains the final port, a proprietary port for the Surface 2's unique Touch Cover or Type Cover.

The Surface 2's power switch is located on the top-right side of the device. If you press and release the switch, it turns off the Surface 2's screen. If you press and hold the switch for several seconds, it turns off the device entirely.

The Surface 2 is also equipped with two microphones, both of which are positioned along the top edge of the device.

It's Not All Good

Powering Off

It's not recommended that you hold the power switch to turn off the Surface 2 unless you have no other option. When you turn off the device in this way, any work you are doing is not saved, and you increase the chances of losing data.

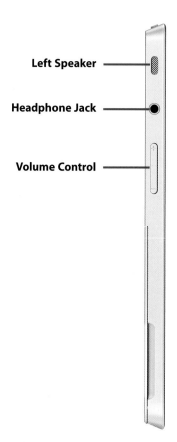

Left Speaker

Headphone Jack

Volume Control

Power Button

The Kickstand

One of the features unique to the Surface line is the built-in Kickstand. The Kickstand is convenient not only when you are using a keyboard with your Surface 2, but it also perfectly positions the Surface 2 for watching video. The Kickstand flips out from the Surface 2 with a satisfying snap, and despite its thinness, it's tough and solid due to the VaporMg construction.

The Kickstand also is convenient when using the Surface 2 for videoconferencing. In fact, Microsoft expects that you'll use it for that purpose, and that's why the front-facing camera in the Surface 2 is positioned in such a way that it's aiming directly at your head when the Surface 2 is tilted at a slight angle by the Kickstand.

The Kickstand on the original Surface locked you into one particular angle. Microsoft found that people didn't like this angle when using the tablet on their lap, so they developed a dual-position Kickstand for the Surface 2. Your Surface 2's Kickstand flips out to the same angle as the original Surface's, but it also has a second position that's more comfortable for people who are using the Surface 2 as a laptop replacement.

Type Cover and Touch Cover

Another feature unique to the Surface 2 is the Touch Cover and the Type Cover. These covers attach to the bottom side of the Surface 2 using strong magnets. If you get the cover close to the bottom, the strong magnets pop it into proper position easily. When the cover is folded over the Surface 2's screen, the screen is automatically turned off. When the cover is folded away from the screen, the screen turns on automatically.

It's Not All Good

Covers Not Included

The Surface 2 does not come with a cover. If you want a Touch Cover or a Type Cover, you're going to have to pay for it. The Touch Cover will run you about $120, and the Type Cover will run you about $130. Even so, I highly encourage you to buy one. It is a great addition to the Surface 2, especially if you plan on using Office 2013 RT apps on your device.

The truly unique thing about the Touch Cover and Type Cover is that they both double as a quality keyboard, complete with a touch pad. The Touch Cover has touch-sensitive keys that are slightly raised from the cover's surface. The Type Cover is slightly thicker and uses physical keyboard keys.

Microsoft improved both the Touch Cover and the Type Cover with the second iteration of the Surface devices. The keys are now backlit and the Touch Cover has many more touch sensors, making it a much more sensitive keyboard. Both the original Surface and the Surface 2 can use the new covers.

Touch Cover

It is worth noting, however, that the Touch Cover and Type Cover only attach to the Surface 2 at the bottom of the device. When you fold the cover over the display, it doesn't attach in any way to the top of the device. Therefore, if you hold the Surface 2 upside down, the cover will open. I don't find it to be a problem, but it's worth mentioning.

Fast Typing

I'm a pretty fast touch-typist, and I find typing on the Touch Cover to be fast and accurate

Windows RT 8.1 Basics

Windows RT 8.1 is a brand-new version of the popular Windows operating system. Although it might look just like the version of Windows 8.1 that's running on your notebook or desktop computer, it's not the same. Windows RT 8.1 is designed to run on ARM processors, whereas Windows 8.1 that you run on your notebook or desktop is designed to run on Intel processors. Is that important? Yes! You can't install software (including drivers for printers and other hardware) onto Windows RT 8.1 unless that software is specifically designed for ARM processors. Regarding the Surface 2 for Windows RT 8.1, that means you can't install apps unless they come from the Windows Store, and unless Windows RT 8.1 comes with a driver for your printer or other hardware, there's a good chance that you can't use it in Windows RT 8.1.

With all of that said, Windows RT 8.1 has a huge advantage in that it is extremely power-efficient, enabling you to squeeze about 10 hours of battery life out of the device. Also, unlike your notebook computer, the Surface 2 for Windows RT 8.1 is capable of transitioning into a very low power state instead of going to sleep. That means that even when the device looks like it's asleep, it's still running and will notify you of appointments, new emails, and so forth.

Those of you who are using Windows RT on the original Surface also benefit from the many improvements in Windows RT 8.1. Microsoft offers the Windows RT 8.1 upgrade free to existing users. Some of the many improvements you'll get in Windows RT 8.1 are Internet Explorer 11, the inclusion of Microsoft Outlook 2013 on the RT devices, great photo editing features in the Photos app, an enhanced Mail app, and much more.

The Start Screen

Windows RT 8.1 has a Start button just like Windows 7 and earlier versions, but pressing it launches the Start screen and not a Start menu like you might be used to. The Start screen is the launching point for your apps, which are laid out across the Start screen as brightly colored tiles. Some of these tiles are what Microsoft calls Live Tiles that display useful information about the app they represent.

Live Tile   The Start Screen

For full information on using the Start screen, see Chapter 3, "Using and Customizing the Start Screen."

App Switching and Charms

You can have multiple apps running at the same time in Windows RT 8.1, and you can easily switch between them by swiping in from the left side of the screen. You also can display two at the same time on the screen.

More on App Switching

For full details on how app switching works in Windows RT 8.1, see "Switching Between Recent Apps" in Chapter 3.

To access settings for an app or to search within an app (or across apps), you swipe in from the right side of the screen. When you do, you'll see a series of vertical icons that you can use to interact with your apps and with Windows (Microsoft calls these *charms*).

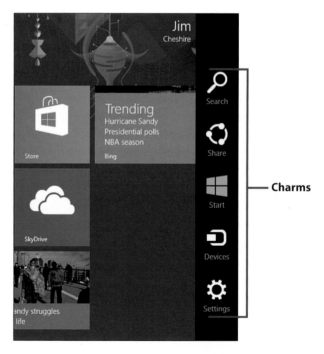

Charms are context-sensitive. For example, if you tap the Settings charm while on the Start screen, you pull up settings for Windows, and if you tap the Settings charm while in the Music app, you pull up settings for the Music app, and so forth.

Printing from Windows RT 8.1
The Device charm is used to print in Windows RT 8.1.

Typing in Windows RT 8.1

For the most part, you type in Windows RT 8.1 just as you would on any other computer. However, there are some shortcuts to make things a bit easier. For example, Windows RT 8.1 has a spell checker across the entire operating system that underlines misspelled words in a red squiggly underline. Windows RT 8.1 also shows suggestions while you type in many areas, and there are other minor conveniences, such as the ability to add a period at the end of a sentence by simply double-tapping the spacebar.

You can control many of these features in the General settings of your Surface 2.

1. From the Start screen, swipe in from the right side of the screen and tap the Settings charm.

2. Tap Change PC Settings.

3. Tap PC and Devices.

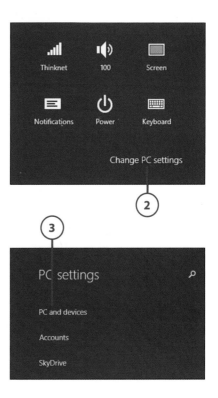

4. Tap Typing.

5. Tap Autocorrect Misspelled Words to turn off that feature.

6. Tap Highlight Misspelled Words to turn off that feature.

7. In the Typing section, tap Show Text Suggestions as I Type to turn off that feature.

8. Tap Add a Space After I Choose a Text Suggestion to turn off that feature.

9. Tap Add a Period After I Double-Tap the Spacebar to turn off that feature.

10. Tap Play Key Sounds as I Type to turn off that feature.

11. Tap Capitalize the First Letter of Each Sentence to turn off that feature.

12. Tap Use All Uppercase Letters When I Double-Tap Shift to turn off that feature.

13. Tap Add the Standard Keyboard Layout as a Touch Keyboard Option to enable a full-size keyboard as an option for your touch keyboard.

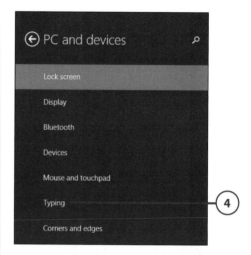

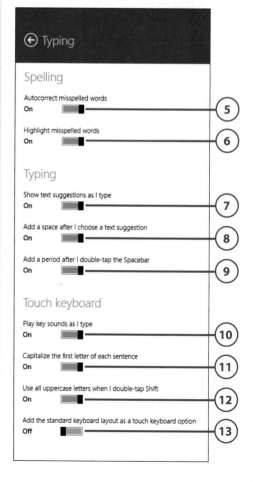

Adding Devices

You can add new devices, such as a printer, a multimedia device, and so forth.

1. From the PC Settings screen, tap PC and Devices.

2. Tap Devices.

3. Tap Add a Device.

4. Tap your device from the list to add it to your Surface 2.

Device Not Visible

If your device is not visible after going through these steps, make sure it's connected to your Surface 2 or connected to the network your Surface 2 is connected to.

Adding Bluetooth Devices

If you are adding a Bluetooth device, follow the steps in "Adding a Bluetooth Device" later in this chapter.

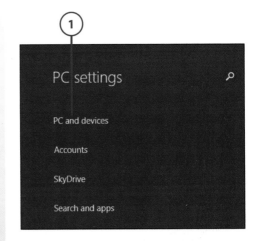

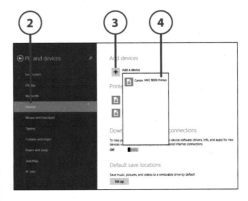

Adding a Bluetooth Device

You can add a Bluetooth device such as a Bluetooth mouse or headset.

1. From the PC and Devices settings screen, tap Bluetooth.

2. If Bluetooth is currently off, tap Bluetooth to turn on Bluetooth.

3. Tap your device to pair your device.

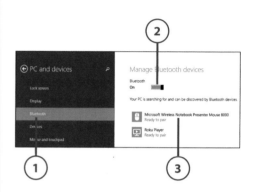

Bluetooth Pairing
Adding a Bluetooth device is referred to as pairing. You might be asked to enter a numeric code in order to pair the device.

Removing Devices

If you no longer need a device that you added, you can remove the device from your Surface 2.

1. From the Devices settings page, tap the device you want to remove.

2. Tap Remove Device.

3. Tap Yes to remove the device.

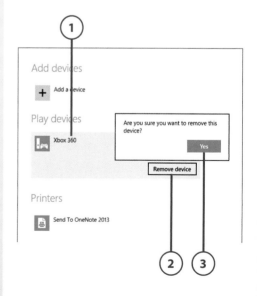

Removing Bluetooth Devices
Bluetooth devices can be removed from the Bluetooth settings screen.

Notifications

Windows RT 8.1 displays notifications in a pop-up in the upper-right corner of the screen. Notifications are displayed for calendar reminders, emails, and more. When you install additional apps from the Windows Store, these apps can also display notifications.

You can control whether notification pop-ups are displayed, whether apps can display notifications on the lock screen, and whether a sound plays when a notification is displayed. You also can specify whether individual apps are allowed to display notifications.

1. From the PC Settings screen, tap Search and Apps.

2. Tap Notifications.

3. Tap Show App Notifications to change the setting to Off and disable all notifications.

4. Tap Show App Notifications on the Lock Screen to change the setting to Off and disable notifications on the lock screen.

5. Tap Play Notification Sounds to change the setting to Off and disable sounds when notifications are displayed.

6. Tap Turn On My Screen When I Get a Call to disable the screen from automatically turning on when you get a call.

7. Slide up to view additional notification options.

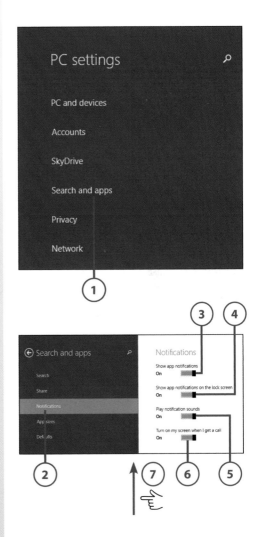

Receiving Calls

The Surface 2 can receive calls using Skype. Other telecommunication apps such as Microsoft Lync are available from the Store.

8. Tap Quiet Hours to turn off quiet hours. When the Quiet Hours feature is enabled, notifications are disabled during the times specified.

9. Tap From and To to set a time range for quiet hours.

10. Tap Receive Calls During Quiet Hours to enable or disable call reception during quiet hours.

11. Tap the slider for an individual app to change it to Off and disallow notifications for that app.

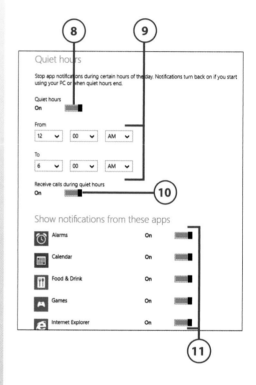

The Lock Screen

The lock screen is displayed when your Surface 2 starts and when you turn on the display after it has been turned off. To get to the sign-in screen or the Start screen, swipe up on the lock screen or press a key on your keyboard.

Signing In

For information on signing in to Windows RT 8.1, see "Securing Your PC" in Chapter 4, "Security and Windows RT 8.1."

You can customize the lock screen with one of your own pictures. You also can decide which apps are allowed to show a status on the lock screen, choose one app to show detailed status, choose an app to show alarms, and choose whether or not the camera is available from the lock screen without logging in.

1. From the PC and Devices settings screen, tap Lock Screen.

2. Tap a picture, or tap Browse to browse to one of your own pictures. A preview of the lock screen appears above the picture tiles.

3. Slide up to reveal Lock Screen Apps options.

4. To add an app that can display status on the lock screen, tap +.

5. Tap an app.

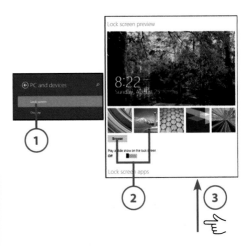

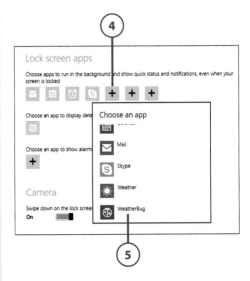

6. To change an app or remove an app from the lock screen, tap the icon for the app.

7. Tap a different app to display, or tap Don't Show Quick Status Here to remove the app's status from the lock screen.

8. To choose an app that displays detailed status on the lock screen, tap the calendar icon. (The Calendar app shows detailed status by default.)

9. Tap an app, or tap Don't Show Detailed Status on the Lock Screen to remove all detailed app statuses from the lock screen.

10. Tap Swipe Down on the Lock Screen to Use the Camera to disable camera access on the lock screen.

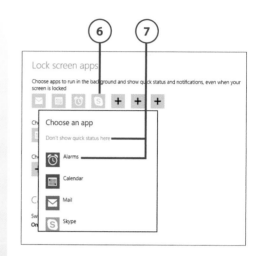

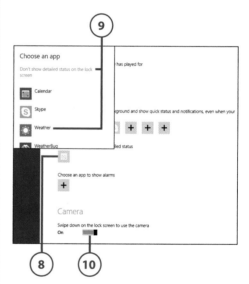

App Status

When an app shows a status on the lock screen, it consists of the app's icon and a numerical indicator showing how many notifications are available for the app. For example, the Mail app would display an envelope icon and a numeric indicator showing how many new mail messages you have.

A detailed status shows additional information. For example, if the Calendar app is selected as the app to show detailed status, you will see details on your next appointment on the lock screen.

Playing a Slide Show on the Lock Screen

You can play a slide show on your lock screen. This feature turns your Surface 2 into a digital picture frame. You can use pictures from your Pictures library on the device, from SkyDrive, and from another folder of your choice. (By default, the slide show uses pictures from your Pictures library and from SkyDrive.)

1. From the Lock Screen settings screen, tap Play a Slide Show on the Lock Screen to enable the slide show.

2. To remove a folder from the slide show, tap the folder and tap Remove.

3. To add a new folder, tap Add a Folder and browse to the desired folder.

4. Tap Include Camera Roll Folders from This PC and SkyDrive to include pictures in the camera roll.

5. Tap Only Use the Pictures That Will Fit Best on My Screen to use all pictures in your slide show regardless of the picture's size.

6. Tap Play a Slide Show When Using Battery Power to play a slide show when your Surface 2 is not plugged in.

7. Tap When My PC Is Inactive, Show the Lock Screen Instead of Turning Off the Screen to turn off the PC instead of playing the slide show after the PC has been inactive for a period of time.

8. Tap Turn Off Screen After Slide Show Has Played For to set the amount of time the slide show should display.

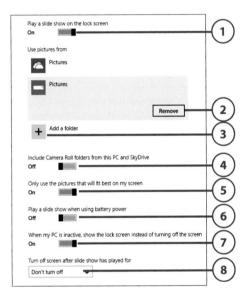

Additional Settings

There are a few other settings in Windows RT 8.1 that you should know about before we dive into the details of using your Surface 2.

Volume and Mute

You can control the volume of your Surface 2 using the volume rocker on the left side of the case, but you also can adjust volume by touch, including muting the sound altogether.

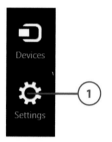

1. From the Start screen, swipe in from the right side of the screen and tap the Settings charm.

2. Tap the speaker icon.

Networks

Ignore the Network icon just to the left of the speaker icon for now. I show you how to join networks in the next chapter.

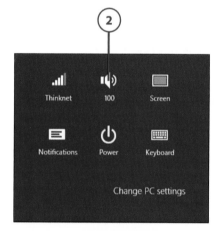

3. Drag the slider down to decrease volume and up to increase volume.

4. Tap on the speaker to mute your Surface 2. Tapping it again unmutes it.

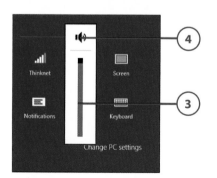

Screen Brightness and Rotation Lock

Your Surface 2 will adjust screen brightness based on battery life and current lighting levels. However, you can adjust the brightness to your liking manually.

1. From the Settings pane, tap the Screen icon.

2. Drag the slider down to decrease brightness and up to increase brightness.

3. Tap the rotation icon to toggle the rotation lock and prevent the screen from rotating when you rotate the device.

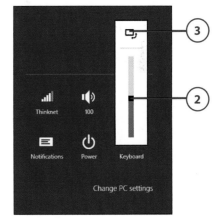

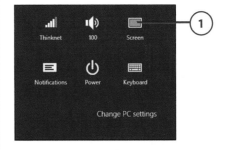

Hiding Notifications Temporarily

You might decide that you want to temporarily hide notifications. For example, if you are in a meeting for an hour and you want to make sure that your Surface 2 doesn't pop up a notification, you can disable notifications for a specific time period.

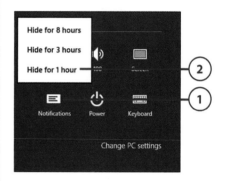

1. From the Settings pane, tap the Notifications icon.

2. Tap a time period during which notifications are hidden.

Shutting Down, Sleeping, and Restarting

If you want to shut down your Surface 2, put it to sleep, or restart it, you can do so from the Settings screen.

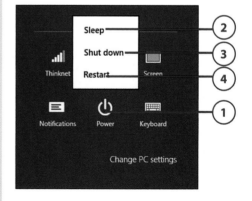

1. From the Settings screen, tap the Power icon.

2. Tap Sleep to put your Surface 2 into a low-power sleep state.

3. Tap Shut Down to turn off your Surface 2 completely.

4. Tap Restart to shut down and restart your Surface 2.

Synchronizing Settings

One of the benefits of using a Microsoft account when signing in to your Surface 2 is that settings are synchronized across your devices. For example, if you change the background image on your lock screen on one device, then that change is automatically synchronized to other computers running Windows 8.1 or Windows RT 8.1 when you log in with that account.

You can control these synchronization settings or disable synchronization altogether.

1. From the PC Settings screen, tap SkyDrive.

2. Tap Sync Settings.

3. To turn off synchronization of settings, tap Sync Your Settings on this PC to change the setting to Off.

4. To disable synchronization of the Start screen tiles and layout, tap the Start Screen slider to change the setting to Off.

5. To disable synchronization of colors, background, the lock screen, and the account picture, tap the Appearance slider to change the setting to Off.

6. To turn off synchronization of themes, taskbar, high contrast, and other personalization traits of the Desktop, tap the Desktop Personalization slider to change the setting to Off.

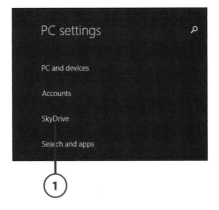

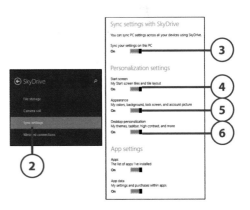

7. To turn off synchronization of installed apps, tap the Apps slider to change the setting to Off.

8. To turn off synchronization of settings and purchases within apps, tap the App Data slider to change the setting to Off.

9. Slide up to reveal additional synchronization options.

10. To turn off synchronization of Internet Explorer favorites, open tabs, home pages, history, and settings, tap the Web Browser slider to change the setting to Off.

11. To turn off synchronization of sign-in info for apps, websites, network locations, and HomeGroups, tap the Passwords slider to change the setting to Off.

12. To turn off synchronization of keyboards, input methods, the display language, personal dictionary, and other language settings, tap the Language Preferences slider to change the setting to Off.

13. To turn off synchronization of the narrator, magnifier, and other accessibility features, tap the Ease of Access slider to change the setting to Off.

14. To turn off synchronization of other settings, such as File Explorer settings and mouse settings, tap the Other Windows Settings slider and change the setting to Off.

15. To turn off backup of your settings to SkyDrive, tap the Back Up Your Settings for This PC slider to change the setting to Off.

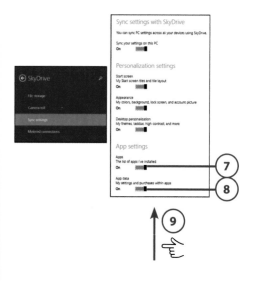

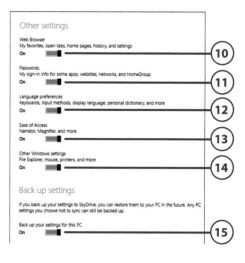

Moving On

Now that you know the basics of your Surface 2 and Windows RT 8.1, it's time to move on to learning all that you can do with your tablet. Along the way, I show you plenty of tips and tricks, and I also warn you when it's needed.

Let's get started learning how to use your Surface 2!

Remote into other
computers.

Connect to wireless
networks.

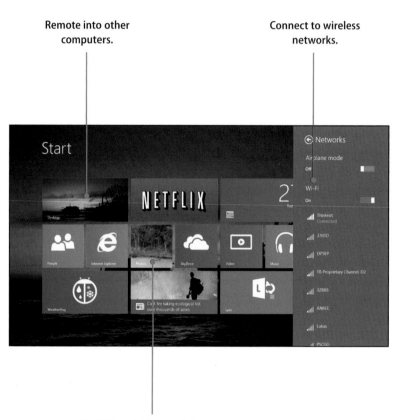

Use Network Sharing to browse
other computers and devices.

2

Connecting to Networks

When you turn on your Surface 2 for the first time, you're walked through a series of steps to get the device ready for use. One of those steps is to connect to a wireless network, and for good reason; Internet access on the Surface 2 is an absolute necessity.

In this chapter, I show you how to connect to wireless networks, how you can share content on your Surface 2 with other computers, and how you can even log in to other computers and remote control them from your Surface 2.

Wireless Networking

Your Surface 2 supports the latest wireless networking standards, so you can connect to any wireless network you might encounter. That includes not only the wireless network in your home, but also wireless access points in public places.

Connecting to a Wireless Network

As long as a wireless network is broadcasting its name (called an SSID), you can connect to it easily.

Connecting to Hidden Networks

You can connect to hidden networks as well. I show you how in the next walkthrough.

1. From the Start screen, swipe in from the right side of the screen and tap the Settings charm.

2. Tap the Wireless icon to see available networks.

3. Tap a network to connect to it. (Networks are listed in order of signal strength.)

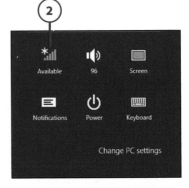

4. Tap to check Connect Automatically if you want your Surface 2 to automatically connect to the selected network when it's in range.

Connecting Automatically

If you choose to connect to multiple networks automatically, Windows RT 8.1 chooses the network to connect to based on signal strength.

5. Tap Connect to connect to the network.

6. If prompted, enter a security key to connect to the network.

7. Tap Next.

8. Tap Yes to enable sharing so that you can see other network devices and connect to them.

Sharing

If you are connecting to a public network, you should choose to not enable sharing. However, if you are using your home network, enabling sharing will allow you to see other network devices.

I cover sharing in the "Network Sharing" section of this chapter.

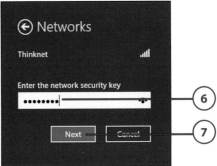

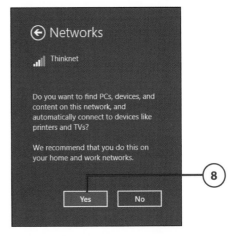

Connecting to a Hidden Network

Some wireless networks are hidden and don't broadcast their SSIDs. You can connect to these networks, but the process is a little more complex.

1. From the Start screen, swipe in from the right and tap the Search charm.

2. Enter **set up a connection** in the text box.

3. Tap Set Up a Connection or Network. Selecting this option takes you to the Windows desktop.

4. Tap Manually Connect to a Wireless Network.

5. Tap Next.

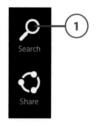

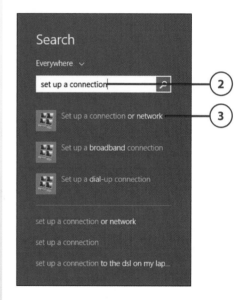

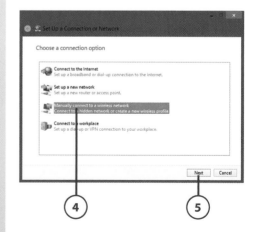

6. Enter the network name.

7. Tap Security Type and select the network's security type.

8. Tap Encryption Type and select the network's encryption type.

9. Enter the security key for the network if necessary.

Network Settings
If you don't know what settings to select for the network, check with the person who runs or administers the network.

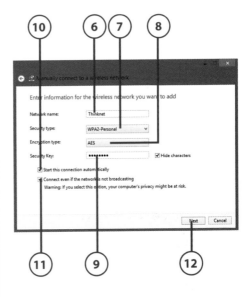

10. Tap to select Start This Connection Automatically to automatically connect to this network when it's in range.

11. Tap to check Connect Even If the Network Is Not Broadcasting to connect to a hidden network.

12. Tap Next.

13. Tap Close.

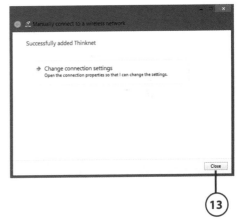

Disconnecting from a Network

If you no longer want to connect to a particular network, you can disconnect from it. If you decide to connect to the network later, you'll have to go through the process of connecting that you followed earlier in this chapter.

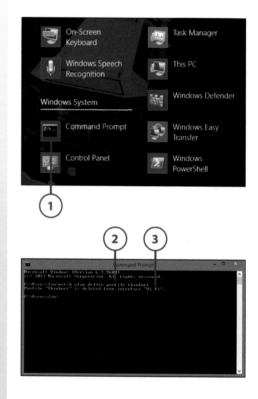

1. From the Apps screen, tap Command Prompt. (You'll find Command Prompt in the Windows System group.)

2. Enter the following command into the Command Prompt window. Replace *SSID* with the name of the network you want to remove:

   Netsh wlan delete profile *SSID*

3. Press Enter to remove the network.

Using Airplane Mode

In some cases (such as when you are Surface 2 in an airplane), you might need to turn off the wireless radio in your Surface 2. When this need arises, you can enable Airplane mode.

1. From the Settings pane, tap the Wireless icon.

2. Tap Airplane Mode to change the setting to On. When Airplane mode is turned on, the Wi-Fi and Bluetooth radios on your Surface 2 are turned off.

3. Tap Airplane Mode again to turn off Airplane mode and turn on the radios again.

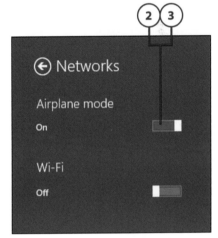

Network Sharing

Windows RT 8.1 includes a network sharing feature that makes it easy for you to share files and devices (such as networked printers) with other computers on your network. For this feature to work, you must modify certain security settings on the computer. Windows RT 8.1 allows you to easily enable and disable sharing.

Sharing and Public Networks

If you are connected to a public network, you should not enable sharing because it can allow others on the network to see your files and devices.

Turning Sharing On or Off

You can easily turn sharing on or off as necessary.

1. From the PC Settings screen, tap Network.

2. Tap the network for which you would like to enable or disable sharing.

3. Tap the Find Devices and Content slider to turn sharing on or off as desired.

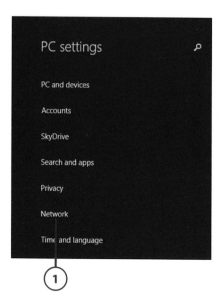

PC settings

PC and devices

Accounts

SkyDrive

Search and apps

Privacy

Network

Time and language

(1)

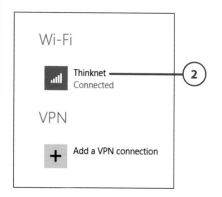

Wi-Fi

Thinknet — (2)
Connected

VPN

+ Add a VPN connection

Find devices and content

Find PCs, devices and content on this network and automatically connect to devices like printers and TVs. Turn this off for public networks to help keep your stuff safe.
On

(3)

Accessing Network Resources

If sharing is turned on, you can use File Explorer in Windows RT 8.1 to view resources on your network.

1. From the Start screen, tap Desktop.

2. Tap File Explorer on the taskbar.

3. In File Explorer, tap Network to see network resources.

4. Double-tap on a resource to connect to it.

5. Enter a username and password if prompted.

6. Tap OK to continue.

7. Browse to the network resource you're interested in.

Other Devices and Resources

In this example, I connected to another computer on my network and was able to browse the folders and files on that computer. You can use the same technique to connect to other resources and devices. For example, if you double-tap on a printer, your Surface 2 will connect to the printer so that you can print to it.

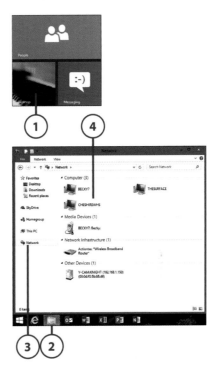

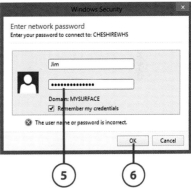

Remoting into Other Computers

Windows RT 8.1 enables you to remotely connect to other Windows computers. When you remote into a computer, what you see on your Surface 2 is exactly what appears on the remote PC, and you can interact with that PC just as though you were using it directly.

Remote connections to other computers are established using a Remote Desktop Connection. By default, Windows does not allow remote connections, so to remote into a computer, you must first enable remote connections.

Enabling Connections on the Remote Computer

These steps should be carried out on the remote computer to which you want to connect. The computer can be running Windows XP, Windows Vista, Windows 7, Windows 8, or Windows 8.1. I show you steps for Windows 8, but the steps are almost identical on other versions of Windows.

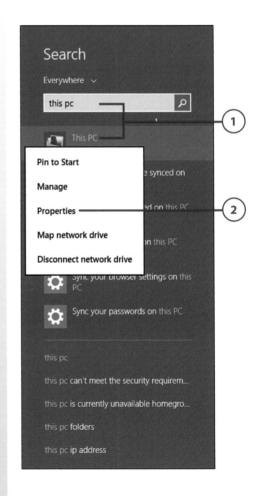

1. From the Start screen, type **this pc** on your keyboard and right-click on This PC from within the search results.

2. Click Properties.

Computer Name

In the Properties window, you'll see the computer name. Make note of it because you'll use it to connect to this computer later.

---

3. Click Remote Settings.

4. Click Allow Remote Connections to This Computer.

5. Click OK.

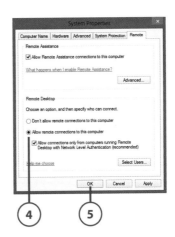

Connecting to Remote Computers

After you've enabled remote connections on your remote computer, you can connect to it from your Surface 2. You should carry out these steps on your Surface 2.

1. From the Start screen, swipe up from the bottom of the screen in order to view all apps.

2. Tap Remote Desktop Connection.

3. Enter the computer name of the remote computer.

4. Tap Connect.

5. Enter your password. If necessary, tap Use Another Account and enter a username and password.

6. Tap to check Remember My Credentials if you want Windows RT 8.1 to remember your username and password.

7. Tap OK.

Use Microsoft Accounts

If you are connecting to a Windows 8 or Windows 8.1 machine, you can make this process much easier by using the same Microsoft account on the remote machine that you are using on your Surface 2.

(2)

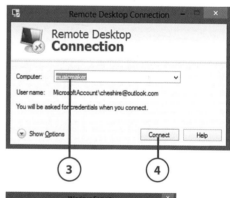

(3) (4)

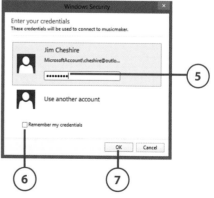

(6) (7)

8. Tap Yes in the certificate errors dialog. (You can safely ignore the certificate problem in this specific case.)

9. To disconnect from the computer, tap the X in the Remote Desktop title bar.

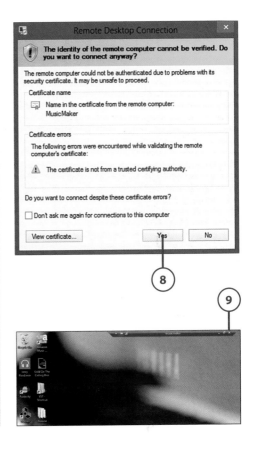

It's Not All Good

One Way

Windows RT 8.1 enables you to use Remote Desktop to connect to a remote computer, but you can't use Remote Desktop on another PC to connect to your Surface 2. If you want to remote into a Surface 2, you'll have to use Surface 2 for Windows 8.1 Pro.

Add a name to a group of tiles.

Change your Start
screen background.

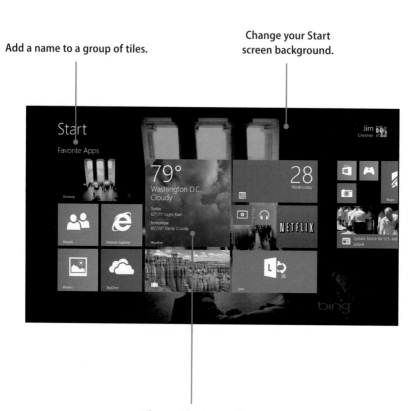

Change tile sizes and
reorganize tiles.

Using and Customizing the Start Screen

If you're coming to Windows RT 8.1 from the world of Windows 7 or prior versions, RT represents a significant departure, a fact that is obvious from the moment you power on your Surface 2. Instead of a desktop filled with icons, the Windows RT 8.1 Start screen offers a rich and colorful environment for interacting with and launching your apps. This environment is built specifically to allow you to customize it to fit your work, life, and play style.

Locating and Launching Apps

The Start screen consists of a series of tiles arranged within groups. Tiles can launch an app or link to content within an app, such as a web page in Internet Explorer.

In addition to the tiles that you see on the Start screen, many apps available in Windows RT 8.1 aren't on the Start screen by default. You can launch these apps using a special Apps view or by searching for a desired app.

Launching Apps from the Start Screen

You can easily locate an app from the start screen and launch it.

1. If necessary, swipe left or right to locate the app you would like to launch.

2. To see more of your Start screen, pinch to zoom out. (This view is called *semantic zoom.*)

3. To locate apps not represented by a tile on the Start screen, tap and hold on a blank part of the Start screen and slide up to reveal the Apps screen.

4. Tap By Name to change the sort order of apps on the Apps screen if desired.

5. Tap By Date Installed to sort apps by the date they were installed.

6. Tap By Most Used to sort apps by most-used apps to least-used apps.

7. Tap By Category to sort apps by category.

8. If the app you want doesn't fit on the screen, you can swipe to locate your app.

App Categories

When you sort apps by category, apps will be sorted by categories from the Windows Store. You cannot define your own categories.

9. You can also pinch and tap a letter to quickly scroll to apps beginning with a particular letter, or tap a group name to quickly scroll to a particular app or group of apps.

Returning to the Start Screen

While displaying the Apps screen, you can return to the Start screen by pressing the Windows button on your Surface 2 (or the Windows key on your keyboard) by swiping up, or by swiping in from the right of the screen and tapping the Start charm.

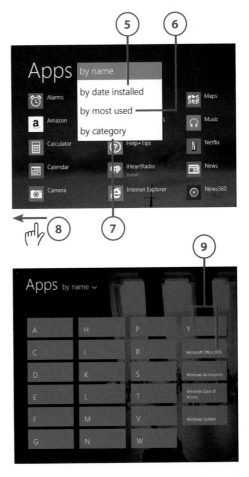

Searching for Apps

If you have any trouble finding a particular app, you can easily search for apps.

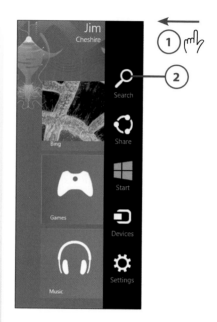

1. From the Start screen or Apps screen, swipe in from the right side of the screen, or press Winkey+C to reveal the charms.

2. Tap Search.

3. If you aren't using a Smart Cover or Type Cover, tap inside of the textbox to open the on-screen keyboard. Enter a search phrase.

4. Apps that match your search phrase appear as you type.

Quick Access to Search

To quickly access the Search charm, press Winkey+Q while on the Start screen.

Switching Between Recent Apps

Windows Store apps are designed to take up the entire screen. When you switch back to the Start screen after launching an app, the app usually remains running even though it's no longer visible. However, you can switch back to apps that you've previously run and, in most cases, the app resumes right where you left off when you last used it.

Closing Apps

Even though multiple apps might be running at once, Windows RT 8.1 controls what resources are available to apps in the background to ensure long battery life; therefore, you don't have to worry about closing apps. However, if you do want to close an app, you can. Simply activate the app, and then swipe down from the top of the screen all the way to the bottom of the screen to close it. If you're using a keyboard, Winkey+F4 closes the active app.

Switching Between Running Apps

You can switch between all the apps that are currently running.

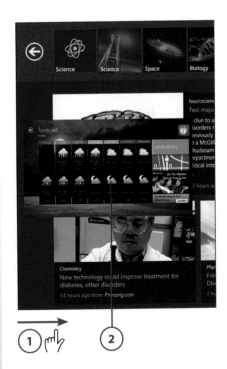

1. Swipe from the left side of the screen.

2. Lift your finger from the screen when the thumbnail of the previous app is fully visible.

3. Repeat the process to cycle through the apps that are currently running.

Activating the Last Run App

You can switch between the Start screen and the last app that you've used by pressing the Windows button on your Surface 2 or by pressing Winkey on the keyboard.

Displaying a List of Running Apps

Windows RT 8.1 provides a quicker way to switch to an app of your choice when multiple apps are running at once. You can display thumbnails of the six most recently started apps along the left edge of the screen. You can then switch to an app by tapping the thumbnail.

1. Swipe from the left side of the screen until the thumbnail of another running app is visible, but don't remove your finger from the screen.

2. Drag the thumbnail of the app back to the left edge of the screen until thumbnails display along the left edge of the screen, and release your finger.

3. Tap one of the app thumbnails to activate the app or tap Start at the bottom of the pane to go to the Start screen.

Tip

Each subsequent press of Winkey+Tab highlights the next app in the list. Release the Windows key to switch to the highlighted app.

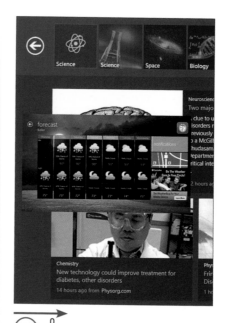

Displaying Two Apps Simultaneously

You might encounter situations in which you want to use two different apps simultaneously. For example, you might be pulling numbers from one app that you are using in a Microsoft Excel spreadsheet. In such situations, being able to display two apps on screen at the same time can be quite helpful.

1. Activate the first app by either launching it from the Start screen or by switching to it as previously described.

2. Swipe from the left side of the screen just until a thumbnail of the second app appears but not so far that the entire thumbnail is visible.

3. Hold your finger on the screen until you see the separator bar.

4. Remove your finger from the screen to dock the second app next to the original app.

5. Drag the separator bar to change which app takes more space on the screen.

6. To remove one app from the screen and return to single-app mode, drag the separator bar to the edge of the screen.

Displaying More Than Two Apps

Windows RT 8.1 has the ability to display more than two apps on the same screen. However, your Surface 2 does not have enough screen resolution to support this feature. If you hook up a sufficiently high-resolution external monitor to your Surface 2, you should be able to display more than two apps on the same screen.

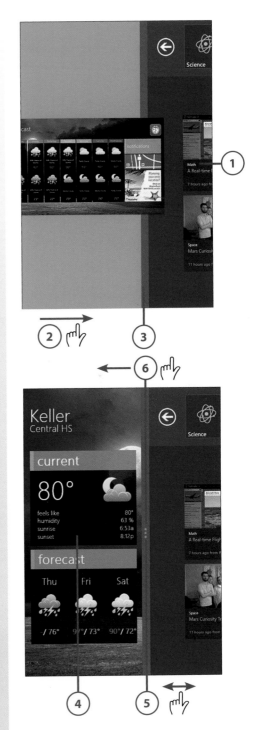

Organizing the Start Screen

You can bring more order to your Start screen by organizing tiles into groups.

Automatic Groups

Windows RT 8.1 groups your Start screen tiles automatically, but you can rearrange these groups any way you choose.

Rearranging Tiles

You can move a tile to a new location by dragging it.

1. Tap and hold the tile to release it from its current location.

2. Drag the tile to a new location. Other tiles will move to accommodate the tile you are moving. Release the tile when it is in the desired location.

3. To create a new tile group, drag the tile to a blank area at the right edge of the Start screen or to the left of an existing group and release it when a highlighted group separator appears.

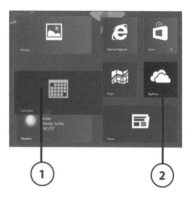

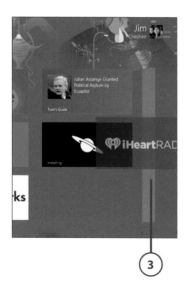

Naming Groups

Naming groups of tiles is another way of providing additional organization to your Start screen.

1. Swipe up from the bottom of the Start screen to reveal the Command bar.

2. Tap Customize.

3. Tap Name Group to add a name to an unnamed group or tap the existing group name to rename a group.

4. Enter a name for your group (or tap the X to remove a group name) and press Enter to apply the name to your group.

5. Tap a blank area of the Start screen to return to the Start screen.

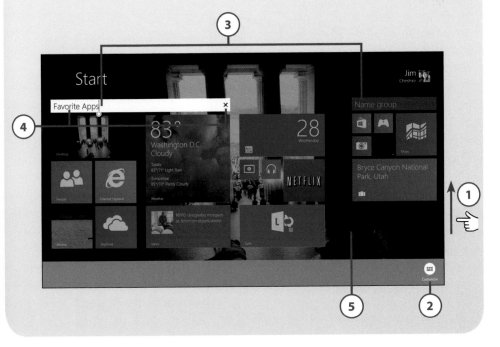

Customizing the Start Screen

Many options are available for customizing your Start screen so that it offers a personalized experience that fits your own tastes and preferences.

Changing the Start Screen Color Scheme and Background Picture

You can change the color scheme and the background picture that is displayed on your Start screen. When you change these settings, your changes are synchronized across all PCs that use your Microsoft account, assuming you have synchronization enabled. For information on synchronization of settings, see "Synchronizing Settings" in Chapter 1, "An Introduction to Surface 2."

1. Swipe in from the right of the Start screen to reveal the charms, and then tap Settings.

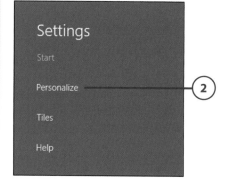

Tip

You can also access the Settings charm by pressing Winkey+I.

2. Tap Personalize.

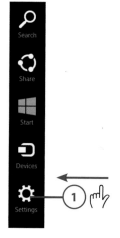

3. Tap a background picture to change the background.

4. Tap the thumbnail of your Windows Desktop background to set the Start screen background to match your Windows Desktop background.

5. Drag the Background Color slider to select a color scheme for the background.

6. Tap a color hue to set the specific background color.

7. Drag the Accent Color slider to select a color scheme for the accent color.

Accent Color

The accent color is used to highlight selected items.

8. Tap a color hue to set the specific accent color.

Changes Happen Immediately

Changes to the background picture or color scheme take place immediately. You don't have to click a button to save these settings.

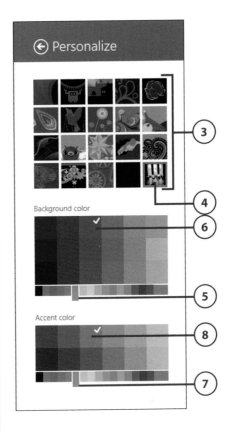

Showing Administrative Tools

Power users might want to display tiles for Administrative Tools in Apps view. Administrative Tools consist of tools used to troubleshoot Windows and get detailed information about the system.

1. Swipe in from the right of the Start screen to reveal the charms, and then tap Settings. (Remember that you can also press Winkey+I on your keyboard.)

2. Tap Tiles.

3. Tap the Show Administrative Tools slider to change the setting to Yes.

4. Tap the Back arrow to return to the Settings charm. (This step is necessary in order to refresh the icons in Apps view.)

5. Swipe up on the Start screen to view the Administrative Tools icons in Apps.

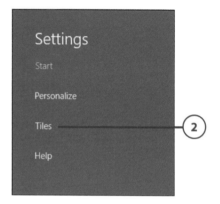

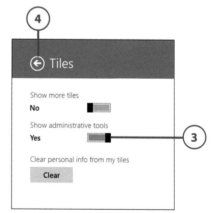

Showing Additional Tiles

You can show an additional row of tiles on the Start screen if you would like to see more tiles.

1. From the Settings screen, tap Tiles.

2. Tap the Show More Tiles slider to change the setting to Yes.

3. Tiles are made slightly smaller and an additional row of tiles is now available on the Start screen.

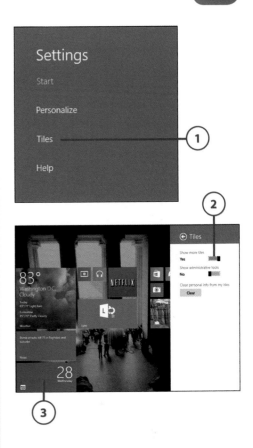

Removing Tiles from the Start Menu

You can remove a tile from the Start screen by unpinning it. You can unpin any tile that you no longer want displayed on your Start screen, including those that are included on the Start screen by default.

1. Tap and hold on the tile that you want to remove from the Start screen. (You can tap additional tiles if you want to remove more than one tile.)

2. Tap Unpin from Start on the Command bar.

Unpinning Tiles

You can also tap and hold an app in the Apps screen and tap Unpin from Start to remove the app's tile from the Start screen.

Pinning Apps to the Start Menu

You can pin any app to the Start menu from the Apps screen.

1. From the Start screen, swipe up to display the Apps screen.

2. Tap and hold on the app you want to pin to the Start screen.

3. Tap any additional apps you want to pin to the Start screen.

4. Tap Pin to Start to pin the apps to the Start screen.

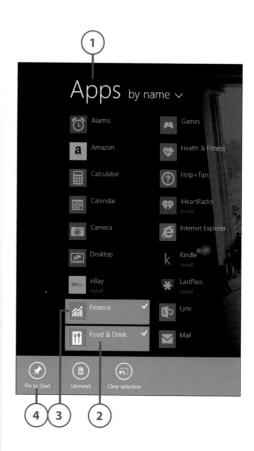

Changing Tile Sizes

Tiles can appear in up to four different sizes. Because Windows RT 8.1 uses Live Tiles (tiles that display useful information directly on the tile), making a tile larger can display more information on the tile.

1. Tap and hold on a tile for which you would like to change the size.

2. Tap Resize.

3. Tap a size from the popup menu.

Tile Sizes

An app must be written to support a particular tile size. You cannot resize a tile to a size that an app does not support.

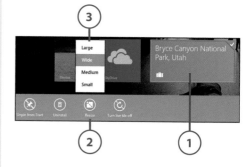

Controlling Live Tiles

Live Tiles allow for useful information to be displayed directly on a tile. For example, a weather app can display a local forecast on its tile and a news app can display news headlines on a tile. You can turn on or off Live Tile functionality.

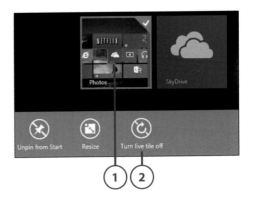

1. Tap and hold on a tile to select it.

2. Tap Turn Live Tile Off to turn off a Live Tile.

3. Tap Turn Live Tile On to turn on a Live Tile.

Live Tile Content

An app developer controls whether an app supports the Live Tile feature and what information is displayed on a Live Tile. Tiles that support the Large size will often display even more information as a Live Tile.

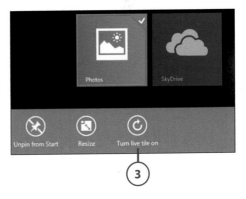

Removing Personal Information from Live Tiles

Live Tiles might display personal information that you don't want visible. For example, the Calendar app displays your next appointment on its Live Tile. If you would prefer to never have this information displayed, you can turn off the Live Tile, but if you simply would like to remove the personal information until you log off and back on again, you can do so.

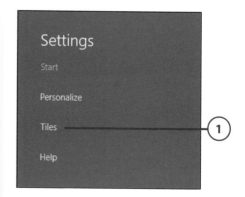

1. From the Settings screen, tap Tiles.

2. Tap Clear to remove personal info from all tiles.

Personal Information Restoration

After you clear personal information from your tiles, it will be removed until you log off and back on again.

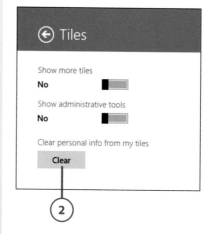

Manage your account and add a Microsoft account.

Create a picture password.

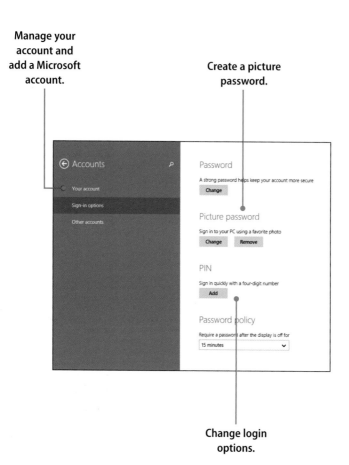

Change login options.

Security and Windows RT 8.1

Your Surface 2 device is quite secure by design. All files are encrypted by default, and apps you run are isolated to their own environment and aren't allowed to access sensitive information stored on the device. Windows RT 8.1 also contains many features deep under the hood that are designed to prevent infections from viruses and other malware. It's not at all hyperbolic to say that Windows RT 8.1 is the most secure version of Windows ever made.

With that said, you will still want to take steps to secure your Surface 2. Today's connected devices offer access to more information than ever before, and it's more important than ever to ensure that access to your PC is controlled. You also might want to let your kids play a game on your Surface 2 without worrying that they are going to delete your emails or get access to information that should be kept private.

Securing Your PC

You secure Surface 2 using a password. If I were to ask you what it is, you obviously wouldn't tell me (I hope), but even so, if your password is a weak one, you might as well. What do I mean by a "weak" password? I mean a password that consists of a word that appears in the dictionary or is the name of your pet, spouse, or some other word that someone, or some hacking tool, might easily guess. You should protect your password vigilantly, and that means choosing one that's impossible to guess and challenging for an automated tool to figure out.

Creating a Strong Password

A good password would be something like this: h028w5y358j3. Believe it or not, remembering this password is pretty easy. It's simply "now is the time" on my keyboard with the spaces removed and with my fingers shifted up one row when I typed it. I use that trick often to create strong passwords.

Changing Your Password

If reading this chapter's introduction made you realize that your password needs to be stronger, you can easily change it. Changing your password periodically as a security precaution is not a bad idea.

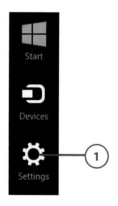

1. From the charms, tap Settings or press Winkey+I on your keyboard.

2. Tap Change PC Settings.

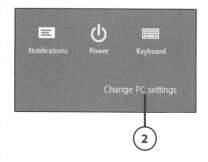

3. Tap Accounts.

4. Tap Sign-in Options.

5. Tap Change to change your password.

6. Enter your current password.

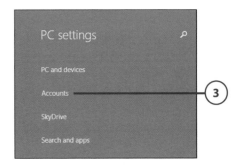

See Your Password Characters

As you enter passwords in Windows RT 8.1, dots are displayed instead of the password's actual characters. If you want to see the actual characters instead, tap and hold on the eye icon at the right edge of the password field.

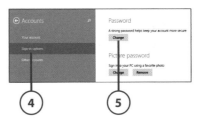

7. Tap Finish.

Signing In to Your Account

You might not have to complete steps 6 and 7 if you have already signed in to your Microsoft account.

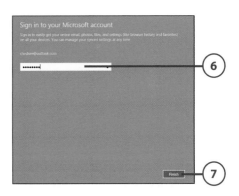

8. Enter your old password. (This is the same password you entered in step 6.)

9. Enter your new password.

10. Reenter your new password.

11. Tap Next.

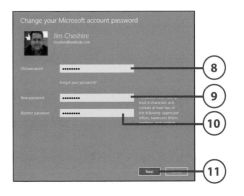

12. Tap Finish.

Tip

If you're using a local account, you'll need to tap Next after entering your current password and enter a password hint.

Locking Your PC

When you're not using your PC, it's a good idea to lock it. When your PC is locked, your password must be entered to access the apps and information on it.

Your PC locks automatically when the screen has been off for 15 minutes, but you can also explicitly lock it immediately. (You can change the time interval for the automatic locking feature, and I'll show you how later in this chapter.)

1. From the Start screen, tap your user name.

2. Tap Lock on the menu to lock your PC.

Locking Faster

You can lock your PC by pressing Winkey+L on your keyboard.

Signing Out of Your PC

You can also sign out (log off) of your PC. Signing out is similar to locking the PC except that it closes all apps you are using and completely signs you out of the PC.

1. From the Start screen, tap your user name.

2. Tap Sign Out.

Configuring Auto-Lock

You can configure Windows RT 8.1 so that a password is required after a particular time period has elapsed. Doing so provides an extra level of security if you fail to explicitly log out or lock your PC.

1. From the Sign-in Options screen in Accounts (refer to the previous section, "Changing Your Password"), tap the Require a Password After the Display Is Off For drop-down box.

2. Select a time interval after which a password will be required. (You can also choose to always require a password or to never require a password.)

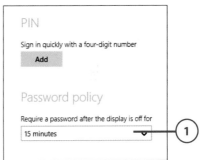

Using Picture Passwords

One of the unique features of Windows 8.1 (both the RT version and the Pro version) is the picture password feature. This feature enables you to use a series of gestures (taps, circles, and lines) on a picture instead of entering a password. The location, size, and direction of your gestures are all part of your picture password.

Security and Picture Passwords

It's worth mentioning that Microsoft considers picture passwords to be secure enough to allow Microsoft employees to use them on the Microsoft corporate network.

Creating a Picture Password

You can create a picture password using a picture that is included with Windows RT 8.1, or you can use one of your own pictures.

1. From the Picture Password section of Sign-in Options, tap Add.

2. Enter your current password.

3. Tap OK.

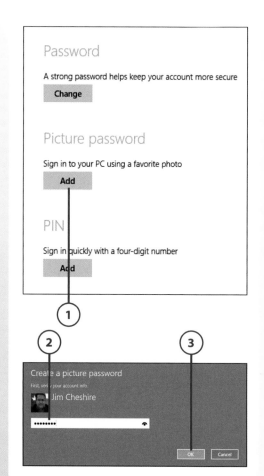

Password

A strong password helps keep your account more secure

Change

Picture password

Sign in to your PC using a favorite photo

Add

PIN

Sign in quickly with a four-digit number

Add

Create a picture password

First, verify your account info.

Jim Cheshire

●●●●●●●●

OK   Cancel

4. Tap Choose Picture.

5. To change to a new folder, tap This PC and select a new folder.

6. Tap the picture you would like to use for your picture password.

7. Tap Open.

8. Drag to position the picture the way you want it.

9. Tap Use This Picture.

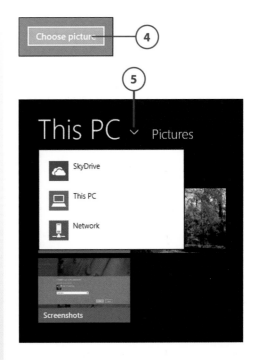

10. Draw three gestures on your picture using the guidelines provided.

11. Repeat your gestures to confirm them.

12. Tap Finish to complete your picture password.

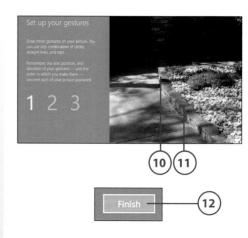

Changing Your Picture Password

If you want to change the picture that is used for your picture password, you can do so. You might also want to change the gestures used while keeping the same picture.

1. From the Sign-in Options screen in Accounts, tap Change.

2. Enter your password to confirm it.

3. Tap OK.

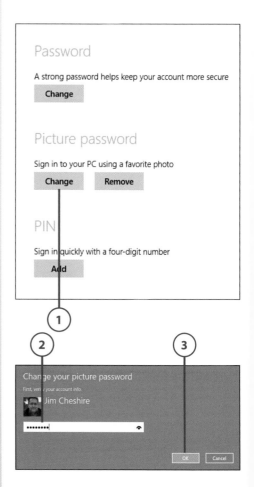

4. Tap Use This Picture to keep using the existing picture or Choose New Picture to select a new picture.

5. Enter the desired gestures for your picture password.

6. Reenter your gestures.

7. Tap Finish.

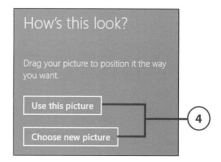

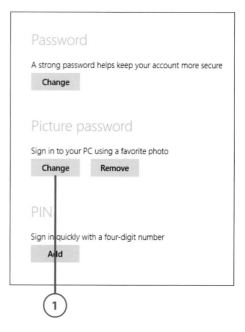

Replaying Your Picture Password

If you've forgotten the gestures you used for your picture password, Windows RT 8.1 can play them back for you.

1. From the Sign-in Options in Accounts, tap Change.

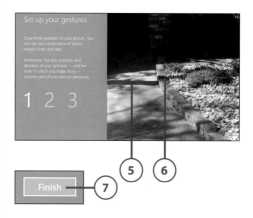

2. Enter your password and tap OK.

3. Tap Replay.

4. Trace the gestures that are displayed on the screen.

5. Repeat your three gestures.

6. Tap Finish.

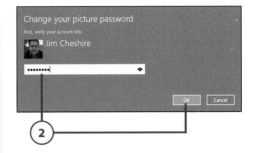

Removing Your Picture Password

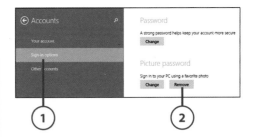

You can remove your picture password, after which point you must enter your textual password when signing in.

1. From the Accounts screen, tap Sign-in Options.

2. Tap Remove to remove your picture password.

Using PINs

Typing a long, complex password into a tablet without a keyboard attached is a hassle. While not as secure as a password, you can use a four-digit PIN to sign in to your Surface 2 instead of using a password.

Creating a PIN

You create a PIN by entering a series of four numbers you want to use when signing in or when unlocking your Surface 2.

1. From the Sign-in Options screen, tap Add under the PIN section.

2. Enter your password to confirm it before creating your PIN.

3. Tap OK.

4. Enter four numerals for your PIN.

5. Confirm your PIN.

6. Tap Finish.

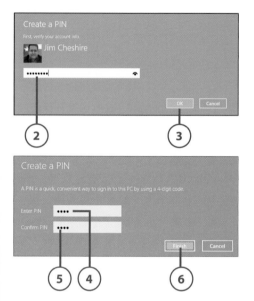

Changing a PIN

You can change your PIN easily.

1. From the PIN section on the Sign-in Options screen, tap Change.

2. Enter your password to confirm it before changing your PIN.

3. Tap OK.

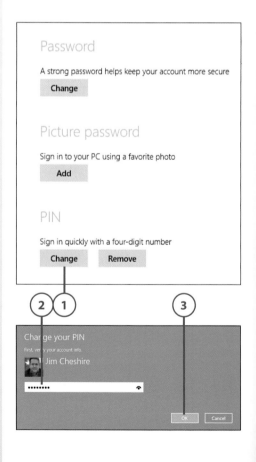

4. Enter a new PIN.

5. Confirm your new PIN.

6. Tap Finish.

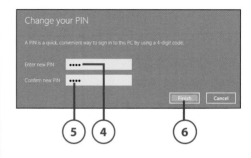

Removing a PIN

You can remove a PIN so that it can no longer be used to sign in.

1. From the Accounts screen, tap Sign-in Options.

2. Tap the Remove button in the PIN section to remove your PIN.

Signing In with a PIN

When a PIN is set for your account, signing in will prompt you for your PIN instead of a password.

1. Swipe up from the lock screen.

2. Enter your PIN to sign in.

PINs and Picture Passwords

If you have a picture password set, it will always be the method used to sign in when you swipe up on the lock screen. If you would like to use your PIN, you'll need to use the method that I describe in the next step-by-step.

Using a PIN When a Picture Password Is Set

If you have a picture password set, you'll need to use these steps to use your PIN for the first time.

1. Swipe up from the lock screen.

2. Tap the Switch to Password button.

3. Tap Sign-in Options.

4. Tap the PIN keypad button.

5. Enter your PIN to sign in.

Changing Sign-in Options

When you tap Sign-in Options, you'll see various buttons depending on whether you've configured a picture password or a PIN. Tap the appropriate button to choose your sign-in option.

Managing User Accounts

User accounts are used to identify particular people using a PC. Windows not only gives each user a unique sign-in ID, but it also separates each user's data into folders that are accessible only by that user or by an administrator.

Administrators

Administrators have the ability to access any folder on the system, change any system setting, and so forth. By default, users that you add are not administrators. If you want to make a user an administrator, see "Changing an Account Type" later in this chapter.

You can add local accounts and Microsoft accounts to your Surface 2. A local account is tied to the particular PC where it was created. A Microsoft account is tied to a particular Microsoft ID and automatically synchronizes settings and other information via the Internet.

Microsoft Accounts

If you don't already have a Microsoft account, you can find out more information by browsing to http://home.live.com.

Adding a Local Account

You can add a new local account that isn't associated with a Microsoft account. This is a convenient way of adding an account for a child or someone else who doesn't have a Microsoft account.

1. From the Accounts screen, tap Other and tap the Add an Account button to add a user account.

2. Tap the Sign In Without a Microsoft Account link.

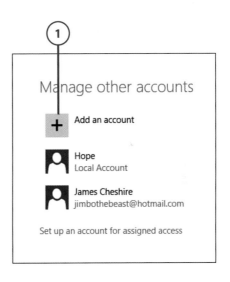

Why a Local Account Is Not Recommended

You might notice that Microsoft doesn't recommend the option to sign in without a Microsoft account. The reason is because that account will not be able to synchronize settings across multiple Windows 8 systems and devices.

3. Tap the Local Account button.

4. Enter a user name.

5. Enter a password for the new user.

6. Reenter the password to confirm it.

7. Enter a password hint. (A user can display this when signing in if he or she forgets the password.)

8. Tap Next.

9. If the account is for a child, check the box to enable Family Safety for the account.

10. Tap Finish.

Family Safety

You can find out more about the Family Safety feature in Chapter 5, "Using Family Safety."

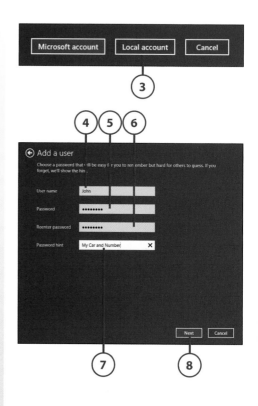

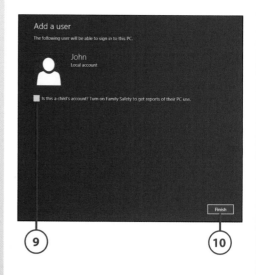

Adding a Microsoft Account

A Microsoft account enables the user to have a more consistent experience across multiple PCs. Settings made on one PC are synchronized to any other Windows 8 PC or device to which that account logs In.

1. From the Other Accounts screen, tap the Add an Account button to add a user account.

2. Enter the email address for the new user.

3. Tap Next.

Using an Existing Microsoft Account

If the email you enter in step 2 is associated with an existing Microsoft account, you will be taken directly to step 20 while creating the account.

4. Enter an email for the Microsoft account. This can be the same email used in step 2 or a different one. (This is the email address the user will use to sign in.)

5. Enter a password.

6. Reenter the password.

7. Enter a first name.

8. Enter a last name.

9. Select a country or region.

10. Tap Next.

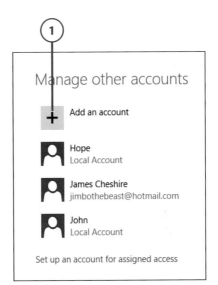

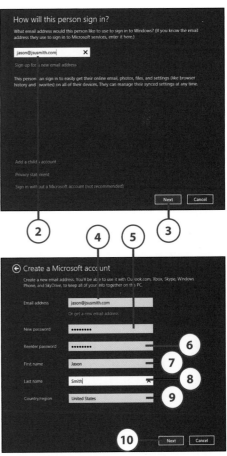

11. Enter a birth day.

12. Select a country for the phone number and enter the number.

13. Enter an alternate email address.

14. Select a secret question.

15. Enter the answer to the secret question.

16. Tap Next.

17. Uncheck Enhance My Online Experiences by Letting Microsoft Advertising Use My Account Information to opt out of the setting.

18. Uncheck Send Me Promotional Offers from Microsoft to opt out of the setting.

19. Enter the CAPTCHA characters to confirm that you are a real person and not an automated system attempting to create a phony account.

20. Tap Next.

21. Check the box to enable Family Safety for the account if desired.

22. Tap Finish.

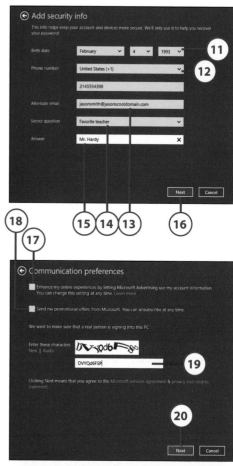

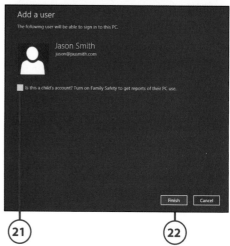

Removing a User Account

If you no longer want to allow an account access to your PC, you can remove the account.

1. From the Other Accounts screen, tap the account you want to remove.

2. Tap Remove to remove the account.

3. Tap Delete Account and Data to delete the account.

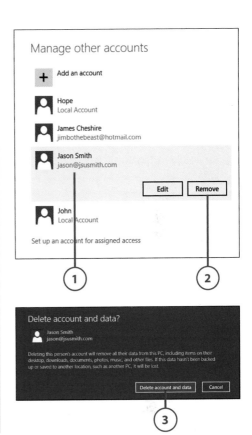

It's Not All Good

Removing an Account Removes Data, Too

When you remove an account, it also removes data for the account. In other words, if the user has stored documents, pictures, or other files, those files are permanently deleted from your Surface 2 when you remove the account.

Changing an Account Type

You can change an account type and make a standard account into an administrator account or a child account. An administrator account has full access to the PC. A child account has limited access based on Family Safety settings. (I cover Family Safety in detail in Chapter 5, "Using Family Safety.")

1. From the Other Accounts screen, tap the account for which you would like to change the type.

2. Tap Edit.

3. Tap Account Type.

4. Tap the desired account type.

5. Tap OK.

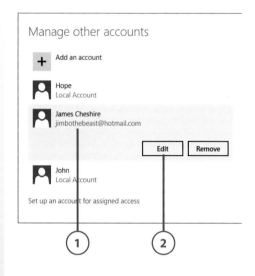

Setting an Account for Assigned Access

There might be times when you want to allow a user access to only one app on your Surface. You can configure an account for assigned access and choose one app that the account can access. When the user signs in, he will be taken directly to the app that you have assigned to him. Access to any other apps or features on your Surface is restricted.

Exiting Assigned Access

If you are logged in with a user who is restricted by assigned access, you can log in with another user by tapping the Windows button on your Surface five times. Microsoft says to tap the button five times quickly, but you actually need to tap it about once per second so that all the taps are recognized. When you do that, Windows returns you to the sign-in screen where you can sign in with a user who is not restricted by assigned access.

1. From the Accounts screen, tap Other Accounts.

2. Tap Set Up an Account for assigned access.

3. Tap Choose an Account.

4. Tap the account that you want to configure for assigned access.

5. Tap Choose an App.

6. Tap an app to assign the app to the user. (Only Windows Store apps are available.)

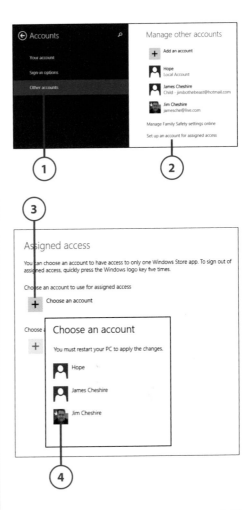

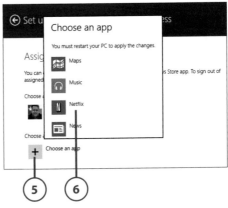

Rebooting for Assigned Access

Windows tells you that you must reboot for assigned access to take effect. That's actually not true when enabling assigned access. However, if you clear assigned access for a user, a reboot is required in order to return the user to an unassigned state.

Clearing Assigned Access

If you want to clear assigned access for a user, you can easily do so. However, after going through these steps, you will need to reboot your Surface.

1. From the Manage Other Accounts screen, tap Set Up an Account for Assigned Access.

2. Tap the account you want to clear.

3. Tap Don't Use Assigned Access.

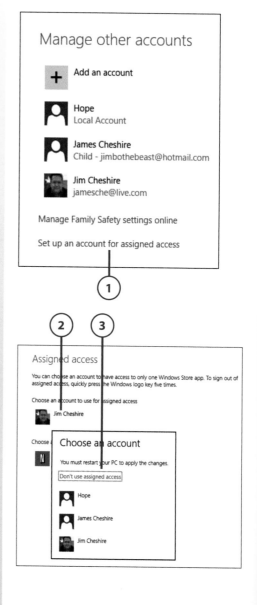

It's Not All Good

Stuck in Assigned Access

If you clear assigned access for an account and then log in on that account before rebooting your Surface, you'll get stuck in the assigned access mode. Pressing the Windows key five times will not take you back to the sign-in screen. If this happens to you, press Winkey+L on a keyboard and then tap the back arrow to return to the sign-in screen. You can then sign in with another account and reboot your Surface.

Switching Accounts

After you create a new account, you might want to switch to one of the other accounts while leaving the original account signed in. For example, you might be working on a Word document and the kids might ask to play a game. If you decide to take a break and indulge them, it's convenient to simply switch to the account used by the kids without having to close Word and sign out of your session.

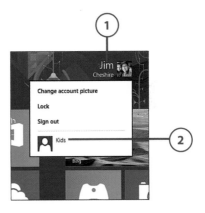

1. From the Start screen, tap your name.

2. Tap the other account from the menu.

3. Enter the password for the other account, and press Enter to sign in.

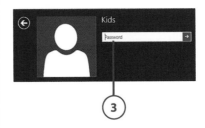

Changing from a Local Account to a Microsoft Account

If you are using a local account, you might decide at some point that you want to enjoy the advantages of using a Microsoft account instead. You can easily switch your local account to a Microsoft account.

1. From the Accounts screen, tap Your Account.

2. Enter the password for your local account.

3. Tap Next.

Moving to a Microsoft Account

When you switch to a Microsoft account, your files and settings will be transferred over to your Microsoft account so that you won't lose them.

4. Enter the Microsoft ID that you would like to use on your PC.

5. Enter the password for your Microsoft account.

6. Tap Next.

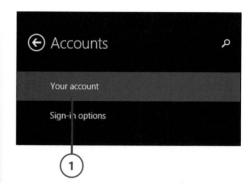

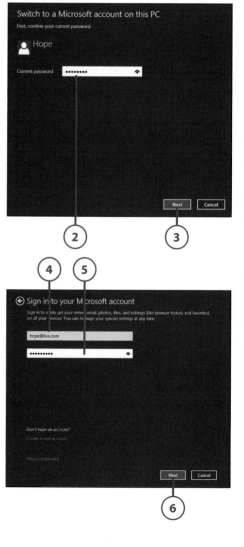

7. Select an option for receiving a confirmation code from Microsoft.

8. Tap Next.

9. Enter the code that Microsoft sends to you.

10. Tap Next.

11. If you choose, tap Turn Off These SkyDrive Settings to disable automatic backup of your files to SkyDrive.

12. Tap Next.

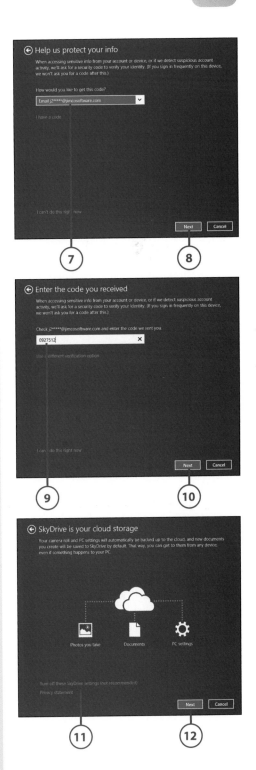

13. Tap Switch.

Creating a New Microsoft Account

If you don't already have a Microsoft account, you can create one by tapping on Create a New Account after you tap Next in step 3.

Trust Your PC

After you switch to a Microsoft account, you'll need to add the PC to your list of trusted PCs for your Microsoft account. You can do so by tapping Trust This PC from the Your Account screen.

Switching to a Local Account

You can switch from using your Microsoft account to a local account. Before you do this, you'll want to save anything you're working on and close your applications because Windows RT 8.1 requires you to log off of your computer to complete this process.

Backing Up Your Recovery Key

Your Surface uses Microsoft BitLocker to encrypt the contents of your device. BitLocker uses a recovery key to decrypt your data, and that recovery key is stored with your Microsoft account. Before you disconnect your Microsoft account and switch to a local account, you should back up your recovery key. These steps walk you through backing up the recovery key as well.

1. From the Start screen, swipe in from the right and tap Search.

2. Enter **back up your recovery key** in the search box.

3. Tap Back Up Your Recovery Key.

4. Tap Back Up Your Recovery Key.

5. Tap Save to a File to save the recovery key to a file. (You can choose to print the key if you prefer.)

6. Browse to a location where you would like to save the backed-up recovery key.

7. Tap Save.

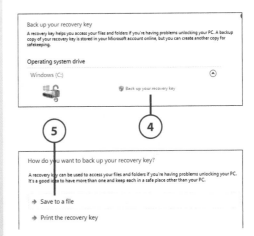

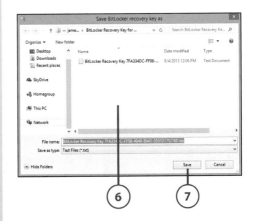

8. Tap Finish.

9. From the Accounts settings screen, tap Your Account.

10. Tap Disconnect.

11. Enter your password.

12. Tap Next.

13. Enter a user name. (This is the new user name that you will use when logging in.)

14. Enter a password.

15. Reenter the password.

16. Enter a password hint.

17. Tap Next.

18. Tap Sign Out and Finish.

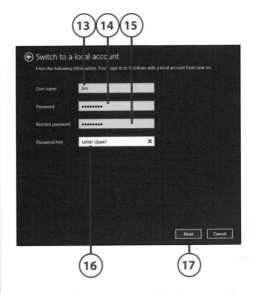

Control which websites a
user can visit.

Enable Family Safety
for any of your family
members who use
your PCs.

Control the apps
and games that
a user can use.

Using Family Safety

Computers are quite popular with kids. They use them for playing games sure enough, but they also use them for school and many other purposes. For the past few years, my kids have used a desktop computer that sits in a common family area, but the advent of tablet PCs has made supervision of their computer use a bit trickier.

Family Safety is designed to solve that problem. Using the Family Safety feature built in to Windows RT 8.1 (and other editions of Windows 8 and 8.1), you can easily monitor your child's use of your PC. You can even set time and other restrictions so that you can control when and how the PC is used.

Configuring Family Safety

As you saw in Chapter 4, "Security and Windows RT 8.1," when you create a user, you are provided with the option to specify that the account is for a child. When you configure an account as a child account, Family Safety is automatically enabled for the account. However, you can enable and disable Family Safety for any user on your PC at any time.

Enabling and Disabling Family Safety for a User

If you need to enable or disable Family Safety for a user, you can do so easily.

1. From the Accounts screen in PC Settings, tap Other Accounts.

2. Tap the account for which you would like to enable Family Safety.

3. Tap Edit.

4. Tap Account Type.

5. Tap Child.

6. Tap OK.

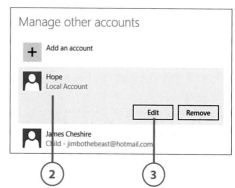

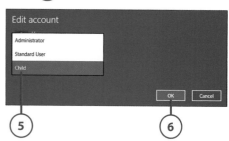

Configuring Activity Reporting for a User

Family Safety can collect detailed information on what a user does while using a PC. You can turn this type of reporting on or off for a user.

1. From the Start screen, tap Internet Explorer.

2. In the address bar, enter **https:// familysafety.microsoft.com** and press Enter.

3. Tap the child for which you want to configure activity reporting.

4. Tap Activity Reporting.

5. Tap the slider to change the setting to Off to disable activity reporting or On to enable activity reporting.

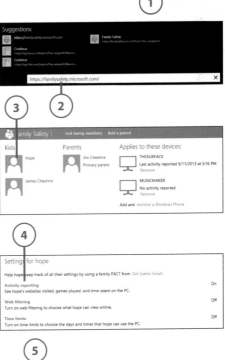

Viewing Activity Reports

You can view activity reports on users from the Family Safety website. Activity reports show when each user used the PC, what apps they used, websites they visited, and much more.

Viewing Activity Reports

You can visit Microsoft's Family Safety website to view activity reports for all PCs and all users you are monitoring.

Determining Whom You See

When you visit the Family Safety website, you can see any account that you created on any of your PCs.

1. From the Family Safety website (https://familysafety.microsoft.com), tap the kid you want to review.

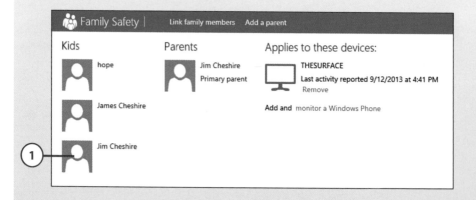

2. Tap Activity Reporting.

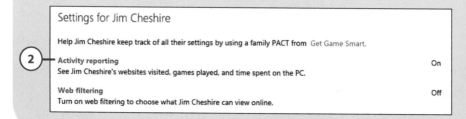

3. Tap the slider to enable or disable activity reporting for this user.

4. Drag up to see more summary information.

5. Tap Web Activity to see details on web browsing activity.

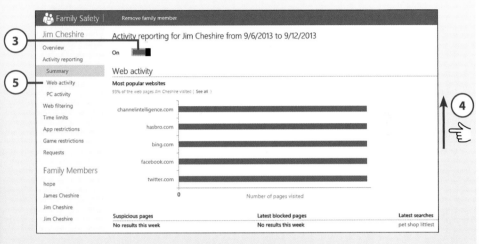

6. Tap the slider to enable or disable web activity reporting for this user.

7. Select a new date range and tap Show Activity to see data for a different range of dates.

8. Tap Show Sites Accessed by Non-Browser Apps to see websites that were accessed by apps and not a web browser.

9. Tap a column header to sort by that column.

10. Tap the filter icon for a column to apply a column filter.

11. Tap an arrow button to see individual pages visited at a site.

12. Tap Report to report a page to Microsoft as inappropriate for children.

13. Tap Block to block future visits to a page or site for this user.

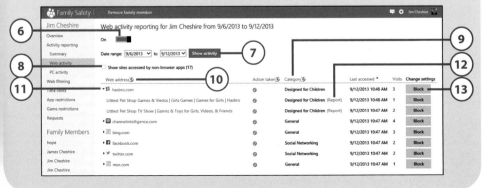

14. Tap PC Activity to see user activity on the current PC.

15. Tap the slider to enable or disable PC activity reporting for this user.

16. Select a new date range and tap Show Activity to see data for a different range of dates.

17. Review the chart to see days and times that the PC was used by this user.

18. Swipe up to see additional details.

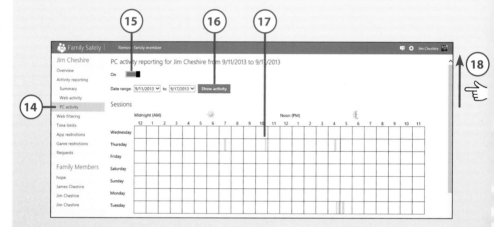

19. Review the list of apps and games to see which apps and games have been used or blocked. (Blocked apps and games will display a red circle with a line through it in the Action column.)

20. Tap a column header to sort by that column.

21. Review the list of downloaded files to see which files have been downloaded.

22. Tap a column header to sort the downloaded files list by that column.

23. Windows Store downloads are displayed in the Windows Store Downloads section.

24. Family Safety Filter activity displays any activity (either blocked or allowed) that was imposed by the Family Safety Filter. (The Family Safety Filter installs on Windows 7, Windows Vista, and Windows XP.)

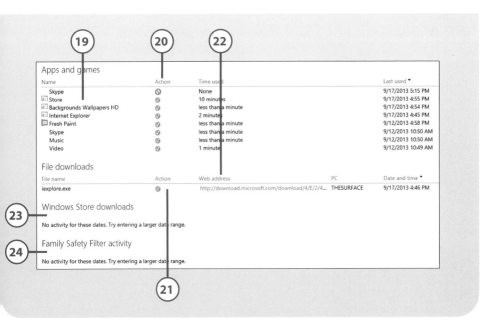

It's Not All Good

Apps and Games

When dealing with Family Safety, "apps" are applications that run in Desktop mode on your Surface and "games" are any apps that run in the modern UI interface.

Using Web Filtering

Web filtering provides a way for you to gain some control over which websites a child is allowed to visit. In the most basic sense, web filtering enables you to set one of four different levels of automatic protection, but you can also configure specific sites that a user is allowed to visit, and you can also block one or more sites.

Enabling Web Filtering

You can enable Web Filtering from the Family Safety website at familysafety.microsoft.com.

1. From the Family Safety site, tap the kid for whom you would like to enable Web Filtering.

2. Tap Web Filtering.

3. Tap the slider to turn on Web Filtering.

4. Select a filtering level for the user.

5. Check the Block File Downloads from the Web box if you want to prevent the user from downloading files.

No Shortcut to Supervision

Family Safety is quite effective at blocking most inappropriate content, but as with any technology, it isn't perfect. Even with Web Filtering enabled, there's a chance that your child might access content that you consider inappropriate. The activity reporting in Family Safety can help you to identify when this happens, but there's really nothing better than keeping a parental eye on what your kids are doing.

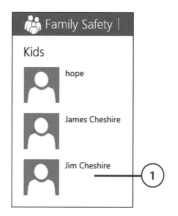

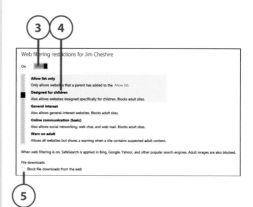

What Gets Blocked or Allowed

When you add an entry to the Allow or Block list, it applies to all subdomains of the site you add. For example, if you add a filter that blocks www.badsite.com, Family Safety will block anything on the badsite.com domain. That means that pics.badsite.com, www.badsite.com/evenbadder, and news.badsite.com will all be blocked.

Modifying the Allow or Block List

You can control which websites are blocked or allowed by editing the Allow or Block list at the Family Safety website.

1. From the Web Filtering view for the user, tap Allow or Block List.

2. Enter a web address that you want to block or allow.

3. Select whether you want to block or allow the site for this user only, for all children, or for everyone.

4. Click Allow to allow the site or Block to block the site.

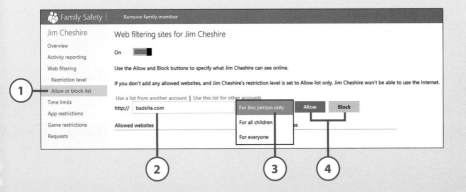

5. To remove a site, tap the trash can icon next to the entry.

It's Not All Good

Cannot Modify Filtering Settings

There isn't a way to modify settings for a site. If you want to change the scope of the filtering rule that you set in step 3, you'll have to remove the site and add it back with the new scope.

Blocking Sites from the Activity Report

You can also block users from a site directly from the Activity Report. This is useful in cases where you happen to notice that a user has visited a questionable site and you want to prevent future visits.

1. Tap Web Activity to view web activity for the user.

2. Tap the Allow button to allow a blocked site.

3. Tap Block to block a site that was visited.

4. Tap Yes, All Children to block a site for all children.

5. Tap No, This Child Only to block the site only for this child.

Using Time Allowances and Curfews

You can control how long a user can use the PC each day. You also can control a time range that the user is allowed to use the PC.

Setting an Allowance

You can configure an allowance for a user in order to enforce a certain number of hours and minutes each day that the user can use the computer. (This setting is applied only on PCs running Windows 8 or Windows 8.1.)

1. From the user's settings page on the Family Safety website, tap Time Limits.

2. Tap Allowance.

3. Tap the slider to turn on time allowance.

4. To set the same time allowance on all weekdays, select the number of hours and minutes that the user can use the PC on each weekday.

5. Tap the arrow to set a different number of hours and minutes for individual weekdays.

6. To set the same time allowance on each weekend day, select the number of hours and minutes that the user can use the PC on each weekend day.

7. Tap the arrow to set a different number of hours and minutes for individual weekend days.

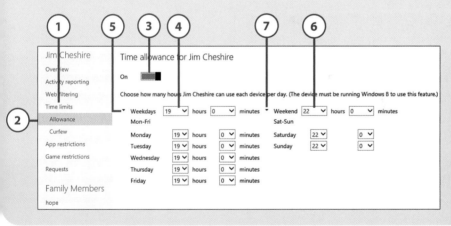

Setting a Curfew

You can set a curfew in order to control what hours of the day a user can use PCs. You can set different curfew hours for different days.

1. From the user's settings page on the Family Safety website, tap Time Limits.

2. Tap Curfew.

3. Tap the slider to turn curfew hours on.

4. Using a mouse or the trackpad on a Touch Cover or Type Cover, click and drag over the hours and days that you want to block the user's use of the PC.

5. Click and drag over selected hours to deselect them and allow them for the user.

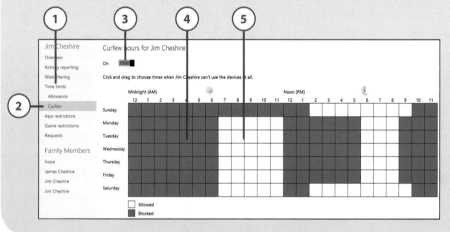

It's Not All Good

Tap and Drag Doesn't Work

It would be nice if you could tap and drag your finger to set curfew hours, but you can't. You can tap and select or deselect 30-minute periods.

Configuring App and Game Restrictions

App and game restrictions enable you to control the apps and games that a user can download from the Windows Store and that the user can run on a PC. You can control which apps and games a user can see in the Windows Store and use on the PC based on a rating system (using the ESRB at www.esrb.org by default), and you can also set specific restrictions for apps and games that are already installed.

Configuring App Restrictions

You can configure app restrictions from the Family Safety website at familysafety. microsoft.com.

1. From the user's settings on the Family Safety website, tap App Restrictions.

2. Tap the slider to enable App Restrictions.

3. Enter an app name in the search box to search for an app.

4. Tap Allow to allow the use of an app.

5. Tap Block to block the use of an app.

6. Tap the Allow header to allow all apps.

7. Tap the Block header to block all apps.

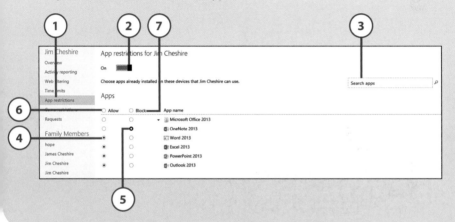

It's Not All Good

Only Microsoft Office 2013 Apps

Family Safety uses the term "apps" to refer to applications that run in Desktop mode and "games" to refer to apps from the Windows Store that run in the modern UI. Because you cannot install desktop apps on Windows RT 8.1, the only apps that are listed in App Restrictions are Microsoft Office 2013 apps that come with your Surface. If you want to block other apps, use Game Restrictions.

Configuring Game Restrictions Using Ratings

Game restrictions allow you to restrict a user from using games and other apps that run in the modern UI. You can configure game restrictions using any one of a number of rating systems.

Rating System Choice Applies to All Users

The selected rating system will apply to all users you manage. You cannot use different rating systems for different users.

---

1. From the user's settings screen in Family Safety, tap Game Restrictions.

2. Tap the slider to enable game restrictions.

3. Tap a rating level to restrict the user to that level and below.

4. Tap Allow Games That Aren't Rated to allow any apps that have not been rated by your selected rating system.

5. To change your selected rating system, tap Rating System.

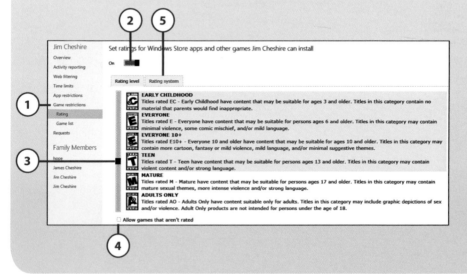

6. Tap your desired rating system.

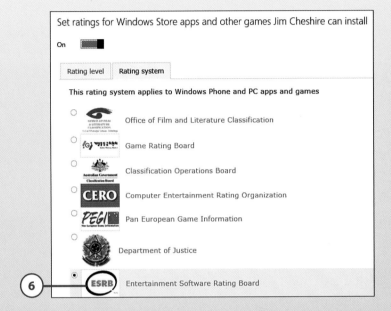

Set ratings for Windows Store apps and other games Jim Cheshire can install

On

| Rating level | **Rating system** |

This rating system applies to Windows Phone and PC apps and games

○ Office of Film and Literature Classification

○ Game Rating Board

○ Classification Operations Board

○ **CERO** Computer Entertainment Rating Organization

○ *PEGI* Pan European Game Information

○ Department of Justice

◉ **ESRB** Entertainment Software Rating Board

6

ESRB Is Best for United States

The ESRB rating system is the best choice for United States users. Other rating systems are typically used for other countries.

Blocking or Allowing Specific Apps

You can explicitly block or allow specific apps. You can use this method to control access to apps that might not have a rating. You can also override a restriction imposed by an app's rating.

1. From the Game Restrictions screen, tap Game List.

2. Tap the slider to enable game restrictions.

3. Enter an app name in the search box to search for an app.

4. Tap Allow to allow a specific app.

5. Tap Block to block a specific app.

6. Tap Use Game Rating to control access to the app based on rating.

7. Tap the Allow header to allow all apps.

8. Tap the Use Game Rating header to use the rating to control access to all apps.

9. Tap the Block header to block all apps.

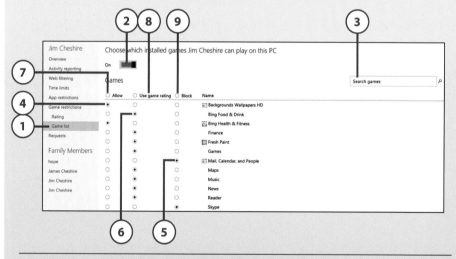

Visibility of Blocked Games in the Windows Store

Any game that is restricted due to the settings you have selected will be invisible to the user in the Windows Store. If the user has already downloaded a game that is restricted by your settings, he or she will still see it on the PC but will be unable to play it.

Blocked visibility only applies to games. Nongame apps that are blocked will still be visible in the Windows Store, but the user will not be able to install them without asking for permission.

Handling Requests

If you've blocked access to a website or an app using Family Safety, the blocked user can request access. You can grant or deny this request from the PC the child is using or from the Family Safety website.

Responding to a Request from the User's PC

You can approve or deny a request directly from the user's PC.

1. Have the user ask for permission.

2. Have the user tap My Parent Is Here.

3. Enter your password and tap OK.

4. Tap Allow.

Responding to a Request from the Website

If you are not available when the user requests access, you can review the request and allow or deny it from the Family Safety website.

Web Requests
Requests that you see in Family Safety are generated by the user tapping Send a Request when requesting access to a blocked app or website.

1. From the user's settings screen on the Family Safety website, tap Requests.

2. Tap Allow to approve a request. Otherwise, tap Ignore.

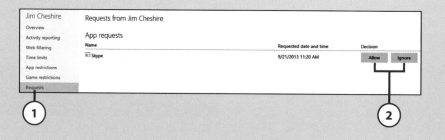

Managing Users in Family Safety

The Family Safety website at familysafety.microsoft.com lists all users for whom you've enabled Family Safety while signed in with your Microsoft account. Users are added by adding them to Family Safety on one of your PCs as you did earlier in this chapter.

You can add a new parent or make an existing user a parent from the Family Safety website. (Parents are authorized to respond to requests from users, view activity reports, and otherwise manage a user's Family Safety settings.) You can also remove users or link multiple users to one user account.

Adding a New Parent

If you would like to give another adult permission to respond to Family Safety requests and that user doesn't have an account on one of your PCs, you can add his or her account from the Family Safety website.

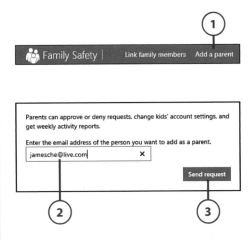

1. From the Family Safety website, tap Add a Parent.

2. Enter the email address for the parent.

3. Tap Send Request.

Linking Accounts

If you have different accounts on different PCs and you would like to manage them as one account, you can link the accounts. For example, suppose my son Bobby has an account on one of my PCs under the name Bobby and another account on another PC under the name Robert. By linking the two accounts, I can manage them in Family Safety as one account. (You can link more than two accounts.) After two accounts are linked, you will only see the primary account listed in Family Safety.

1. From the Family Safety website, tap Link Family Members.

Linked Accounts Require Separate PCs

You cannot link accounts on the same PC. Accounts that you link must be on separate PCs.

2. Tap the checkbox for the users you would like to link.

3. Tap OK.

4. Select the account you would like to use for the primary account. The settings shown for the selected account will be applied to all accounts you are linking.

5. Tap Combine Accounts.

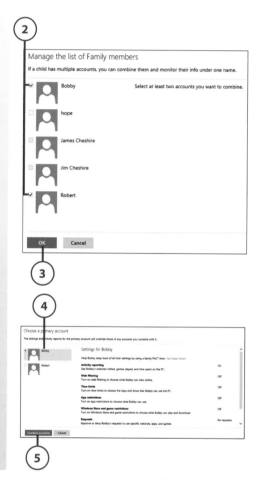

It's Not All Good

Unlinking Accounts

You cannot unlink accounts after you've linked them. If you want to remove the account linking, you have to remove the accounts from Family Safety entirely and add them back on the PC on which the account is configured.

Configuring Email Notifications

By default, you will receive weekly email notifications regarding the activities of those users you manage in Family Safety. You also will receive emails daily when users you manage have made requests to use or view content blocked by Family Safety settings.

The Family Safety website enables you to configure the emails that Family Safety sends you.

Changing Frequency of Request Emails

You can modify when you receive emails detailing user requests. You can also unsubscribe from emails so that you won't receive them.

1. From the Family Summary screen, tap a parent.

2. Tap Request Frequency.

3. Tap Immediately to receive emails immediately when requests are made.

4. Tap Daily Per Child to receive a daily email when requests are made.

5. Tap Off to unsubscribe from Family Safety request emails.

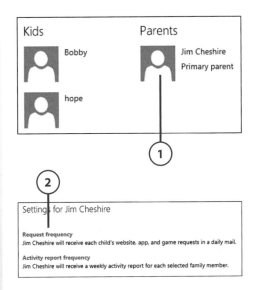

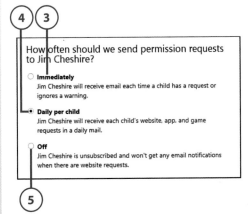

Changing Activity Report Email Settings

You can control which users you receive a summary for regarding PC activity. You can also unsubscribe from activity reports.

1. On the settings screen for a parent, tap Activity Report Frequency.

2. Tap Weekly and select the users for whom you would like to receive activity reports.

3. Tap Off to unsubscribe from activity reports on all users.

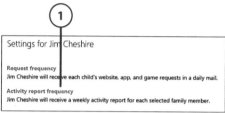

Settings for Jim Cheshire

Request frequency
Jim Cheshire will receive each child's website, app, and game requests in a daily mail.

Activity report frequency
Jim Cheshire will receive a weekly activity report for each selected family member.

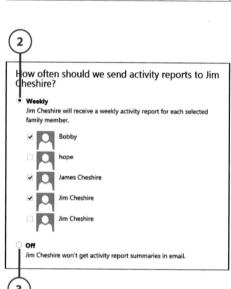

How often should we send activity reports to Jim Cheshire?

• **Weekly**
Jim Cheshire will receive a weekly activity report for each selected family member.

☑ Bobby

☐ hope

☑ James Cheshire

☑ Jim Cheshire

☐ Jim Cheshire

○ **Off**
Jim Cheshire won't get activity report summaries in email.

Restore your files when bad things happen.

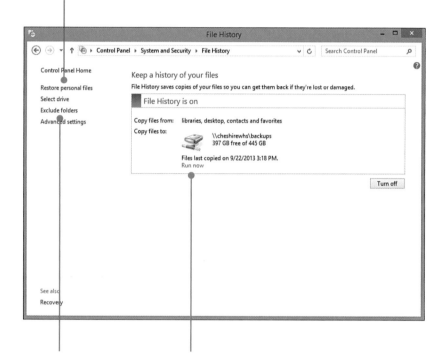

Control what gets backed up and when it happens.

Easily back up your important files to another PC or a network drive.

Backing Up Your Data

Your Surface uses a solid-state hard drive. That means that it has no moving parts and, because of that, it's faster and more mechanically reliable than a traditional hard drive. However, solid-state drives don't even approach 100% reliability. That means that the chances of losing data stored on your Surface at some point is higher than you might think. Because most of us store irreplaceable data on our PCs these days (things such as priceless photographs), the importance of a good backup strategy simply cannot be overstated.

Configuring and Starting File History

File History is a feature in Windows RT 8.1 that makes it easy to automatically save backups of critical files to an external drive or a network drive. If something happens to damage your critical files, you can easily restore them from the backed-up source.

It's Not All Good

File History Is Not a Full System Backup

File History backs up only your personal data files; it doesn't back up system files. If you want to back up folders that exist outside the folders backed up by File History, you'll need to add those folders to a library in Windows RT 8.1 and File History will back them up.

For more information on using Libraries in Windows RT 8.1, see Chapter 12, "HomeGroups and SkyDrive."

Starting Your First Backup

You start your first backup by opening File History in Control Panel and pointing it to a removable drive.

Quickly Backing Up to a Removable Drive

When you insert a removable drive, such as a USB thumb drive, Windows RT 8.1 displays a notification asking you to tap to choose what to do when the removable drive is inserted. If you tap that notification, you can then choose to use the drive to back up your files in one step.

Note that the option to use the drive for File History backups appears only if File History is turned off when the drive is connected.

1. Make sure that you either have a USB thumb drive or another removable drive plugged in to your PC.

2. Press Winkey+W and enter **File History** into the search box.

3. Tap File History in the search results.

4. After your drive is found, tap Turn On to enable File History and back up your files.

5. Wait until the first backup of your files is complete before you remove the drive.

Selecting a Different Drive

After you've set up File History for the first time, you can change to a different drive for your backups. For example, you might want to back up to another machine on your network.

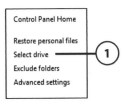

1. From File History in Control Panel, tap on Select Drive.

2. Select a drive from the list if your desired drive appears.

3. To add a network location for backup, tap Add Network Location.

4. Browse to the network location or enter a network path.

5. Tap Select Folder.

Existing Backups

If a backup already exists on the drive you choose, you will have an option to choose an existing backup. If you do, files backed up on the original drive will remain on that drive.

6. Tap OK to confirm the new drive.

7. Tap Yes to move your previously backed up files to the new drive; otherwise, tap No. (If your selected drive contains a previous backup, this step will be skipped.)

Unavailable Drives

File History is designed to accommodate situations where a backup drive becomes unavailable. If you unplug a removable drive, shut down a PC that you're backing up to, put your PC to sleep, and so on, File History will recognize that and will quietly wait until the drive is available again. When it sees the drive again, it will pick up right where it left off.

OK	Cancel

⑥

File History ×

Do you want to move your existing files, too?

We found some files you previously copied using File History. We can move them to your new drive so they'll still be available.

Yes	No	Cancel

⑦

Excluding Folders

You might want to exclude some folders from being backed up. For example, if you have temporarily saved some videos to your Videos library, you might want to exclude them from being backed up to save space in your backup drive.

1. From File History, tap Exclude Folders.

2. Tap Add.

Restore personal files
Select drive
Exclude folders ①
Advanced settings

Exclude from File History
If you don't want to save copies of specific folders or libraries, add them here.
Excluded folders and libraries:

No excluded items.

Add   Remove

②

3. Select the folder you want to exclude.

4. Tap Select Folder.

5. Tap Save Changes.

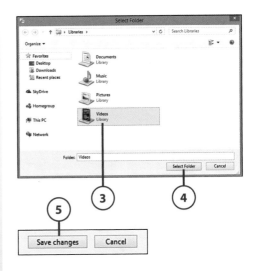

Choosing When Backups Happen

By default, your backups happen once per hour. You can change how often backups occur so that they occur more frequently or less frequently.

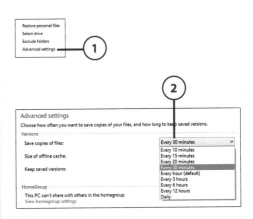

1. From File History, tap Advanced Settings.

2. Tap the Save Copies of Files dropdown and select a time interval for backups.

3. Tap Save Changes.

Backups Only When Changes Happen

File History, backs up a file only if the file has changed since the last time it was backed up.

Controlling Local Disk Usage

If your backup drive isn't available, File History still stores backups of files that change. It does so by using a portion of your local drive to store file changes in a cache. When the backup drive is available again, File History uses this cache to transfer backups made while the backup drive was unavailable.

By default, File History uses 5% of disk space on your local drive for caching. You can change how much disk space is used on the local drive for caching.

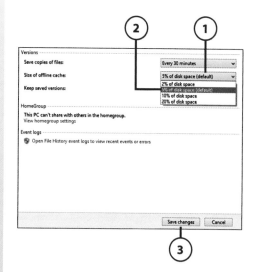

1. From the Advanced Settings screen, tap the Size of Offline Cache drop-down.

2. Choose a percentage of disk space that your backup cache should use on the local drive.

3. Tap Save Changes.

Controlling How Long Backups Are Kept

By default, File History saves your backups forever; however, this can quickly fill up your backup drive. You can control how long File History saves backups.

1. From the Advanced Settings screen, tap the Keep Saved Versions drop-down.

2. Choose a new value to set how long File History keeps your backups.

3. Tap Save Changes.

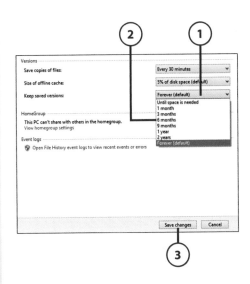

Restoring Files

File History makes it easy to locate the backed-up copies of your files and restore them. You can restore files to the same folder where they were located when File History backed them up, but you can also choose to restore files to a different location if you prefer.

Restoring Files to the Original Location

You can browse your backed-up files and easily restore one or more of them to the original file location.

1. From File History, tap Restore Personal Files.

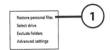

2. Double-click on a folder to browse files inside the folder.

3. Tap the up arrow to go back to the parent folder.

4. Select a previous path from the drop-down to quickly navigate to that path.

5. Tap the Gear icon, and then tap the View menu to change the view.

6. Tap Previous Version to see an earlier version of backed-up files.

7. Tap Next Version to see later versions of backed-up files.

8. Select one or more files or folders, and tap Restore to restore them to the original location.

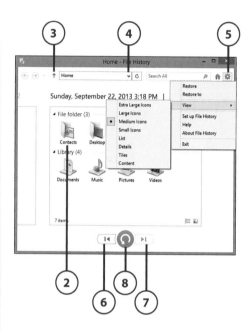

Resolving File Conflicts

If you attempt to restore a file to your local drive and that file already exists in the same location, File History enables you to overwrite the existing file, skip the file restore, or view information about the original file and the backed-up file so that you can decide what you would like to do.

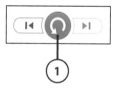

1. Tap Restore to restore one or more existing files.

2. Tap Replace to overwrite the existing file or files.

3. Tap Skip to skip the file or files.

4. Tap Compare Info for Both Files if only one conflict exists or Let Me Decide for Each File if multiple conflicts exist to compare the files and select those that you want to keep.

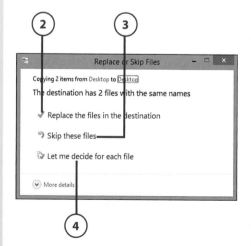

5. Check a location to keep all files in that location. (Files from the backup are listed on the left.)

6. Check individual files to keep specific files.

7. Check Skip to skip all files that have the same date and size.

8. Tap Continue to perform the actions you selected.

Resolving Conflicts

File History tries to help you resolve conflicts by bolding differences in file attributes. If one version of a file has a larger file size than another, File History displays the larger size in a bold font. If one file has a later date than another, the one with the later date appears bolded.

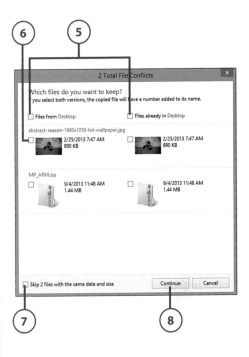

Restoring to a Different Location

If you would like to restore files to a location other than their original location, you can easily do that. This is useful in cases where you want an additional copy of a file on your local machine or if you want to restore files to a USB thumb drive or another removable device.

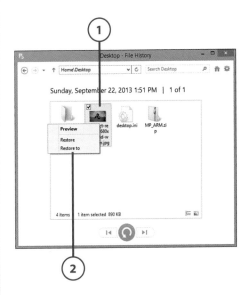

1. Select the files or folders you want to restore.

2. Tap and hold on one of the files to show the context menu, and tap Restore To on the context menu.

3. Select a location where you would like to restore the files or folders.

4. Tap Select Folder to restore the files.

Cleaning Up Files

By default, File History saves your backed-up files forever. In many cases, you will want to keep all versions of your files, but if you have files that change often, keeping all versions might mean that your backups use more disk space than you would like. Fortunately, you can clean up backed-up files so that you can free disk space on your backup drive.

Performing a Clean Up

When you clean up file versions, you can specify to clean up files older than a certain time frame, or you can clean up all versions except the most recent version. In no cases will cleaning file versions remove the latest version of a file.

1. From the Advanced Settings dialog in File History, tap Clean Up Versions.

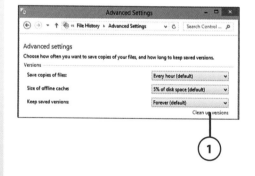

2. Select an option from the Delete Files drop-down. By default, a cleanup will remove all files older than one year, but you can modify that as desired.

3. Tap Clean Up to delete the file versions in the backup as per your selection.

File History Might Not Find Files to Delete

If File History cannot find any files in your backups that are old enough to be deleted given your selected timeframe, it will notify you and ask you to choose a shorter period of time.

It's Not All Good

Grab a Snack

If your backups are on a network location, it could take quite a while for File History to parse through your files and clean things up. Start the process, and then go grab a snack.

Troubleshooting File History

If you see error messages that don't provide enough detail for you to figure out what went wrong, or if you notice that files you expect to be backed up aren't getting backed up, you can view detailed logs from the Windows Event Viewer.

Viewing File History Event History

You can view details of all File History events in the Windows Event Viewer.

1. From the Advanced Settings screen in File History, tap the Open File History Event Logs link.

2. If prompted, enter your password for User Account Control.

3. Select an event to see more details about it.

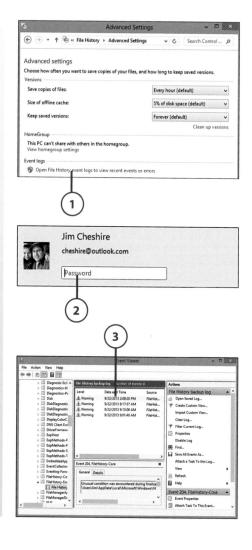

Search the Internet with
new search features in
Windows RT 8.1.

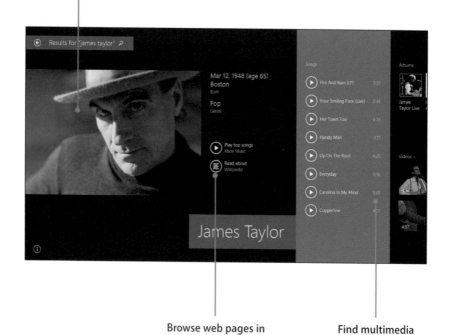

Browse web pages in
Internet Explorer 11.

Find multimedia
content easily.

Searching and Browsing the Internet

The Internet is a wonderful source of information, and your Surface makes it a pleasure to explore that information in many ways. In this chapter, I show you how you can search the Internet using Smart Search and how you can browse the content that you find using Internet Explorer, both in the Modern user interface and on the Windows Desktop.

Using Search

You can search the Internet by browsing to your favorite search engine and entering a search term, but you can get a better experience by using the integrated search experience in Windows RT 8.1. Search returns Internet search results in an easy-to-navigate view much like the Bing app that was included in Windows 8. However, Windows 8.1 adds many new features, including visually attractive and functional curated views (sometimes referred to as "hero search") of Internet content.

Smart Search

When you search in Windows RT 8.1, Windows provides search results from the Internet and from your PC. Windows also chooses how results are displayed based on your search topic. The internal Microsoft term for this feature is Smart Search, which is also how many outside of Microsoft also refer to it.

Searching for Web Pages with Smart Search

Searching the Internet using Smart Search presents you with search results in an easy-to-navigate view. Smart Search is used when your search scope is set to Everywhere.

1. Swipe in from the right side of your screen and tap the Search charm.

2. Enter your search term. (Make sure to leave the search scope set to Everywhere.)

3. Tap a suggestion or tap the magnifying glass to search the Internet. (You can also press Enter on your keyboard.)

4. Tap a search result to visit that page in your web browser.

5. Swipe right and left to view additional search results.

6. Tap See All Images (if available) to view all images related to your search term.

7. Tap the magnifying glass to start a new search.

8. Tap the Back arrow to see a previous search result.

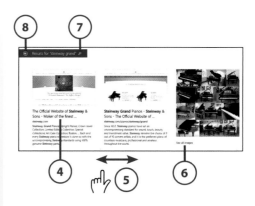

Copying a Search Result Link

You might want to copy the URL to a search result link so that you can send it to someone in email or use it in another app.

1. Search the Internet for a search term.

2. Swipe down on a search result.

3. Tap Copy Link to copy a link to the web page to your clipboard.

Searching for Images

When using Smart Search, image results are available for most searches. However, you can also explicitly search for images. Windows RT 8.1 has enhanced capabilities that make it easy to find images of a certain size, color hue, type, or layout, and you can even search for images that contain people.

SafeSearch

Internet searches for images and videos might turn up results that are inappropriate or offensive. SafeSearch is a feature built into Smart Search that does a great job of filtering out inappropriate and offensive results. I show you how to use SafeSearch later in this chapter.

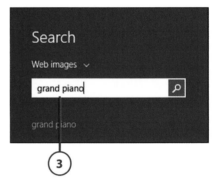

1. From the Search charm, tap Everywhere to change your search scope.

2. Tap Web Images.

3. Enter a search term and press Enter.

4. Swipe right and left to view search results.

5. Swipe up to filter your search results.

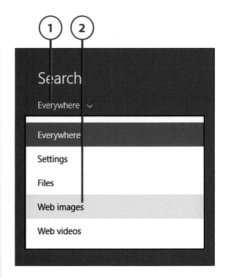

6. Tap Size and tap an image size to see only images of a certain size.

7. Tap Color and select a color option to see images of a certain hue, black-and-white images, or color images.

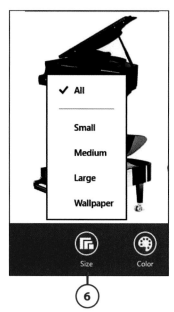

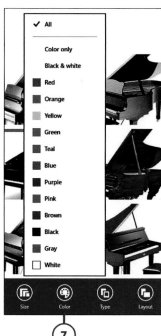

8. Tap Type and tap an image type to see images that are photos, clipart, or line drawings.

9. Tap Layout and tap a layout option to see images that are square, wide, or tall.

10. Tap People and tap Just Faces or Head & Shoulders to see images of people.

11. Tap an image to see a larger image.

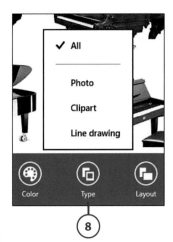

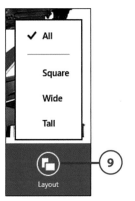

12. Tap the source URL to visit the web page that contains the image.

13. Tap the image to remove the title banner from the screen. (Tap again to display it again.)

14. Swipe up from the bottom of the screen to view additional options.

15. Tap Copy Link to copy a link to the image to your clipboard.

16. Tap Copy Image to copy the image itself to your clipboard.

17. Tap Save As to save a local copy of the image.

18. Tap Set as Lockscreen to set the image as your lock screen image.

19. Tap Back to return to the search results.

Searching for Videos

You can search for videos on any topic. Video results can be filtered by length or by resolution.

1. From the Search charm, change your search scope to Web Videos.

2. Enter a search term and press Enter.

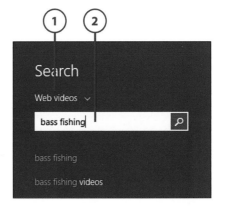

3. Tap a result to view the video.

4. Swipe left and right to see additional search results.

5. Drag down on a video to select it and then tap Copy Link to copy a link to the video to the clipboard.

6. Swipe up from the bottom of the screen and tap Length to filter on length.

7. Tap the desired length to apply the filter.

8. Tap Resolution to filter on video resolution.

9. Tap the desired resolution to apply the filter.

Video Categories

When searching for videos, search results will often include links to categories of videos based on your search term. Tapping one of those categories will refine your search.

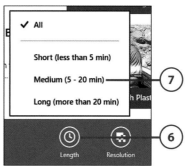

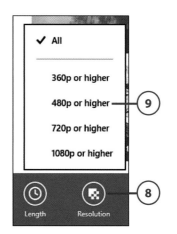

Using Hero Search

If you search for a popular location or person, you might find your search results returned to you in a style more like its own web page than a list of links. This kind of search result is called a hero search result. Microsoft created these results especially for Windows 8.1, and they make it incredibly easy to enjoy all that the Internet offers on these types of searches.

1. Enter a search for a popular location or person.

2. Tap an icon to see more information.

3. Swipe left to see additional Bing search results.

4. Tap on a search result to navigate to the page in Internet Explorer.

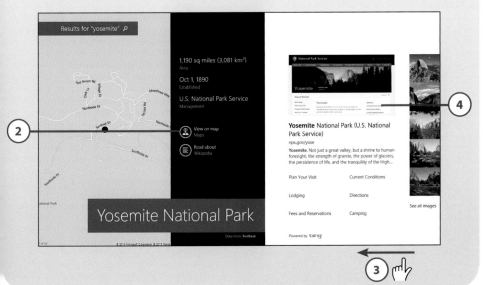

Experiment with Hero Search

Different types of hero searches present you with a different type of experience. For example, in the search results I show, you can tap to see Yosemite National Park in the Maps app or read about it in Wikipedia. However, if I search for a music artist, I can tap on a song from a list of popular songs to play the song in Xbox Music. Experiment with hero search to get a better feel for all that it offers.

Disabling Bing Search

If you would prefer that the Search charm only search for items on your PC and not search for Internet content, you can disable Bing search.

1. From the PC Settings screen, tap Search and Apps.

2. Tap Search.

3. Tap the Get Search Suggestions and Web Results from Bing slider to change the setting to Off.

Disabling Bing

When you disable Bing search, you are essentially removing any Internet results from your searches. If you want to search the Internet after disabling Bing search, you must launch a web browser and search from there.

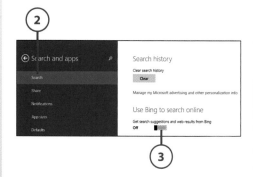

Clearing Your Search History

As you enter search terms, things that you've searched for in the past will appear as suggestions. You can clear this search history at any time.

1. From the Search and Apps settings screen, tap Search.

2. Tap Clear to clear your search history.

3. Tap Clear to confirm that you want to delete your search history.

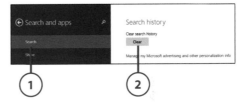

Clearing History

When you clear your search history, it clears the history only for searches made from within Windows. It does not clear your search history from the Bing website at www.bing.com.

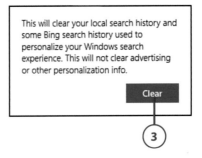

Changing Personalization Settings

By default, Bing returns results that are personalized for you using your search history, information from your Microsoft account, and your current location. You can control how much of your information is available to Bing when providing search results.

1. From Search settings, tap Get Personalized Results from Bing that Use My Location to share your history, Microsoft account information, and your current location to Bing for use in search results.

2. Tap Get Personalized Results from Bing to share your history and Microsoft account information but not your current location.

3. Tap Don't Get Personalized Results from Bing to prevent Bing from accessing any information about your search history, your Microsoft account, or your location.

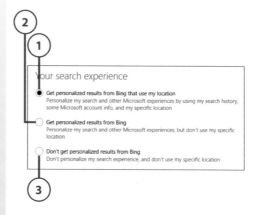

Controlling SafeSearch

SafeSearch is a feature in Windows that filters search results in an attempt to prevent inappropriate content (whether images, videos, or text) from appearing in your results. You can control how SafeSearch filters your search results and you can also turn off SafeSearch entirely.

1. From the Search settings screen, swipe up to access SafeSearch settings.

2. Tap Strict to filter out any inappropriate text, images, and videos from your search results.

3. Tap Moderate to filter out inappropriate images and videos, but not filter any text in your search results. (This is the default setting.)

4. Tap Off to disable SafeSearch entirely.

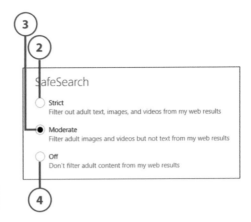

It's Not All Good

SafeSearch Isn't Perfect

Microsoft uses complex mechanisms to filter search results using SafeSearch, but it isn't perfect. There are still times when search results will contain content you might feel is inappropriate. It's also important to realize that SafeSearch only filters search results. Browsing directly to inappropriate websites when SafeSearch is enabled is still possible.

If you want to use a more robust system to protect users of your PC from inappropriate content, Family Safety is a great option. I cover Family Safety in detail in Chapter 5, "Using Family Safety."

Browsing Sites with Internet Explorer

Windows RT 8.1 comes with Internet Explorer 11, the latest version of Microsoft's web browser. Internet Explorer 11 is designed to work well with all modern websites, and it's also designed to be fast and powerful. In fact, Internet Explorer 11 is reported to be almost 45% faster than previous versions of Internet Explorer.

Two different versions of Internet Explorer are actually on your Surface. One runs in the Modern user interface (UI) and the other runs on the Windows Desktop. One of the main reasons why there are two versions is because most add-ons for Internet Explorer won't work on the Modern UI version, so the Desktop version is available for compatibility. Another reason is that compatibility mode (a special mode that fixes rendering problems with some websites) isn't available in the Modern UI version of Internet Explorer.

It's Not All Good

Websites and Touch

In my experience, some websites just don't work well with touch. Menus might not activate correctly, and other parts of the site might not work correctly.

Opening a Site in the Modern UI Internet Explorer

The Modern UI version of Internet Explorer provides a full-screen experience for viewing websites.

1. From the Start screen, tap the Internet Explorer icon.

2. Tap inside the textbox and enter a website address.

3. Tap a website suggestion to immediately navigate to the site.

4. Tap a link to follow it.

5. Reverse pinch to zoom in on a page.

6. Pinch to zoom out on a page.

7. Double-tap to quickly zoom in on part of a page.

8. Double-tap again to zoom out.

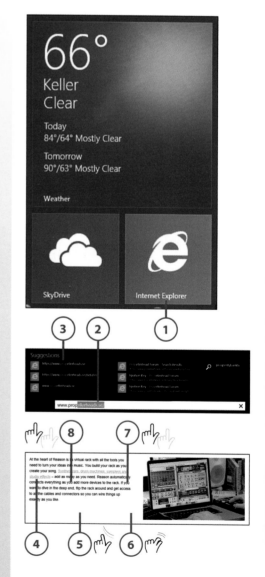

9. Swipe up from the bottom of the screen, and tap Back to go to the previously viewed page.

10. Tap Reload to reload the current page.

11. Tap Forward to move to the next page in your history.

Moving Forward

The Forward button is active only if you've tapped the Back button to go back in your browsing history. You can also move backward and forward through your browsing history by swiping left and right on a web page.

Using Reading View

Internet Explorer can reformat a web page for easier reading. This feature is called Reading view, and it's a great way to view a page that contains text and images in a column format.

1. While viewing a page, swipe up from the bottom of the screen and tap Reading view.

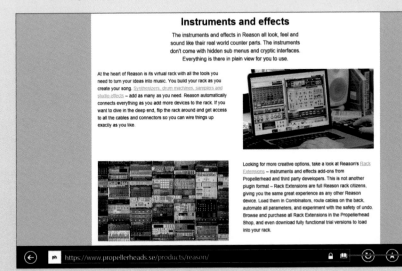

2. Swipe left and right to view the page's content.

3. Tap on a link to follow it.

4. Reverse pinch to zoom in.

5. Pinch to zoom out.

6. Double-tap to zoom in on a portion of the page.

7. Double-tap again to zoom out.

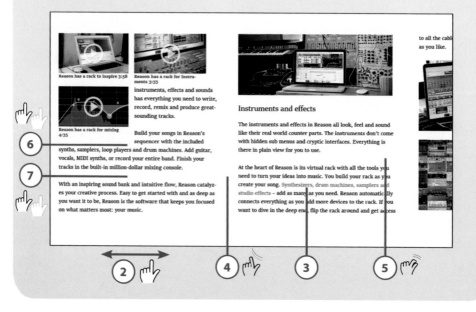

It's Not All Good

Limitations of Reading View

Some pages are quite a bit easier to read using Reading view, but some items on a page might not be available in Reading view. For example, there are videos embedded on the page I show in Reading view. You can see the Play button on the video, but it doesn't actually play the video. That's because Internet Explorer converted the video to a static image when it switched to Reading view.

It's also worth noting that when you click a link in Reading view, the new page opens back in Internet Explorer and does not open in Reading view. When you navigate back in your history to the page you were viewing in Reading view, it will also not return to Reading view automatically.

Changing Reading View Style and Font Size

If you want to change the textual style and the font size in Reading view, you can do so. You can choose a style that has more contrast and you can increase or decrease the font size.

1. From Internet Explorer's Settings charm, tap Options.

2. Tap a style to change the background color in Reading view.

3. Tap Font Size to select a new font size for the text in Reading view.

Viewing a Site in Desktop Internet Explorer

In rare cases, you might have a problem viewing a website in the Modern UI version of Internet Explorer. You might want to try viewing a page in the Desktop version of Internet Explorer if you see errors on a page, if parts of a page aren't visible, and so forth.

1. While viewing a web page, swipe up from the bottom of the screen and tap the Page Tools button.

2. Tap View in the Desktop.

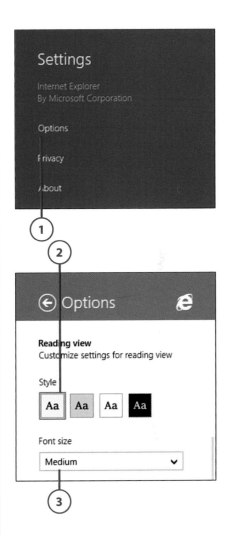

Pinning Web Pages to the Start Screen

If you find a particular useful web page, you might want to pin a link to that page to the Start screen so that you can access it quickly.

1. While viewing the page that you want to pin to the Start screen, swipe up from the bottom of the screen and tap Favorites.

2. Tap Pin to Start.

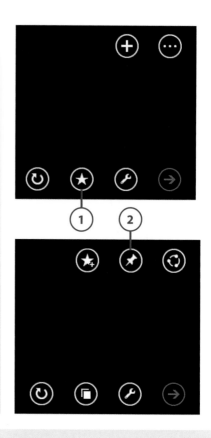

Searching a Web Page

You can search for a particular word or phrase on a web page.

1. While viewing the web page you want to search, tap the Page Tools button.

2. Tap Find on Page.

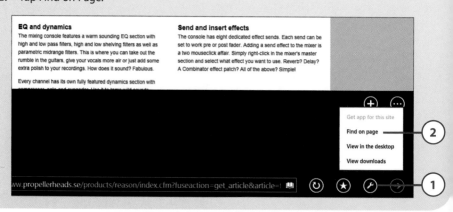

3. Enter a search term. All occurrences of the term are highlighted in yellow and the currently selected occurrence is highlighted in blue.

4. Tap Next to select the next occurrence.

5. Tap Previous to select the previous occurrence.

6. Tap Close to close the Find pane.

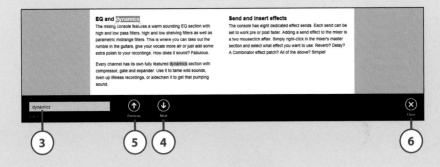

Setting the Zoom Level

You might find that increasing the zoom level in Internet Explorer makes it easier to read websites. On the other hand, if you have excellent vision, you can always decrease the zoom level to fit more content on the screen.

1. With Internet Explorer open, swipe in from the right of the screen and tap Settings.

2. Tap Options.

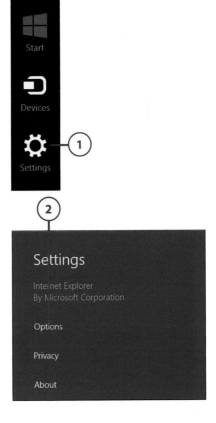

3. Drag the Zoom slider to the right to increase the zoom level.

4. Drag the Zoom slider to the left to decrease the zoom level.

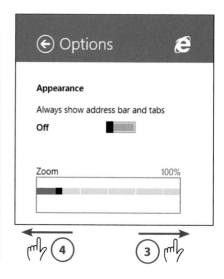

Protecting Your Privacy

Internet Explorer 11 provides several features designed to protect your privacy when browsing the Internet. You can also add capabilities to help prevent your Web activities from being tracked.

Adding a Tracking Protection List

As you browse the Internet, information regarding the pages you visit and what you're searching on can be sent to third-party companies. These companies use this information to track your browsing habits for marketing purposes. By adding a tracking protection list (TPL) to your browser, you can prevent most of these third-party companies from tracking your information.

1. From the Settings pane for Internet Explorer, tap Privacy.

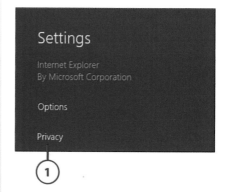

2. Tap Add Tracking Protection Lists.

3. Tap Add next to the TPL that you would like to add.

4. Tap Add List.

Enabling Do Not Track

Internet Explorer can send a special code to websites when you're browsing that lets third-party companies (such as advertising companies, social networks, and so forth) know that you do not want your activity to be tracked. As long as the third-party company honors the "do not track" code, your information will not be collected by the third party.

1. From the Privacy pane in Internet Explorer (access it through IE's Settings charm), tap the Do Not Track slider to change the setting to On.

2. Restart Internet Explorer.

It's Not All Good

Do Not Track Is Voluntary

Although "do not track" sounds like a great idea, it's a voluntary system. That means that only those third-party companies that have decided they will honor "do not track" are impacted by it. The truth is that most advertising companies and other companies that track your activities on the Web have not agreed to participate, so as of now, "do not track" is not as useful as it could be.

Blocking Third-Party Cookies

Cookies are small files that contain information about what you're doing on a web page. Although cookies don't typically contain any personally identifiable information, many people are concerned about advertising companies and information-collecting companies using cookies to track what they're doing on the Internet. Blocking all cookies would break most websites, but you can block cookies from sites other than the site you're visiting (referred to as third-party cookies) without impacting your Web experience.

1. From the Privacy panel in Internet Explorer (within IE's Settings charm), swipe up to locate the Cookies section.

2. Tap the Block All Third-Party Cookies slider to enable the setting.

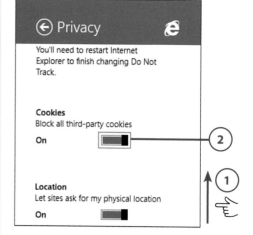

Disallowing Location Services

Some websites will request to use your current location to provide you with a more customized experience. When this happens, you'll be prompted. You can, however, configure Internet Explorer so that sites are not allowed to ask you for your location at all.

1. From the Privacy panel in Internet Explorer (within IE's Settings charm), tap the Let Sites Ask for My Physical Location slider to move it to the Off position.

2. To clear any previous permissions to use your location, tap the Clear button.

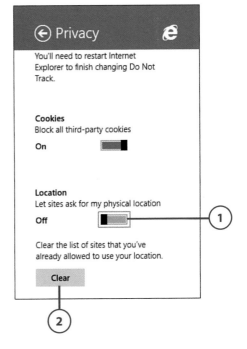

Controlling Web Services

Internet Explorer offers several web services from Microsoft to enhance your browsing experience. Each of these services sends information about your browsing session to Microsoft in order to work correctly. If you want, you can disable these services so that no information is sent to Microsoft.

1. In the Privacy panel in Internet Explorer (within IE's Settings charm), swipe up to reveal the Web Services section.

2. Tap the Flip Ahead with Page Prediction slider to disable the ability to swipe left on a web page to change pages in a multi-page story.

3. Tap the Suggestions slider to disable enhanced search and website suggestions as you type.

4. Tap the SmartScreen slider to disable Internet Explorer's security scan of websites and downloaded files.

5. Tap the Protected Media Playback slider to disable the automatic download of any required licenses for protected audio and video files.

6. Swipe up to reveal additional settings.

7. Tap Delete to delete any previously downloaded licenses for protected media.

8. Restart your PC to complete the deletion of licenses.

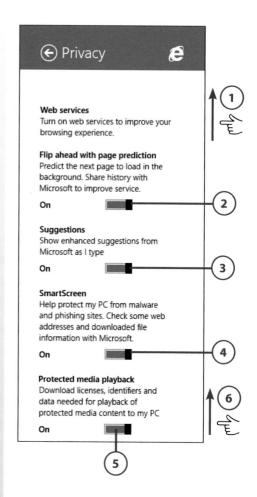

Using Tabs

Tabs enable you to have multiple web pages open at the same time. You can easily switch between tabs, open new tabs, and close tabs as desired.

It's Not All Good

Tabs Aren't Shared Between Modern UI and Desktop

Tabs that you open in the Modern UI version of Internet Explorer are not shared with the Desktop version. Therefore, if you open a series of tabs and then choose to view a site in the Desktop version of Internet Explorer, you won't see your tabs when you switch to the Desktop version.

Opening a Link in a New Tab

You can open a link on a page in a new tab. This is a convenient way to follow links on a page you're viewing while making it easy to return to the original page.

1. While viewing a page, tap and hold on the link you want to open in a new tab.

2. Tap Open in New Tab.

3. Tap the icon for the new tab that you've just created to activate the tab and view the page.

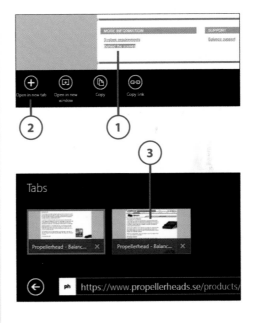

Creating a New Blank Tab

You can add a new blank tab if you want to enter a URL for a new site without closing the current site.

1. Swipe up from the bottom of the screen.

2. Tap New Tab to create a new tab.

3. Enter a URL to browse to a page in the new tab.

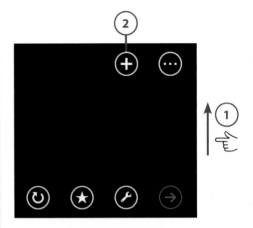

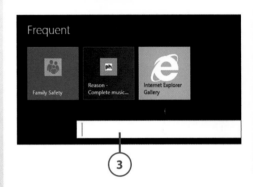

Closing a Tab

You can close individual tabs if you no longer want to leave them open.

1. Swipe up from the bottom of the screen.

2. Tap Close on the tab or tabs that you want to close.

3. Tap and hold and release on a tab and tap Close Other Tabs to close all other tabs.

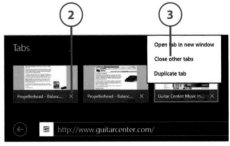

Opening an InPrivate Tab

InPrivate mode is a special mode of Internet Explorer. When you are browsing in InPrivate mode, Internet Explorer does not save your history, it doesn't save any temporary files while visiting websites, and it doesn't save any cookies. In other words, when you close an InPrivate tab, no evidence remains on your PC that you visited the sites you visited while InPrivate mode was active.

Keep Things Private

I frequently use InPrivate mode when I'm browsing the Internet looking for gift ideas for my wife and kids. By using InPrivate browsing, my wife won't find any clues about her gift if she happens to use my Surface to browse the Internet.

1. Swipe up from the bottom of the screen.

2. Tap the Tab Tools button.

3. Tap New InPrivate Tab.

4. Enter a URL to browse privately.

Ensuring You're InPrivate

When you are browsing using InPrivate mode, a blue InPrivate indicator appears in the address bar and at the bottom of the tab's icon.

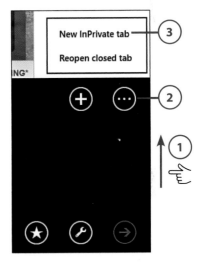

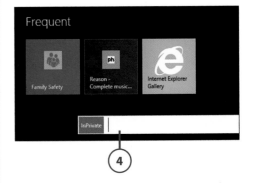

Reopening a Closed Tab

If you close a tab by mistake, you can easily reopen it. This only works for the last tab that was closed.

1. Swipe up from the bottom of the screen.

2. Tap the Tab Tools button.

3. Tap Reopen Closed Tab.

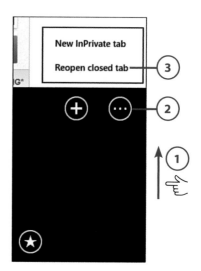

Favorites and Frequent Sites

Favorites make it easy to return to your favorite website. Internet Explorer also keeps track of the sites you visit so that you can easily return to them. Unlike tabs, favorites are shared between the Modern UI version and the Desktop version of Internet Explorer. If you add a favorite in one, the favorite is also added to the other.

Adding a Favorite

You can add a favorite while viewing a web page.

1. While visiting the page that you want to add as a favorite, swipe up from the bottom of the screen.

2. Tap the Favorites button.

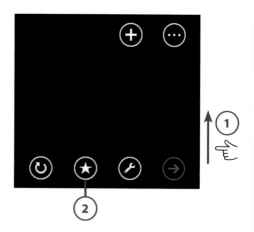

3. Tap the Add to Favorites button.

4. Enter a name for your favorite.

5. Select a folder for your favorite if desired or tap New Folder to create a new folder.

6. Tap Add to add the favorite.

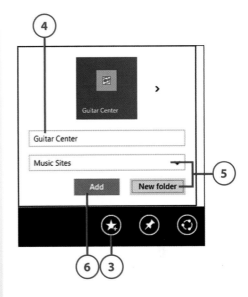

Browsing to a Favorite Page

You can quickly browse to a favorite page by tapping the page's tile in Favorites.

1. In Internet Explorer, swipe up from the bottom of the screen.

2. Tap the Favorites button.

3. Swipe to the left if necessary to scroll to your desired favorite page.

4. Tap the down arrow to select a Favorites folder if necessary.

5. Tap the tile for the Favorite to quickly navigate to the page.

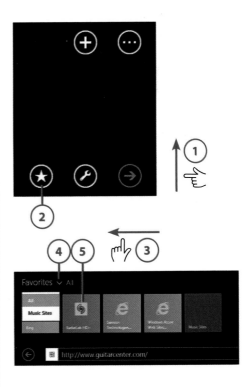

Opening a Favorite in a New Tab

You can also open a favorite page in a new tab.

1. Tap and hold on the tile for your favorite to display the context menu.

2. Select Open in New Tab to open the favorite in a new tab.

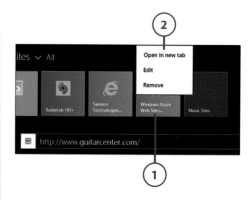

Deleting a Favorite

If you decide you no longer want a favorite, you can remove it from the Favorites list.

1. Tap and hold on the tile for the favorite you would like to delete to display the context menu.

2. Select Remove to delete the favorite.

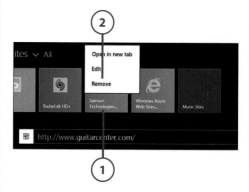

Editing a Favorite

If you would like to edit the name or URL of a favorite, you can edit it.

1. Tap and hold on the favorite you want to edit to display the context menu.

2. Tap Edit.

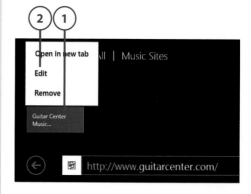

3. Edit the Favorite.

4. Tap Save.

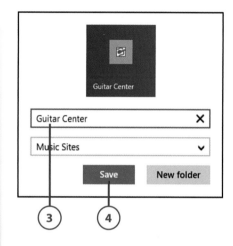

Visiting a Frequent Site

Internet Explorer keeps track of sites that you visit often and provides tiles so that you can quickly return to one of those sites.

1. Tap inside the Internet Explorer address bar.

2. Tap a tile for a frequent site.

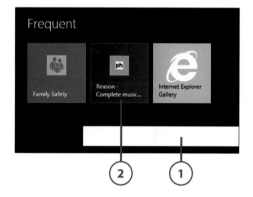

Opening a Frequent Site in a New Tab

You can open a frequently visited site inside a new tab.

1. Tap inside the address bar in Internet Explorer.

2. Tap and hold on a frequent site's tile to display the context menu.

3. Tap Open in New Tab to open the site in a new tab.

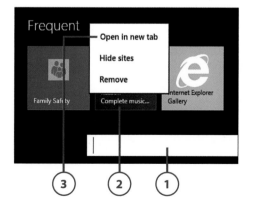

Deleting a Frequent Site Tile

You can remove the tile for a frequently visited site.

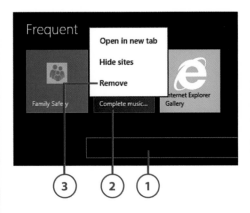

1. Tap inside the address bar in Internet Explorer.

2. Tap and hold on a frequent site's tile to display the context menu.

3. Tap Remove to delete the frequent site's tile.

Managing Website Passwords

Internet Explorer offers to save passwords for you when you log into sites. You can turn off this feature if you want to. You can also manage passwords that have been saved by Internet Explorer.

Saving a Password for a Site

You can save your password after logging in to a website.

1. Browse to a website that requires you to log in.

2. Enter your username and password and log into the site.

Log in

This part of the Propellerhead Software web site is secured and you will need to log in in order to proceed. Please enter your Username and Password below.

Username

Password

☐ Keep me logged in on this computer until I log out.

Log in   Lost password?

3. Tap Yes to save your password.

4. Tap Not for This Site to not save the password and not be asked again for this site.

5. Tap Ask Me Later to not save the password and to be asked again the next time you log into this site.

Your Passwords Are Safe

When you choose to save a password, Windows encrypts the data and saves it so that only your account has access to them. If someone else logs into your PC, that person cannot access your saved passwords.

Disabling the Offer to Save Passwords

You might have another password management tool that you use (LastPass is my personal favorite) and, therefore, might not want Internet Explorer to offer to save passwords. You can disable the feature if you want to.

1. From the Options panel in Internet Explorer, swipe up to see the Passwords section.

2. Tap the slider to change the setting to Off.

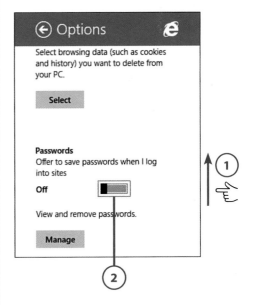

Viewing and Removing Saved Password Entries

You can view and remove password entries that you've saved in Internet Explorer. (The actual password cannot be viewed, but you can view the username.)

1. From the Passwords section in the Options panel, tap Manage.

2. Tap the entry you want to view or remove.

3. Tap Remove to remove the entry.

It's Not All Good

No Warning

There is no warning when you remove a password entry, so make sure you want to remove it before you tap Remove.

**Keep up with your
social networks.**

**Manage your
contacts.**

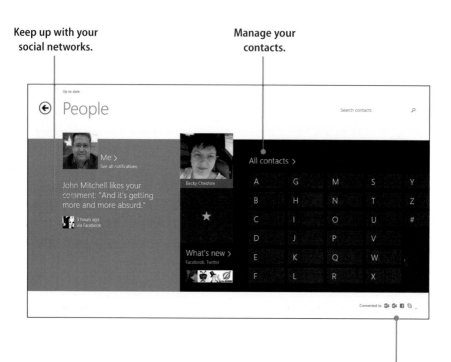

**Connect with
multiple accounts
and services.**

Connecting with People

Social is everywhere. Even if you're not all that into Twitter, Facebook, or other social media services, chances are you still have a core group of friends and family with whom you interact. Windows RT 8.1 is packed with features that make interacting with friends and family easy and convenient. The hub for all of the features is the People app.

Working with Contacts

Before you can connect with your friends and family on Windows RT 8.1, you need to add them as contacts. There are several ways to go about doing that. You can manually add each person, but you also can let Windows RT 8.1 automatically add your contacts from Facebook, Hotmail, Google, LinkedIn, and other websites.

Contacts in the Cloud

Cloud is the buzzword of the day, and for good reason. By using contacts from Hotmail, Facebook, Google, or another such service in the cloud (which really just means that it's on the Internet), you'll be able to maintain only one copy of your contacts. When you update a contact in one place, the update is automatically available everywhere else that contact is shared.

Adding Contacts from the Cloud

Contacts in Windows RT 8.1 are managed using the People app. The People app can pull in your contacts from just about any website where your contacts are stored.

1. From the Windows RT 8.1 Start screen, tap the People app.

People App Live Tile

By default, the People app is a Live Tile that might look different from the one pictured here, which has its Live Tile functionality disabled.

2. While in the People app, swipe in from the right side of the screen and tap the Settings charm.

3. Tap Accounts.

4. Tap Add an Account.

5. Tap an account.

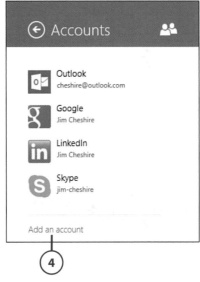

6. Enter any information the service requires (if necessary) and tap Connect.

7. If asked, enter your login information for the service.

Adding Services

Some services ask for your username and password before you see the Connect button. Others ask for your username and password after you tap Connect.

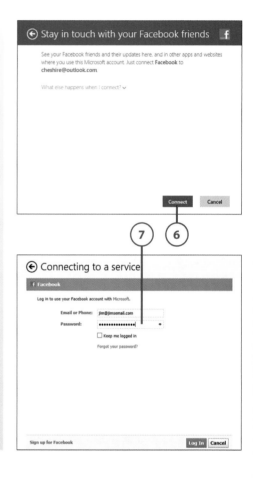

It's Not All Good

How Long?

After you configure a connection with one of your services, you might need to wait for several minutes before the People app synchronizes with the service and updates its content. I have noticed that Facebook is particularly slow, sometimes taking a few minutes to synchronize.

Changing Contact Sort Order

You might notice that, by default, the People app sorts your contacts by first name. If you would prefer, you can change it so that your contacts are sorted by last name.

1. From the Settings charm in the People app, tap Options.

2. Drag the slider to Yes to sort your contacts by last name.

3. Drag the slider to No to sort your contacts by first name.

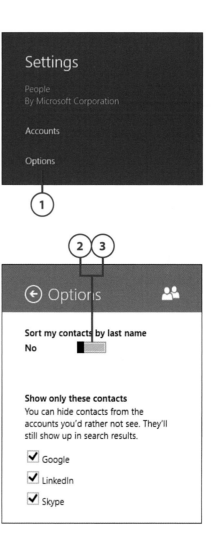

Filtering Your Contacts

You can filter your contacts so that only those contacts from the services you choose are displayed.

1. From the Options screen for the People app, check a service to include contacts from the service in your contacts list.

2. Uncheck a service to hide contacts from that service.

Linking Contacts

If you add contacts from more than one service, you might have some contacts that appear twice in your list. In most cases, Windows RT 8.1 is smart enough to display duplicate contacts as one contact, but if the name is slightly different, you might need to manually link duplicates.

1. Tap one of the contacts you want to link from your list of contacts.

2. Tap Link Contacts.

3. Windows RT 8.1 will suggest a contact to link in some cases. Select the contact if it's correct, or tap Choose a Contact to select a contact to link.

4. Choose one or more contacts to link to the contact that you selected from your list in step 1.

5. Tap Add.

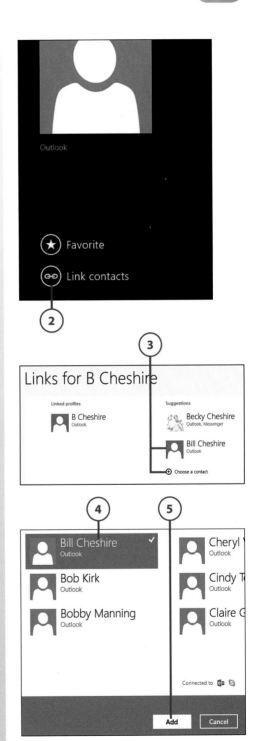

6. Tap Save to save the linked contacts.

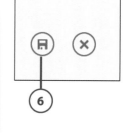

6

Linked Contacts

When you link two or more contacts, your contact list displays one contact entry for the contacts that you select to link together. Contact information for that single entry will be consolidated from all the linked contacts.

Unlinking Contacts

If you no longer want two or more contacts to be linked, you can unlink the contacts.

1. Tap the linked contact.

2. Tap Link Contacts.

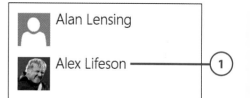

1

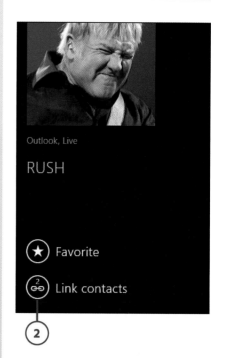

2

3. Tap the contact or contacts that you want to unlink.

4. Tap Save.

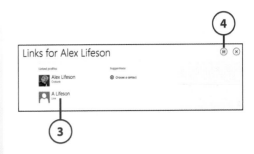

Making a Contact a Favorite

Tiles for your favorite contacts are displayed to the left of your contact list so that you can access them easily. You can easily set a contact as a favorite.

1. Tap a contact that you want to make a favorite.

2. Tap Favorite.

Removing a Favorite

You can easily remove a favorite by tapping the Favorite button again.

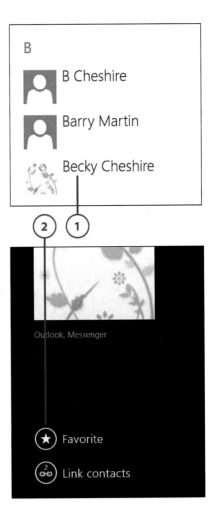

Pinning Contacts to the Start Screen

If you have a contact that you interact with often, you can pin the contact to the Start screen.

1. Tap a contact.

2. Swipe up from the bottom of the screen.

3. Tap Pin to Start.

4. Enter a name to display on the tile on your Start screen.

5. Tap Pin to Start.

Why Pin?

You might be wondering why you would want to pin a contact to your Start screen. As you go through the rest of this chapter and see all that ways in which you can interact with people in Windows RT 8.1, it should become obvious how convenient pinning is for your frequent contacts.

By the way, if you change your mind and want to unpin a contact from your Start screen, go through the same steps and tap Unpin from Start.

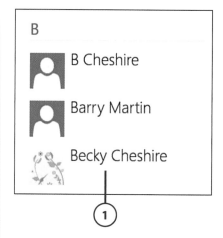

Creating a New Contact

You can create new contacts on your Surface 2. When you create a contact, you can choose an online service for the contact. Any device that synchronizes with the selected online service will have access to the contact that you create.

1. From the People screen, swipe up from the bottom of the screen.

2. Tap New Contact.

3. Select the service for the account.

4. Enter the contact's information.

5. Tap the plus sign to add a new field, such as a new phone number or a business address.

6. Tap Save to save the new contact.

Contacts Are Not Local

It's important for you to realize that when you add a contact on your Surface 2, that contact isn't specific to your Surface 2. You are actually adding an online contact for the service you select, and that contact will be available to all devices that use the service, not just your Surface 2.

Deleting a Contact

You can delete a contact from the contact list in the People app. Deleting a contact removes the contact from all devices that synchronize with the service that originally contained the contact.

1. From the All Contacts screen, tap the contact you would like to delete.

2. Swipe up from the bottom of the screen.

3. Tap Delete.

4. Tap Delete to confirm that you want to delete the contact.

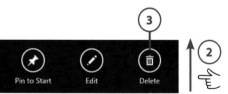

It's Not All Good

Take Care When Deleting Contacts

Contacts in Windows RT 8.1 come from one or more online services. If you delete a contact from your Surface 2, you are actually deleting the contact from the online service, and if you have other computers or devices (such as your smart phone) that use the same online service for contacts, the contact will be removed from those devices as well.

Removing All Contacts from a Service

As you've seen, when you add a connection to Twitter, Gmail, Facebook, or another service, any contacts for that service are added to your contact list. If you want to remove those contacts from your Surface 2, you can simply remove the connection with the service containing the contacts.

1. From the People app, tap any of the service icons in the lower-right corner.

2. Tap the account that you want to remove.

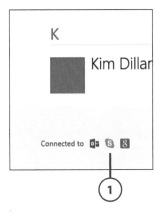

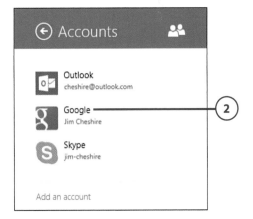

3. Tap the Manage This Account Online link.

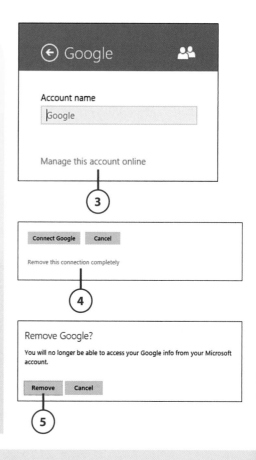

Easier Removal

Some accounts might have a Remove Account button in the Accounts tab that you can click to remove the account in one easy step.

---

4. In the web page for the account, tap the Remove This Connection Completely link.

5. Tap the Remove button to confirm the removal of the service.

Editing a Contact

You can edit a contact in cases where information has changed or where you want to add additional information for a contact.

1. Tap a contact that you would like to edit.

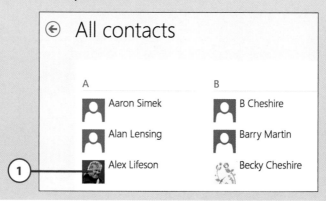

2. Swipe up from the bottom of the screen.

3. Tap Edit.

4. If the contact is a linked contact, select the contact that you would like to edit from the pop-up menu. (Note that the items on the pop-up menu will show the name of the account for the contact but not the name.)

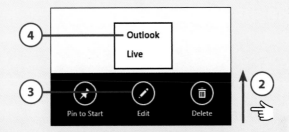

5. Edit the contact's existing information, if necessary.

6. To add additional information, tap a plus sign.

7. Select the information you would like to add, and enter it.

8. To change the name for a field, tap the current field name and select a new name from the list.

9. To delete a value in a field, tap inside the field, and then tap the X to delete the value.

10. Tap Save to save the contact.

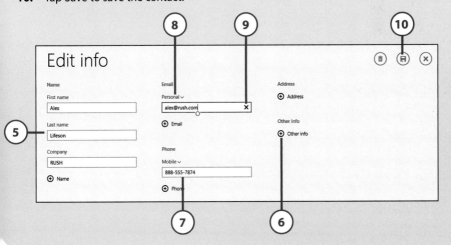

Contacting Someone from the People App

There are various ways that you can contact someone while viewing their information from within the People app.

Options for Contacting People

The communication options available to you in the People app vary based on the contact information available for a particular person.

1. Tap a contact to view the contact's details.

2. To send an email to the contact, tap Send Email to send email to the address that is displayed for the contact.

3. To send an email to an alternative email address, tap the down arrow and tap one of the contact's other email addresses.

4. To send an SMS message to the contact, tap Send Message. (SMS messages are sent using Skype.)

5. To call someone's phone, tap Call. (You might need to select an app to use to call telephone numbers if you haven't done so already.)

Using Email

If you would like detailed information on how to use the Email app in Windows RT 8.1, see Chapter 9, "Using Mail."

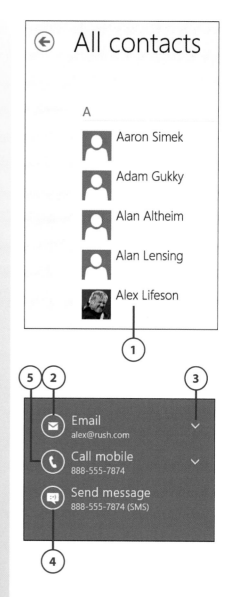

6. To call an alternative number for
the contact, tap the down arrow
and select a number to call.

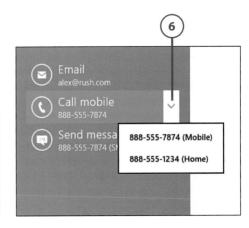

Social Networking

Windows RT 8.1 integrates social networking so that you can easily post to
social networks, see what's new with your friends and family, and get notified
when someone interacts with you on a social network.

Posting to Social Networks

The People app provides a quick and easy interface for posting to social networks to
which you connect.

1. From the People app, swipe down from the top of the screen and tap Me.

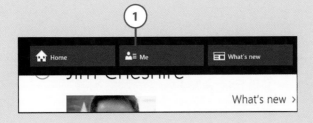

2. Tap the down arrow to select a social network if desired.

3. Enter a status update.

4. Tap Send to post to your social network.

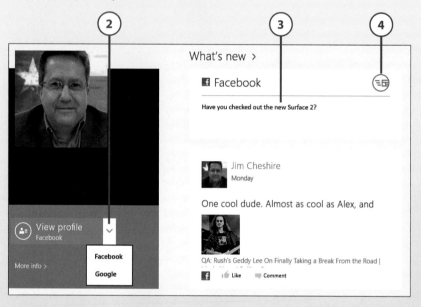

Viewing Updates on Social Networks

You can view all of your status updates, comments, and other interactions with people on your social networks.

1. From the People app, swipe down from the top of the screen and tap What's New.

2. Swipe left and right to see more.

3. Tap Favorite on a tweet to mark it as a favorite.

4. Tap Undo Favorite to unmark a tweet as a favorite.

5. Tap Like on a Facebook post to like it.

6. Tap Unlike on a Facebook post to unlike it.

7. Tap the Twitter icon to see the tweet in Internet Explorer.

8. Tap the Facebook icon to see the post in Internet Explorer.

9. Tap Retweet to retweet a tweet.

10. Tap a tweet, or tap Reply to tweet a reply.

11. Tap a Facebook post, or tap Comment to comment on a post.

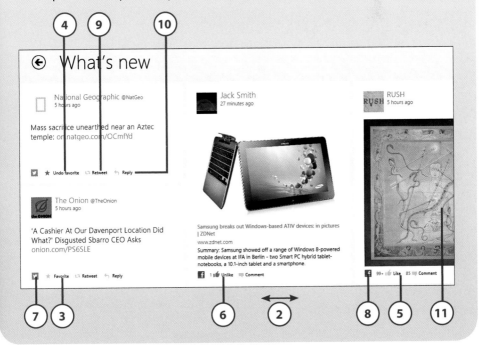

12. Swipe up from the bottom of the screen, and tap Refresh to refresh updates.

13. Swipe up from the bottom of the screen, and tap New Post to post to a social network.

Skype

Skype is a messaging application that supports text, voice, and video. It comes pre-installed on your Surface 2 and you can use it to communicate with people in your contact list. You can see Skype and get a general overview in the "Great Apps for Your Surface 2" section of Chapter 22, "Enhancing Windows with Apps".

Sharing Content with People

Windows RT 8.1 enables apps to share content using what Microsoft calls a sharing contract. Any app that implements this feature shows up on the Share charm. By default, Internet Explorer, the People app, and the Mail app allow for sharing of content, but you can add more apps from the Windows Store.

Sharing App Content with Social Networks

Windows RT 8.1 makes it easy to share information with social networks. In this example, I show you how you can share a website with a social network, but sharing works the same way for any app that supports it.

Share Part of a Web Page

If you would like to share part of a web page rather than a link to the page, select the content you want to share before sharing. Only the content you select will be shared.

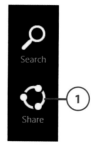

1. From a web page in Internet Explorer, swipe in from the right side of the screen and tap the Share charm.

Shortcut Key for the Share Charm

You can press Winkey+H to quickly access the Share charm.

2. Tap People.

3. Tap the arrow and choose one of your connected social networks.

4. Enter a message you would like to include with your post.

5. Tap Send.

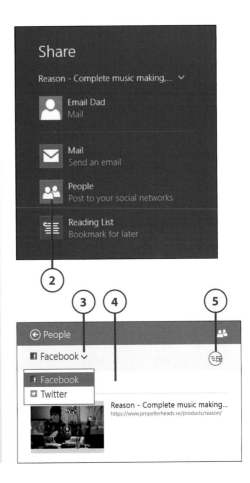

It's Not All Good

Cannot Share from Desktop Apps

You can only share from Windows Store apps. If you are viewing a website in Internet Explorer on the desktop, you will be unable to share the site using the Share charm.

Emailing App Content to Contacts

The Share charm also makes it easy to email information from an app to one or more contacts. Again, this example demonstrates sharing a web link, but other apps enable you to share additional types of information.

1. From the Share pane, tap Mail.

2. Enter one or more email addresses.

3. Enter a message for your email.

4. Tap Send to send the email.

Easily Share with Email

When you share something with an email contact, that contact is added to a shortcut list of email addresses that appears at the top of the Share pane. The next time you want to share something with that contact, you can tap his or her email address in the shortcut list and an email is automatically addressed to the contact.

Sharing a Screenshot

You might want to share an image of your screen with one of your contacts. Windows RT 8.1 makes it easy using the Share charm.

1. While displaying the screen you want to share, swipe in from the right of the screen and tap Share.

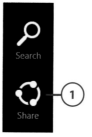

2. In the Share panel, tap the down arrow and tap Screenshot.

3. Tap Mail to share your screenshot. (Screenshots cannot be shared with the People app.)

4. Enter a mail recipient.

5. Change the subject if you want to.

6. Enter a message if you want to.

7. Tap Send.

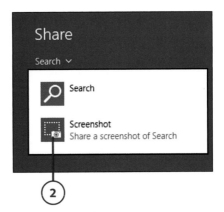

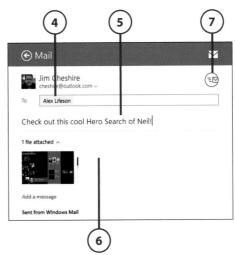

Listing Share Apps in Alphabetical Order

When you access the Share pane, the apps that you use most often when sharing are listed at the top of the list by default. You can turn off this feature so that apps are listed in alphabetical order instead.

1. From the PC Settings screen, tap Search and Apps.

2. Tap Share.

3. Tap the Show Apps I Use Most Often at the Top of the App List slider to change the setting to Off.

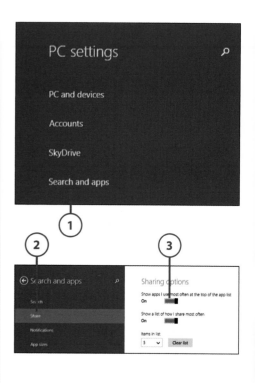

Managing the List of Often-Shared Choices

As I mentioned earlier, when you share an item using email, the email address of the person with whom you shared the item appears on a shortcut list at the top of the Share pane. This shortcut list is populated as you share items, showing the ways in which you share most often so that you can access them quickly. You can control how many items appear in this list (up to 9) and you can clear this list if you want.

1. From the Search and Apps settings screen, tap Share.

2. Tap the Items in List drop-down menu and select the maximum number of items you want to appear in the list.

3. Tap Clear List to clear the list of often-shared methods.

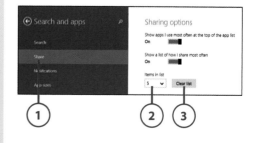

Disabling the Often-Shared Shortcut List

You can turn off the often-shared shortcut list if you don't want to list ways you share most often in the Share pane.

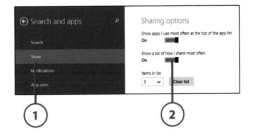

1. From the Search and Apps screen, tap Share.

2. Tap the Show a List of How I Share Most Often slider to change the setting to Off.

It's Not All Good

Disabling the Shortcut List Clears the List

When you disable the often-shared shortcut list, it clears items from the list. If you re-enable the list, you will start fresh again and new shortcuts are added as you share additional items.

Read and send mail from multiple email accounts.

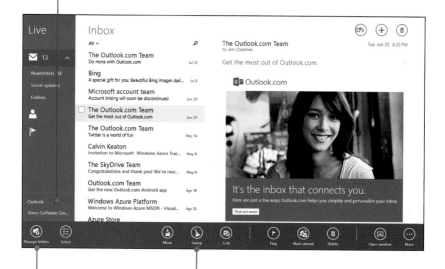

Organize your email with folders.

Manage your inboxes and reduce clutter.

9

Using Mail

Like many Windows Store apps, the Mail app that comes with Windows RT 8.1 seems simple at first glance, but as you dig into it, you soon realize that it is a feature-rich and powerful app for managing your email. It has the capability to connect to online services, so keeping your email synchronized across all of your devices is simple to do.

Adding and Managing Email Accounts

If you sign in to your Surface 2 using your Microsoft account, the Mail app automatically configures itself for your Microsoft email. You can easily add your other email accounts as well. You do so by tapping the Settings charm and then tapping Accounts to get to the Accounts page.

Adding an Outlook.com (Hotmail) Account

You can add your Outlook.com, Live.com, or MSN email account to the Mail app.

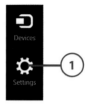

1. From the Mail app, swipe in from the right side of the screen and tap Settings, or press Winkey+I on your keyboard.

2. Tap Accounts from the Settings pane.

3. Tap Add an Account in the Accounts pane.

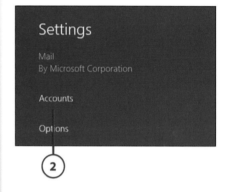

4. Tap Outlook.com.

5. Enter your Outlook.com email address.

6. Enter your password.

7. Tap Connect.

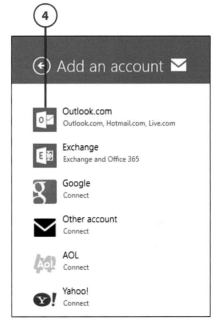

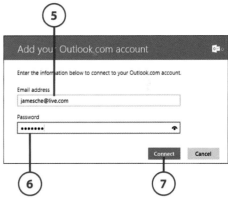

Adding an Exchange Account

Exchange accounts are used for Exchange servers and Office 365 email accounts, which you'll most commonly find in corporate office environments.

1. From the Accounts pane in the Mail app, tap Add an Account.

2. Tap Exchange.

3. Enter your email address.

4. Enter your password.

5. If you are required to enter a server address or domain name information, tap Show More Details.

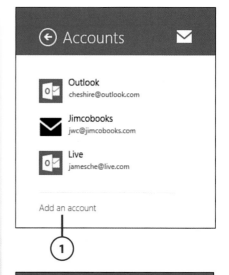

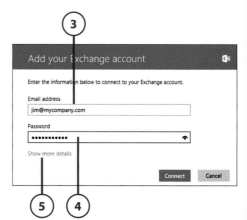

6. Enter your mail server's address.

7. Enter your domain name.

8. Enter your username.

9. Tap Connect.

10. If your network administrator requires it, your PC might need to be made more secure. If so, tap Enforce These Policies to perform the necessary configuration.

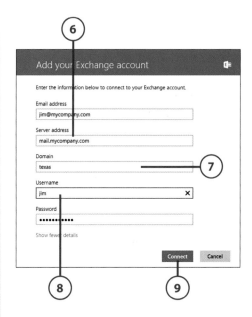

Adding a Google Account

You can add a Google account so that you can read your Gmail in the Mail app.

1. From the Add an Account pane in Mail, tap Google.

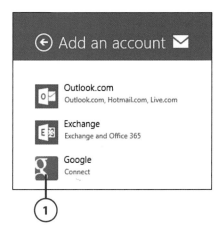

2. Enter your email address.

3. Enter your password.

4. Tap Sign In.

5. Tap Accept.

6. Tap Yes to allow Windows to remember your username and password for Google. Otherwise, tap Skip.

AOL and Yahoo! Accounts

You can add an AOL account or a Yahoo! account following the same procedures outlined for adding a Google account.

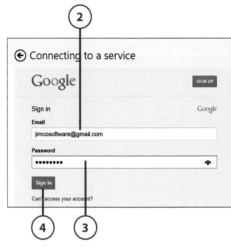

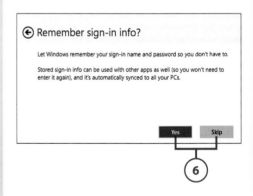

Adding a Custom Account

If you have your own domain name and you want to add email for that account, you can do that easily.

1. From the Add an Account pane, tap Other Account.

2. Select the type of account you are adding. (If you are unsure, ask your email provider.)

3. Tap Connect.

4. Enter your email address.

5. Enter your password.

6. Tap Show More Details if you need to enter additional server information.

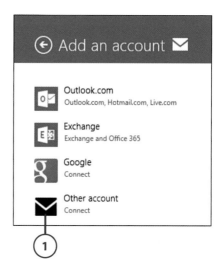

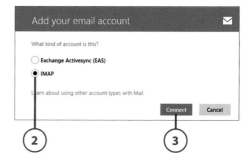

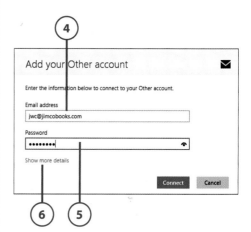

7. Enter your incoming mail server address.

8. If your incoming mail server doesn't support SSL, uncheck the Incoming Server Requires SSL box.

9. Change the incoming mail server port number if necessary.

10. Enter the outgoing email server address.

11. If your outgoing server doesn't support SSL, uncheck the Outgoing Server Requires SSL box.

12. Change the outgoing mail server port number if necessary.

13. If your outgoing server doesn't require authentication, uncheck the authentication check box.

14. If your outgoing server does use authentication and the username and password are the same as the incoming server's, check the Use the Same Username and Password to Send and Receive Email checkbox.

15. Tap Connect.

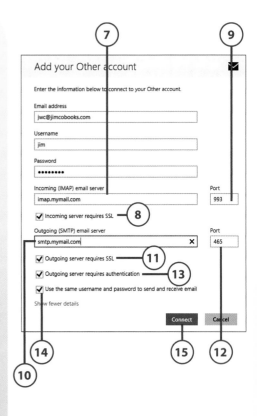

It's Not All Good

IMAP Only

Some email providers only provide what's known as POP email. The Mail app requires that you use IMAP email, and that's not the same as POP. If your email provider doesn't provide IMAP email, you're better off going with a Hotmail or Gmail account. POP is an old method of using email, and IMAP is far superior.

Outgoing Email Port

If you uncheck the box to use SSL for outgoing mail, the Mail app changes the port to 25 automatically. Port 25 is the port typically used for SMTP (outgoing) email, but many Internet providers block that port from being used. If you are using port 25 and you are unable to send email, try changing the outgoing port to port 587.

Setting When and How Much Email Is Downloaded

By default, the Mail app downloads new emails as they arrive on the mail server and downloads all email from the last two weeks. You can modify how often Email downloads email and how much email it retrieves as well.

1. From the Accounts pane, tap an account to change the settings for the account.

2. Tap the Download New Email drop-down and select how often new email should be downloaded from the server.

3. Tap the Download Email From drop-down and select how much email you want to download.

4. Drag the Automatically Download External Images slider to Off if you don't want the Mail app to automatically download images in emails.

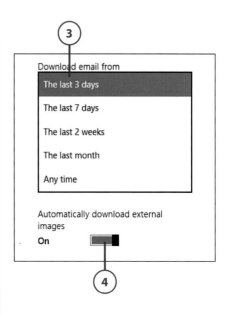

Changes Apply Immediately

When you change the settings for an email account, the change is applied immediately. There is no OK button or anything like that. After you've made the changes you want to make, you can just click outside the Account Settings pane to return to the Mail app.

Manually Syncing Email

You can force a manual email sync by swiping up from the bottom of the screen, tapping the More button, and then tapping the Sync button.

Renaming an Account

The Mail app chooses a name for accounts that you add based on the type of account. You can easily change the name to something more descriptive.

1. From the Accounts pane, tap an account to change the settings for the account.

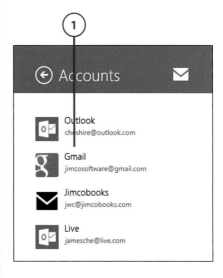

2. Enter a new value for the Account Name.

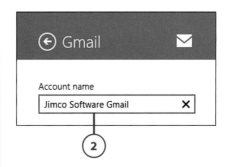

Choosing What to Sync

You can sync email, contacts, and calendars from accounts that you add in the Mail app. (Note that not all of these are available for every service.) However, you don't have to sync all three of these. You can pick and choose what to sync from each account that you add.

1. From the Accounts pane, tap an account to change the settings for the account.

2. Check Email to sync email from the account.

3. Check Contacts to sync contacts from the account.

4. Check Calendar to sync calendars from the account.

Contacts and Calendars

Contacts are synchronized with the People app and calendars are synchronized with the Calendar app. The People app is covered in Chapter 8, "Connecting with People." The Calendar app is covered in Chapter 10, "Using Calendar."

Automatically Organize Your Mail

The Mail app can automatically organize your email by placing emails that appear to be newsletters and emails that appear to be updates from social networks into their own folders for you. If you want to, you can disable this feature. (This feature is only available for Outlook.com accounts.)

1. From the Accounts pane, tap the account that you want to change.

2. Uncheck Show Newsletters Separately to stop the Mail app from automatically organizing newsletter emails.

3. Uncheck Show Social Updates Separately to stop the Mail app from automatically organizing your social network updates.

Changing an Account Password

If you're a security-conscious computer user, you will likely want to change your passwords on a regular basis. After you change your password for an account that you use in the Mail app, you'll need to change the password that the Mail app uses so that you can still synchronize with the account.

1. From the Accounts pane, tap the account you want to change.

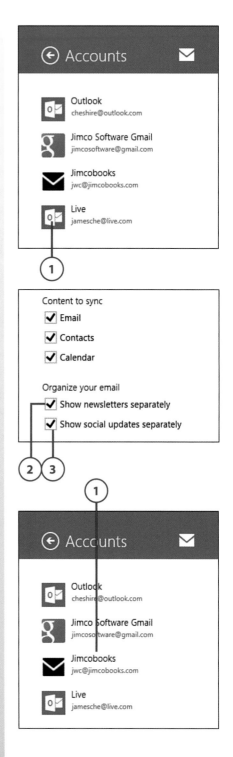

2. Scroll down in the Settings pane and enter your new password.

Controlling Account Email Notifications

By default, you will only see notifications when new email from your favorite people arrives in your inbox; however, you can enable notifications for all contacts or disable notifications entirely if you want. Each of your email accounts has its own notification setting, so you can decide which accounts you want to see notifications for and which ones you don't.

1. From the Accounts pane, tap the account you want to change.

2. Slide up in the Settings pane to reveal the Show Email Notifications setting.

3. Tap the Show Email Notifications drop-down list and select the desired notification setting.

Favorite People

The mail app allows you to create a separate list of favorite people for each of your mail accounts. These favorites are not related to favorite contacts that you create in the People app.

For details on how to add people to the favorite list for an email account, see "Adding and Removing Favorite People" later in this chapter.

Removing an Account

If you decide you no longer want to synchronize with an account, you can remove the account from the Mail app.

1. From the Accounts pane, tap the account that you would like to remove.

2. Slide up to move to the bottom of the Settings pane.

3. Tap Remove Account.

4. Tap All My Synced PCs to remove the account from all of your PCs.

5. Tap This PC to remove the account from only this PC.

Don't Fear Removal

Don't worry about removing an account—you can always add it back again. Because the Mail app uses cloud technology, it's really just a viewer for email that is stored on a server on the Internet. If you remove an account, it simply removes the Mail app's capability to view that account. It doesn't actually delete any email.

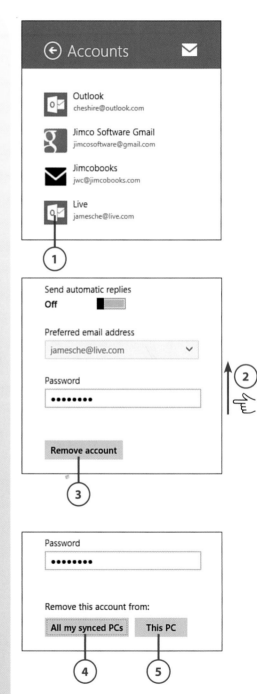

Reading and Organizing Email

The Mail app uses tabs to separate your email accounts. When you tap one of your accounts in the Mail app, you see the folders available for that email account as well as the email messages in the selected folder.

Reading an Email

The Mail app supports HTML emails as well as plain text emails. HTML is the technology used to create websites, and emails created in HTML can contain pictures along with richly formatted text.

1. Tap the desired account.

2. Tap a folder that contains your email.

3. Tap an email from the list to view the email in the reading pane.

Unread Emails
Folders show the number of unread messages in the folder immediately to the right of the folder name. Unread emails in the email list have a bolded subject line.

4. Swipe up and down to scroll in the reading pane.

5. If necessary, you can also swipe right and left to view wider emails.

6. Tap a link in an email to launch your web browser and navigate to the link.

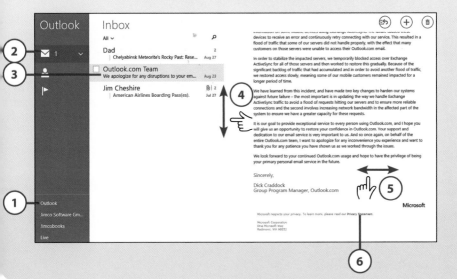

Viewing or Saving Email Attachments

Pictures that are attached to emails will show up as a thumbnail so that you can preview the picture. Other attachments show as file icons. You can save an attachment to your PC so that you can view them.

1. Select an email that includes an attachment. Emails with an attachment display a paperclip icon.

2. Tap the attachment to open it with the app associated with the file type of the attachment.

3. Tap and hold and then tap Open With to open the attachment with a different app.

4. To save the attachment, tap Save.

5. Browse to the location where you want to save the file.

6. Enter a name for the file.

7. Tap Save.

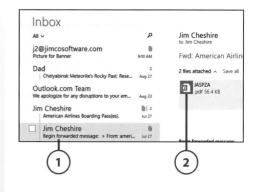

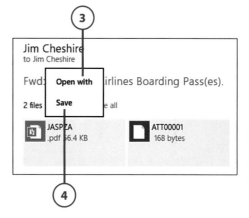

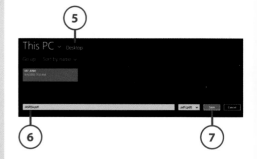

Marking Emails Read or Unread

When you view an email, it is marked as read for you automatically. You can mark one or more emails read or unread in one step without displaying the email.

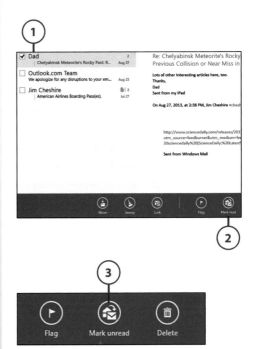

1. Select one or more emails. You can select multiple email messages by swiping left on each message you want to select. (Swiping left on a selected message deselects it.)

2. Tap Mark Read to mark all selected emails read.

3. Tap Mark Unread to mark all selected emails unread.

Tip

If you select both read and unread email messages, you will see the Mark Read button if the last email you selected is unread. You will see the Mark Unread button if the last email you selected has already been read.

Deleting Email Messages

You can delete one or more email messages. When you delete emails, they are moved to the Deleted Items folder. If you delete emails from within the Deleted Items folder, they are deleted permanently.

1. Select one or more email messages that you want to delete.

2. Tap the Delete button. (If you selected multiple emails, you can also tap Delete at the bottom of the screen.)

Deleting with the Keyboard

You can also press the Delete key or Ctrl+D on your keyboard to delete email messages.

Deleting All Messages in a Folder

You can delete all messages in a folder in one step.

1. Tap a folder in which you want to delete all messages.

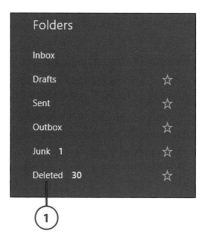

2. Swipe up from the bottom of the screen.

3. Tap Manage Folders.

4. Tap Empty Folder.

5. Tap Yes to delete all messages in the folder.

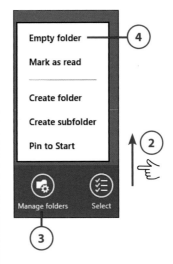

Undeleting Email Messages

If you've unintentionally deleted one or more mail messages and you would like to restore them, you must move them out of the Deleted Items folder.

1. Tap the down arrow for the account's inbox.

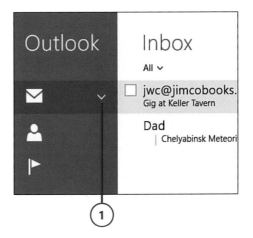

2. Tap Folders.

3. Tap the Deleted folder.

4. Select one or more messages that you would like to undelete.

5. If you selected only one message, swipe up from the bottom of the screen.

6. Tap Move.

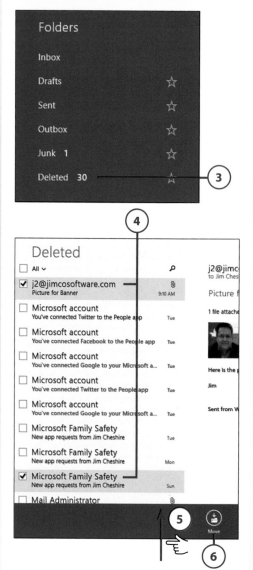

7. Tap the folder into which you want to move the undeleted message or messages.

8. Tap the inbox icon to return to your inbox.

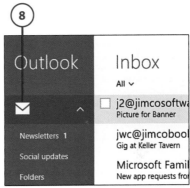

Pinning a Folder to the Start Screen

There is a Mail tile on the Start screen that launches the Mail app. If the Mail app is already running when you tap the Mail tile, it opens to the same folder you were in during your last email session. If the Mail app is not already running, it launches into the inbox of your first email account. You might instead want a tile on the Start screen that will open the Mail app and show you the contents of a specific folder immediately. You can do that by pinning the folder to the Start screen. You can do this for any folder in any account.

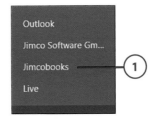

1. Tap the account that contains the folder you want to pin.

2. Tap the down arrow to view folders.

3. Tap the folder that you want to pin to the Start screen. If the folder isn't visible, tap Folders and then tap the folder.

4. Swipe up from the bottom of the screen.

5. Tap Manage Folders.

6. Tap Pin to Start.

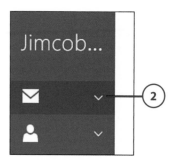

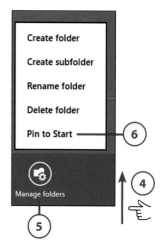

7. Change the name that will display on the pinned tile if you want.

8. Tap the forward and back arrows to select a tile size.

9. Tap Pin to Start.

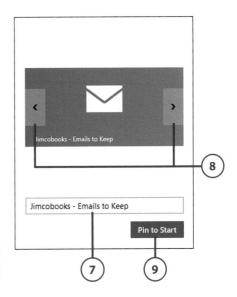

It's Not All Good

Not a Live Tile

The Mail tile on the Start screen is a live tile. However, when you pin a mail folder to the Start screen, it doesn't create a live tile, so you won't see previews of emails displayed on the tile that you pin.

Organizing Mail

The Mail app in Windows RT 8.1 introduces several new features that make it easy to keep your email organized. You can create folders for your mail, create simple rules for automatically organizing incoming mail, sweep your mail to take actions on a lot of messages at once, and more.

Creating a Folder

You can create a new folder for organizing your emails.

1. Tap the account in which you want to create the new folder.

2. Swipe up from the bottom of the screen.

3. Tap Manage Folders.

4. Tap Create Folder.

5. Enter a name for your new folder.

6. Tap OK to create the folder.

7. Tap OK to acknowledge that the folder has been created.

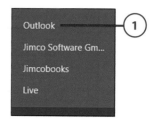

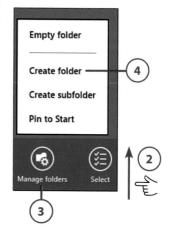

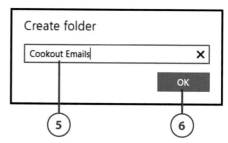

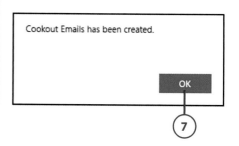

Creating a Subfolder

You can further organize a folder by creating subfolders underneath it. For example, if you have a folder for emails about a party you're having, you might want to have one sub-folder for people who are coming and another for people who have declined the invite.

1. Select the folder under which you would like to create a subfolder.

2. Swipe up from the bottom of the screen.

3. Tap Manage Folders.

4. Tap Create Subfolder.

5. Enter a name for your subfolder.

6. Tap OK to create the subfolder.

7. Tap OK to confirm.

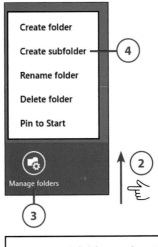

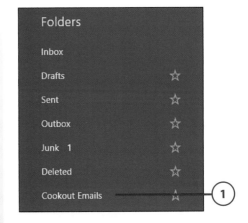

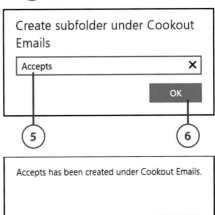

Renaming a Folder

If you want to change the name of a folder, you can easily rename it.

1. Select the folder you want to rename.

2. Swipe up from the bottom of the screen and tap Manage Folders.

3. Tap Rename Folder.

4. Enter a new name for the folder.

5. Tap OK.

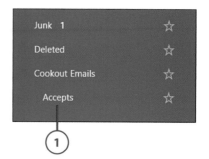

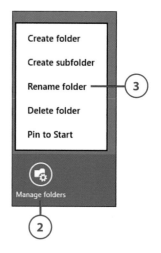

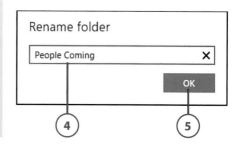

It's Not All Good

Renaming Subfolders Sometimes Doesn't Work

I have encountered several situations where renaming a subfolder for an Outlook.com account failed. When this happens, I had to use the Outlook.com website in Internet Explorer to rename the folder.

Deleting a Folder

If you no longer need a folder, you can delete it. When you delete a folder, it and all messages in it are moved to your trash.

1. Tap the folder you want to delete.

2. Swipe up from the bottom of the screen and tap Manage Folders.

3. Tap Delete Folder.

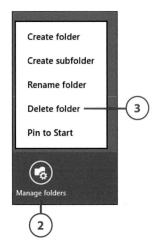

It's Not All Good

No Confirmation

When you delete a folder, there's no confirmation dialog. If you want to restore the folder, you'll have to recreate it. However, you can recover any emails in the deleted folder from your trash.

Adding and Removing Favorite Folders

When you tap the down arrow next to the inbox for a mail account, you see a list of favorite folders. You can add folders to and remove them from this list.

1. Tap the down arrow next to the inbox.

2. Tap Folders.

3. Tap the star icon next to a folder you want to add to the favorites list.

4. Tap the star icon of a folder that is on the favorites list to remove the folder from the list.

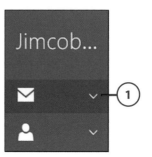

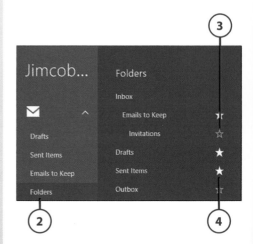

Adding and Removing Favorite People

You can maintain a list of favorite people. You can then quickly see all messages from that person by tapping his name in the People list. As you saw earlier, you can also have Mail configured so that you see new mail notifications only for people on your favorites list.

1. Tap the People icon.

Adding New People

If you've already added one or more people to your favorites list, tap People after tapping on the People icon to add new people.

2. Tap the star next to a frequent contact to add that contact to the favorites list.

3. Tap the star next to a contact on the favorites list to remove that contact from the favorites list.

4. Tap Browse Contacts to browse for a contact to add to the favorites list.

5. Tap one or more people you want to add to the favorites list.

6. Tap Add.

Viewing Mail from Favorites

You can view all messages from a favorite person by tapping them in the People list.

Moving Messages

By default, all mail shows up in your inbox. You can move messages into another folder in order to organize your mail.

1. Select one or more mail messages.

2. Tap Move. (If you only selected one message, you need to swipe up from the bottom of the screen to access this command.)

3. Select a folder to move the messages to that folder.

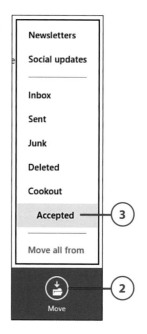

Moving All Messages from Specific People

You can move all messages from one or more people in one easy step. However, this feature is only available for Outlook.com accounts.

1. Select one message from each of the people whose mail you want to move.

2. Tap Move.

3. Tap Move All From.

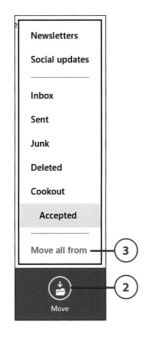

4. Tap Choose a Folder.

5. Tap a folder into which you want to move the messages.

6. Tap Move All from Inbox to move all existing messages from the selected senders from the inbox into the folder you selected.

7. Tap Move All from Inbox and Move All Future Email to move all existing messages and all future messages from the selected senders into the folder you selected.

8. Tap Always Keep the Latest One, Move the Rest from All Folders to keep only the latest email from the selected senders in your inbox. All others will be moved to the selected folder as new messages arrive.

9. Tap Always Move Email Older Than 10 Days from All Folders to automatically move mail older than 10 days old from the selected senders.

10. Tap Yes to move messages based on your selection.

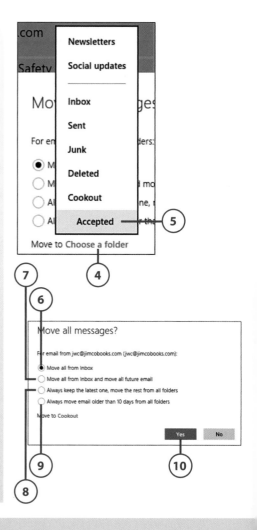

MANAGING RULES

When you follow the steps to always move mail from specific senders, you are creating what's known as a **rule**. The Mail app makes it easy to set up rules, but you cannot remove a rule or edit a rule from within the Mail app. Instead, you must go to the Outlook.com website to manage your rules. I show you how later in this chapter.

>>Go Further

Sweeping Mail

Sweeping mail is a process in which you can quickly deal with many messages from one or more senders and set up rules for future messages. It differs from the rule you created in the previous walkthrough in that you can also delete messages and block messages from specific senders.

Only Available for Outlook.com Accounts

Just as with the "Move All From" feature, the Sweep feature is only available for Outlook.com email accounts.

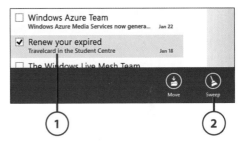

1. Select an email message from one or more senders.

2. Tap Sweep.

3. Tap Delete All from Inbox to delete all messages from the selected senders.

4. Tap Delete All from Inbox and Block Future Email to delete all messages from the selected senders and block any future messages from those senders.

5. Tap Always Keep the Latest One, Delete All the Rest from All Folders to create a rule that only keeps the latest message from the senders and deletes all others.

6. Tap Always Delete Email Older Than 10 Days from All Folders to create a rule that always deletes email from the senders that is older than 10 days old.

7. Tap Sweep.

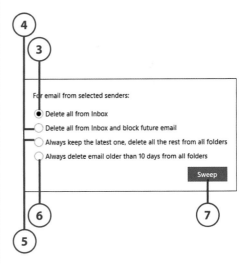

Inbox or All Folders

Notice that the options in steps 3 and 4 act only on messages in your inbox, whereas the options in items 5 and 6 will affect messages in all folders.

Composing and Sending Email

The Mail app provides tools for basic editing of email messages. You can also attach files to an email and share parts of an email with someone easily.

Creating a New Email Message

You can create a new, blank email message.

1. Tap an account to be used to send the email.

2. Tap the + button in the upper-right corner of the Mail app.

3. Tap inside the To or Cc box and enter one or more email addresses. Multiple email addresses should be separated by a semicolon.

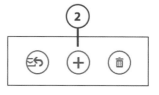

Entering Email Addresses

As you enter email addresses, you will see a pop-up of people that are in your contact list. You can choose one from the list by tapping on it.

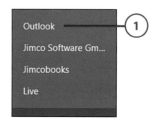

4. Tap More to enter an email address that should be blind copied, to set the priority of the email message, or to select the account to be used to send the message.

5. Tap your email address if you want to change the email address from which the mail will be sent.

6. Tap and enter a subject for your email.

7. Tap and enter your email message. Note that Email automatically creates hyperlinks as you enter web addresses.

8. Spelling errors are underlined with a red, squiggly line. Tap the word to see a menu of corrections.

9. Tap a correctly spelled word from the list to change the misspelled word.

10. Tap Add to Dictionary to add the word to your dictionary so that it won't be marked as misspelled again.

11. Tap Ignore to ignore the spelling error for this mail message only.

12. Tap Send to send your mail message.

13. Tap Delete to delete your message.

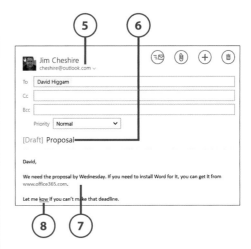

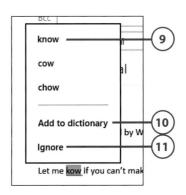

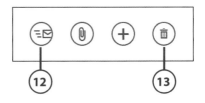

Replying to Email

You can reply to the sender of an email, reply to everyone who received the email, or forward an email to someone else.

1. With the email message selected, tap Respond.

2. Tap Reply to respond only to the sender of the email.

3. Tap Reply All to respond to everyone who received the message, except for those who were blind copied.

4. Tap Forward to forward the email message to someone else.

5. If forwarding a message, enter a recipient's email address. Otherwise, tap Change and enter email addresses of anyone else whom you would like to receive the message.

6. Enter your message text.

7. Tap Send.

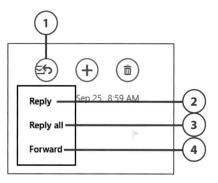

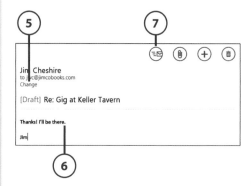

Formatting Text in an Email

You can apply special formatting to text when creating email messages.

1. Select text in your email message to which you would like to apply formatting.

2. Tap Hyperlink to create a hyperlink to a web page.

3. Tap Bold, Italic, or Underline to format the text as you want.

4. Tap List to create a bulleted or numbered list.

5. To change the font typeface or size, tap Font.

6. Tap a typeface and size for the selected text.

7. To change text color, tap Text Color and select the desired color.

8. To highlight the text, tap Highlight and select the desired color.

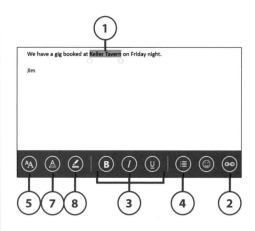

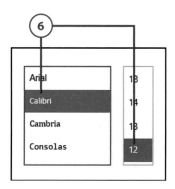

Adding Emoticons to Email

You can add emoticons, such as :), while entering your text. However, the Mail app will not convert these to emoticon images. If you would prefer to use emoticon images instead, you can.

1. Tap where you would like the emoticon to be added.

2. Swipe up from the bottom of the screen and tap Emoticons.

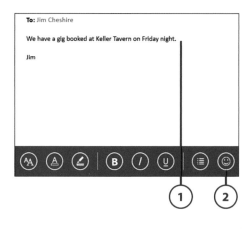

3. Tap an emoticon category.

4. Tap the desired emoticon image to insert it.

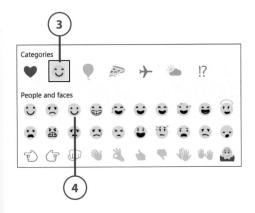

Identifying Emoticons

If you don't know what an emoticon is, you can tap and hold on it to see a description. If you release your finger while still over the emoticon, it will add that emoticon to your message. If you don't want to add the emoticon to your message, drag your finger off the emoticon before releasing.

Attaching Files to an Email

You can attach files to an email.

1. While composing your mail message, tap Attachments.

2. Navigate to the folder that contains the file or files you would like to attach.

3. Tap one or more files that you would like to attach to your message. (If you unintentionally select a file, tap it again to unselect it.)

4. Tap Attach.

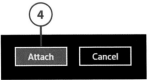

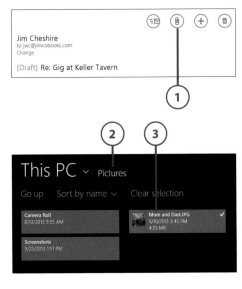

5. To hide the attachment while you are typing your email, tap the up arrow. Tap the arrow again to display the attachment.

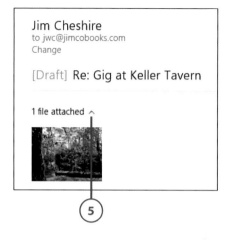

Saving Email Drafts

If you would like to save an email you are writing so that you won't lose your work if the Mail app crashes or something else bad happens, you can save a draft.

1. To save a draft, swipe up from the bottom of the screen.

2. Tap Save Draft.

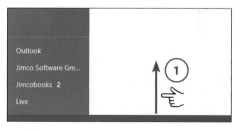

Continuing a Saved Draft

You can continue an email that you saved earlier.

1. Tap the email account that you used when creating the email draft.

2. Tap the email draft to continue it.

Using an Email Signature

You can enter a signature for your email account that will be automatically added to the end of all your email messages sent from that account.

1. From the Accounts pane, tap the account for which you would like to use an email signature.

2. Drag the Use an Email Signature slider to Yes.

3. Enter your desired email signature in the textbox.

Email Signatures

Because email signatures are individually set for each account, you can choose to have a different signature for each of your accounts. You also can use a signature with some accounts and not with others.

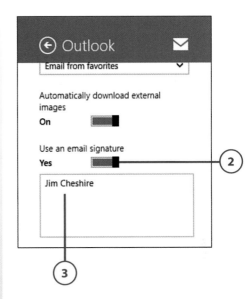

Sending Automatic Replies

If you are away from your PC and you want people who send you mail to get an automatic reply letting them know that you aren't immediately available, you can configure it easily for your Outlook.com account.

1. From the Settings panel for your Outlook.com account, swipe up to reveal the Send Automatic Replies setting.

2. Tap to set the Send Automatic Replies slider to On.

3. Enter the message to be automatically sent to those who send you email.

4. If you only want automatic replies to be sent to people in your contact list, tap to check the Only Reply to My Contacts checkbox.

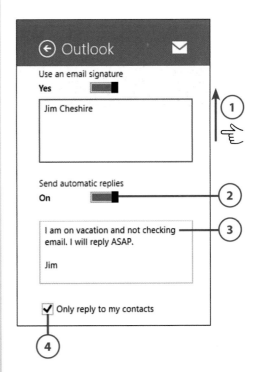

Automatic Replies

When you set up an automatic reply, it's not necessary for you to leave your PC on for the replies to be sent. Your automatic reply settings are stored in the cloud and will apply even if your PC is off. It's also important to note that if someone emails you often, Outlook.com will only send the automatic reply to that person once every 4 days.

It's Not All Good

Sending Automatic Replies to Everyone

Sending automatic replies to people not on your contact list is usually not a good idea. Many spammers send out "feelers" to email addresses to check for good email addresses. If they get a reply to the feeler, it lets them know that your email address is connected to a live person and it makes you much more susceptible to spam.

View your calendars in
multiple ways.

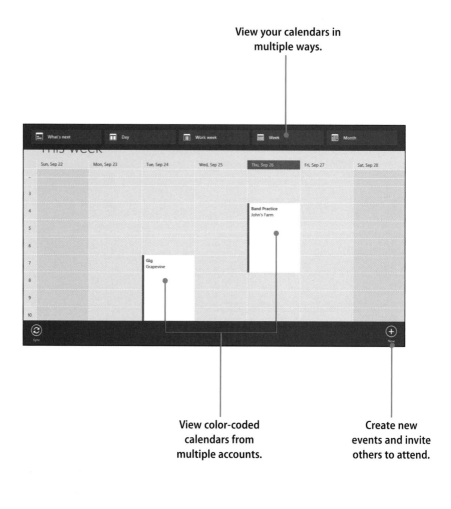

View color-coded
calendars from
multiple accounts.

Create new
events and invite
others to attend.

Using Calendar

There's nothing new about a calendar on your computer, but there is something new about Calendar on your Surface 2. As with other apps on your Surface 2, Calendar is a cloud-enabled app that makes it easy to keep track of multiple calendars in one place.

Connecting Calendars

I use a couple of different calendars. I have a work calendar on my company's Exchange server and we keep a family calendar on Outlook.com. Fortunately, I don't have to re-create all the appointments in all of these calendars on my Surface 2. Instead, I simply connect both of these calendars to the Calendar app, and all my appointments are immediately available to me.

It's Not All Good

No Google Calendar

The Calendar app used to support Google's calendar, but it doesn't anymore because Google decided that it would no longer support the technology that the Calendar app uses to sync appointments. There is a chance that Microsoft might eventually update the Calendar app to support the technologies that Google does support, but no one knows for sure.

You can add your Outlook.com (which includes Hotmail and Windows Live) calendar or an Exchange calendar (which includes Office 365).

Adding an Outlook.com Calendar

You can add a calendar from your Outlook.com, Hotmail.com, or Live.com account.

1. From the Settings pane of the Calendar app, tap Accounts.

2. Tap Add an Account.

3. Tap Outlook.com.

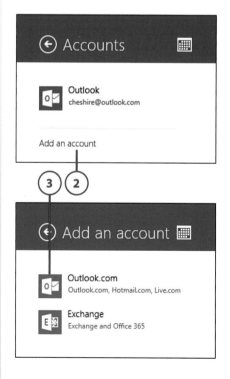

4. Enter your Outlook.com email address.

5. Enter your Outlook.com password.

6. Tap Connect.

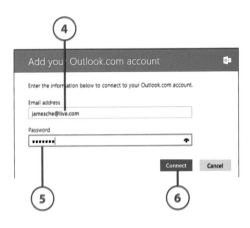

Microsoft Account Added Automatically

To use the Calendar app, you must enter an email and password for your Microsoft account when you first launch Calendar. The calendar for that account is added automatically to the Calendar app.

Adding an Exchange Calendar

You can add a calendar from your company's Exchange server or from Office 365.

1. From the Add an Account pane (refer to "Adding an Outlook.com Calendar"), tap Exchange.

2. Enter your account email address.

3. Enter your account password.

4. If you need to provide additional details such as a mail server address or additional credentials, tap Show More Details.

Exchange Details

You will need to check with your administrator or hosting provider to know what information you need to provide to connect to your Calendar.

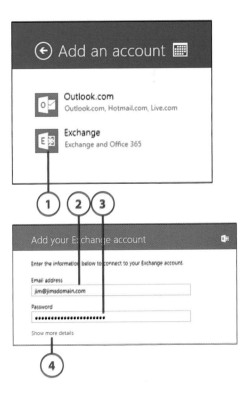

5. Enter your email server address.

6. Enter your domain name.

7. Enter your username.

8. Tap Connect.

9. If your company requires it, tap Enforce These Policies to make your PC more secure.

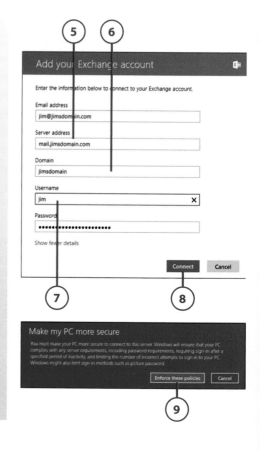

Viewing Calendars

You can choose which calendars to display in Calendar, the color used for each calendar, and which view you would like to see for your events.

Hiding a Calendar

By default, after you connect a calendar to the Calendar app, events from that calendar are displayed. If you don't want to see events from a particular calendar, you can hide it.

1. From the Settings pane, tap Options.

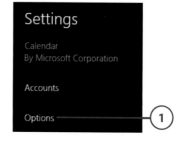

2. Each of your calendars is listed here. Drag the Show slider for the calendar you want to hide to the left to hide the calendar.

Birthday and Holiday Calendars

Note that the Calendar app automatically displays a birthday calendar and a holiday calendar. The birthday calendar displays an event when one of your contacts in the People app has a birthday.

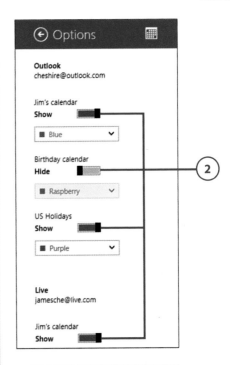

Changing a Calendar's Display Color

The Calendar app chooses a different color for each calendar that you connect. This makes it easy to tell at a glance which calendar contains a specific event. You can customize the color used for each of your calendars.

1. From the Options pane, tap the color drop-down for the calendar you want to change.

2. Tap the desired color for the calendar.

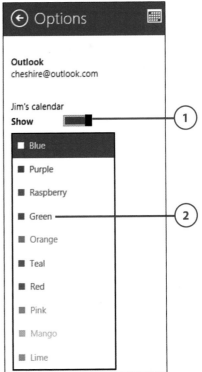

Viewing Events in What's Next View

What's Next view is the default view for the Calendar app. What's Next view shows you a list of upcoming events. Only days for which an event is scheduled appear in What's Next view.

1. Swipe down from the top of the screen and tap What's Next.

2. Swipe right and left to see additional events.

3. Tap on an event to open it for editing.

Editing Events

For details on how you can edit an event, see "Editing an Event" later in this chapter.

Changing the Background in What's Next View

You can change the background for What's Next view so that it displays one of your own pictures.

1. While in What's Next view, swipe up from the bottom of the screen and tap Background.

2. Tap Use Default to use the default background.

3. Tap Browse to browse for one of your own pictures for the background.

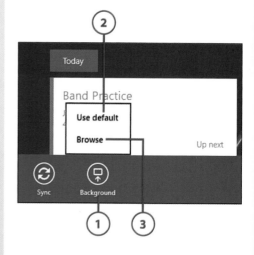

4. Browse to the folder containing your picture and tap the picture file you want to use.

5. Tap Choose Picture.

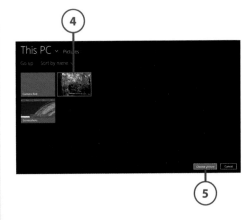

Viewing Events in Month View

You can change the view to Month view so that you can see events for the entire month.

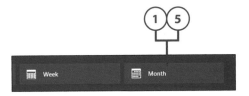

1. Swipe down from the top of the screen and tap Month.

2. Swipe right to see previous months.

3. Swipe left to see future months.

4. Tap an event to see additional details on the event.

5. To quickly return to the current month, swipe down from the top of the screen and tap Month.

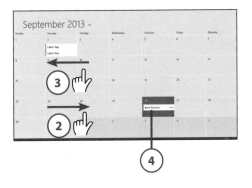

Viewing Events in Week View

Week view is helpful when you want to see an entire week of events on a single screen. In Week view, each column represents a single day and each row represents a 1-hour time slot. Therefore, Week view is a good way to get an idea of how long each event lasts at a glance.

1. Swipe down from the top of the screen and tap Week.

2. Drag up or down to see additional time slots.

3. Swipe right to see previous weeks.

4. Swipe left to see future weeks.

5. Tap an event to see more details of the event.

6. To return to the current week, swipe down from the top of the screen and tap Week.

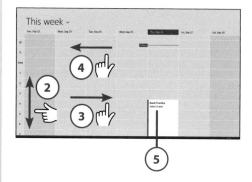

Viewing Only Weekdays

You can change the week view to display only weekdays by swiping down from the top of the screen and tapping Work Week.

Viewing Events in Day View

Day view enables you to see two days of events side by side. Each day can be scrolled individually so that you can view the events you're most interested in.

1. Swipe down from the top of the screen and tap Day.

2. Drag up or down on a particular day to view more times for that day. (Each day can be vertically scrolled independently.)

3. Swipe right to see previous days.

4. Swipe left to see future days.

5. Tap an event to see more details of the event.

6. To return to the current day, swipe down from the top of the screen and tap Day.

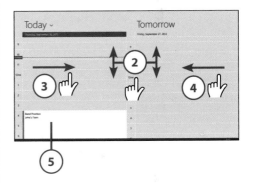

Working with Events

Events in Calendar are automatically synchronized from your online calendars. If you add or modify an event on your smartphone or another computer, Calendar reflects that change automatically. Additionally, events you create or modify in Calendar synchronize with your other devices.

Adding a Basic Event

A basic event is one without any recurrences and that uses the default reminder time and other options.

1. In the Calendar app, swipe up from the bottom of the screen and tap New.

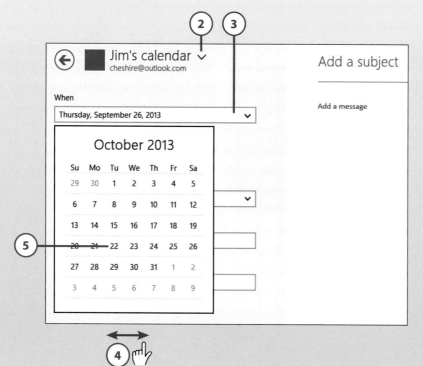

2. Tap the Calendar drop-down and select the calendar account in which you would like the event created.

3. Tap the When drop-down.

4. Swipe left or right to change months.

5. Tap the date for the event.

6. Tap the Start drop-downs and select a start time for the event.

7. Tap the How Long drop-down and select a duration for the event, or select Custom to specify your own start and end times.

8. Enter a location for the event in the Location textbox if applicable.

9. Enter a contact you would like to invite to the event if applicable. (An email invitation will be sent to invitees.)

10. Enter a title for the event.

11. Enter a message for the event if desired.

12. Tap Send Invite to save the event. (If no invitees were selected, tap Save instead.)

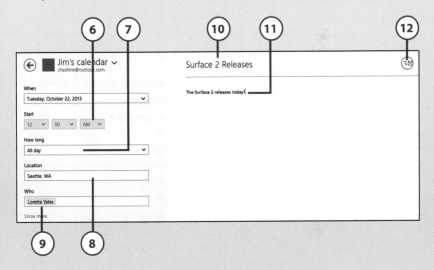

Quickly Creating an Event

You can more quickly create an event by tapping on the date or time for the event.

1. Tap on a date or time for the event.

2. If not in Month view, tap and drag the handles to adjust the times for the event.

3. Enter a subject for the event.

4. Enter a location for the event.

5. Tap the down arrow to select the calendar for the event or to add additional details.

6. Tap a calendar for the event.

7. Tap Add Details to open the event and add details on the event.

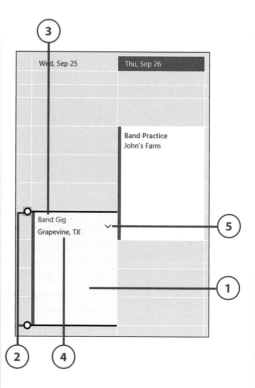

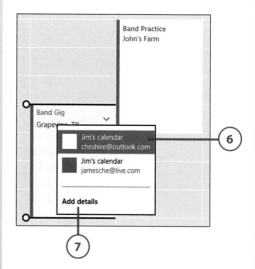

Adding a Recurring Event

You can create an event that recurs at a regular interval.

1. While creating your event, tap Show More.

2. Tap the How Often drop-down and select how often the event will occur.

3. Tap Save to save the event.

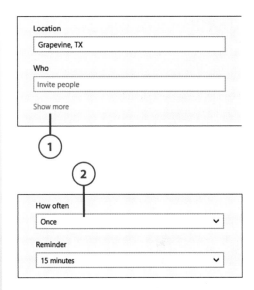

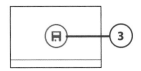

Setting Reminders

Windows RT 8.1 pops up event reminders in the upper-right corner of your screen. By default, you will be reminded of events 15 minutes prior to the start time, but you can choose a different reminder time or choose not to be reminded.

1. While creating your event, tap Show More.

2. Tap the Reminder drop-down and choose a time to be reminded or None to disable the reminder.

Specifying an Event Status

You can specify a status for your event of Free, Busy, Tentative, or Out of Office. Calendar displays a unique colored left edge for the event based on the status you select. Free displays a light-colored edge, Busy displays a darker colored edge, Tentative displays a hashed edge of alternating colors, and Out of Office displays an edge that is slightly darker than the Busy edge.

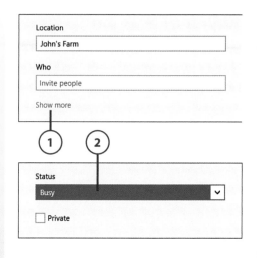

1. While creating an event, tap Show More.

2. Tap the Status drop-down and select a status.

Creating a Private Event

You might want to create an event that only you can see. You can do that by marking an event as private. When you do, the event is actually created only as a local event on the device you are using. You (or others) will not be able to see the event on other devices that synchronize with your calendar.

1. While creating your event, tap Show More.

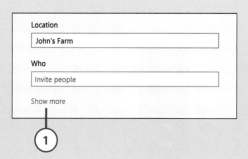

2. Tap the Private checkbox to check it.

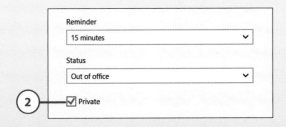

Editing an Event

If you would like to make a change to an event, you can edit it and then resave it.

1. Tap the event you would like to edit.

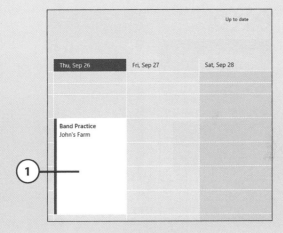

2. Make any changes you want to make.

3. Tap Save to save the edited event.

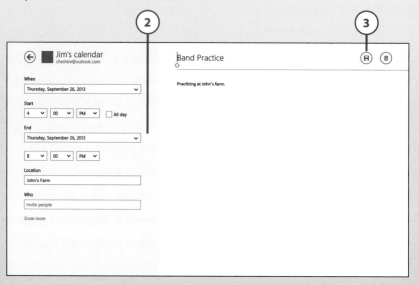

Save or Send

If the event you are editing includes invites to others, you will tap Send to save the edited event and send the changed event to those with whom you've shared the event.

Deleting an Event

If an event has been canceled, you can delete it from your calendar.

1. Tap the event you would like to delete.

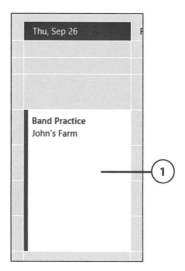

2. Tap the trash can icon to delete the event.

3. Tap Delete to delete the event. (If the event has invitees, tap OK instead to delete the event. An email message canceling the event will be launched in Mail so that you can notify the invitees.)

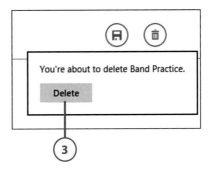

You're about to delete Band Practice.

Delete

Add your own news topics that you find interesting.

Choose from a large collection of news sources.

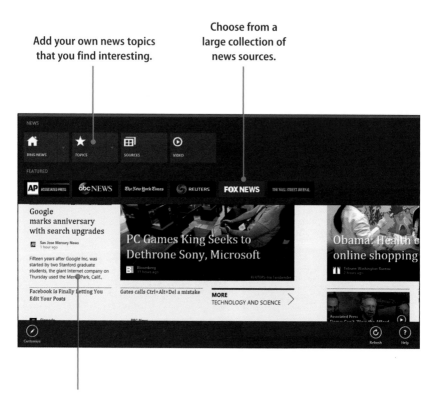

Keep up to date with news that is categorized by section.

11

Keeping Up to Date with News

It's becoming more common for people to turn to computers instead of newspapers, radio, and television to keep up with the news. Using the News app on your Surface 2, you can keep track of news and read Internet articles that interest you in an attractive interface optimized for a tablet.

Reading the News

The News app keeps track of news from sources such as the Associated Press, Reuters, and various other online news sources. Articles are categorized for easy browsing and you can pin a particular category to the Start screen for instant access. When you start the News app, you'll see Bing News, a synopsis of news from many sources. Later in this chapter, I'll show you how to add other news sources and even add your own sources.

Reading an Article

Bing News provides a convenient one-stop way to get up-to-date on all the latest news. You can read top news stories and you can also read stories from several different categories of news.

Info on Pictures

You can tap the "i" icon in the corner of a picture in News to see details on the picture.

1. From the Start screen, tap the News tile to launch the News app.

2. Swipe to see more categories.

3. Tap a category name to see all news stories in that category.

4. Tap a news story to read the entire story.

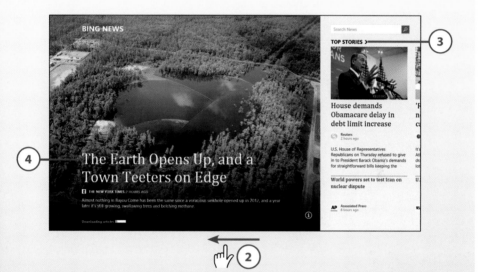

5. Swipe left to move to the next page in an article.

6. Swipe right to move to the previous page.

7. Tap Back to return to the previous screen.

8. Swipe down from the top of the screen or up from the bottom of the screen, and tap Text Style to toggle between a serif and sans serif text style.

9. Tap Text Size and tap a size to change the size of the text.

10. Tap Next Article to go to the next article.

11. Tap Previous Article to go to the previous article.

12. Tap Bing News to return to the Bing News home screen.

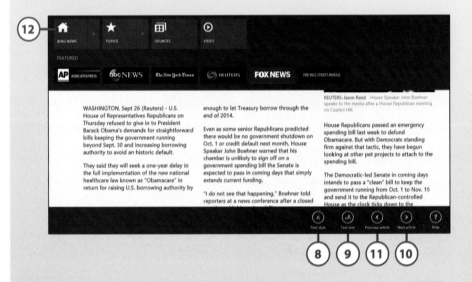

Videos

You can quickly see all the videos that News has to offer by swiping down from the top of the screen and tapping Video.

Pinning a Section to the Start Screen

If you would like a way to quickly return to a particular section in Bing News, you can pin it to your Start screen. You can then return to that section by tapping its tile on your Start screen.

1. While viewing Bing News, tap the section you want to pin to your Start screen.

2. Swipe up from the bottom of the screen.

3. Tap Pin to Start.

4. Tap the arrow to select a tile size.

5. Enter a title for the tile.

6. Tap Pin to Start.

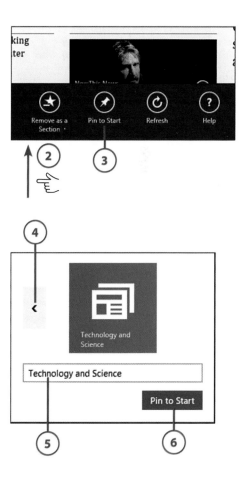

Disabling Offline Reading

By default, News downloads articles so that you can read them when you're offline. If you prefer, you can disable this feature so that News doesn't use your bandwidth.

1. In the News app, swipe in from the right side of the screen and tap Settings.

2. Tap Options.

3. Tap the Read Articles Offline slide to change the setting to Off.

It's Not All Good

Offline Reading

If you disable offline reading, you will have to be online to read any news articles in News. News is also much faster with offline reading enabled. I recommend that you disable offline reading only if you are using a metered cellular data plan and are concerned with bandwidth usage.

Saving an Article for Reading Later

As you are browsing through Bing News or another news source, you might want to select a few articles to read at your leisure at a later time. The News app can share with the Reading List app so that you can save a list of articles to read later.

1. Tap a story that you are interested in reading later.

2. Swipe in from the right side of the screen and tap the Share charm.

3. Tap Reading List.

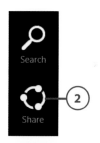

Parents weigh risks, benefits of online family photos

Austin American-Statesman
1 day ago

About five years ago, while interviewing the subject of an article for the Austin American-Statesman, I was asked if I thought parents should post photos of

Microsoft details Windows 8.1 updates ——(1)

4. Tap Add to add the article to your reading list.

Reading List
The next task describes how to use the Reading List app to read articles offline.

Reading Articles Offline with Reading List

When you save a news item for reading later, it gets added to the Reading List app. The reading app stores articles and websites that you want to read later. You can think of the Reading List app as a bookmark list for items that interest you.

Reading List Doesn't Save Content
No content is actually saved to Reading List. Instead, it stores a link to the content that links to the app where you were originally reading the content. If you saved an article to Reading List from the News app, when you read the article from Reading List, it opens the article in the News app.

1. Tap and hold on an empty area of the Start screen and swipe up to show the Apps screen.

2. Tap Reading List to launch the Reading List app.

3. Tap Continue Viewing to continue viewing the last item you were reading.

4. Slide left to view additional items in your reading list. (Items are sorted by the date they were added to Reading List.)

5. Tap an item to read it. The app from which the item originated will open in split screen.

6. Slide up to see additional Reading List items.

7. Tap another item to open it.

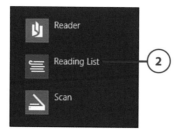

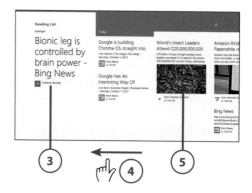

Other News Sources

Reading Bing News is a great way to get caught up on the latest news from the AP, Reuters, and other mainstream news organizations, but if you have an interest in reading information from other sources, you can access those as well. The News app provides news sources for entertainment, tech, science, sports, and much more.

Reading News from Other Sources

No matter what your interests are, you are sure to find something you'll want to read in the News app's news sources. Articles often open directly from a source's website, but even so, the reading experience is better in the News app than it is in a web browser.

1. From the News app, swipe up from the bottom or down from the top of the screen and tap a featured news source or the sources tile to see additional news sources.

2. Type a search term to look for a news source.

3. Enter an RSS URL to add it as a source.

4. Tap a source category to see all sources in that category.

5. Swipe left to see additional sources.

6. Tap a source to list articles from that source.

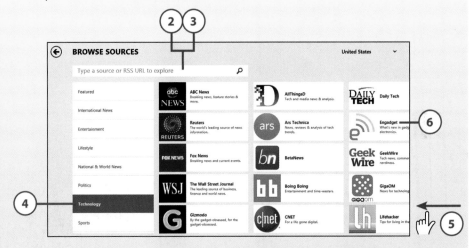

7. Swipe left and right to locate an article you're interested in reading.

8. Tap an article to open it.

9. Reverse-pinch to zoom in on the article.

10. Pinch to zoom out on the article.

11. Tap Back to return to the list of articles.

12. Tap Back to return to the list of news sources.

Pinning a News Source to the Start Screen

If you find that a news source is particularly interesting to you, you can pin it to the Start screen so that you can access it with a single tap.

1. While viewing the list of articles for a news source, swipe up from the bottom of the screen and tap Pin to Start.

2. Edit the name for the pinned tile if you want.

3. Use the arrow to select a tile size.

4. Tap Pin to Start.

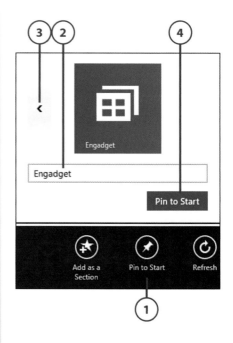

Custom News

Searching for news is a good way to find information on a topic of interest, but each time you want to see the latest news on your topic, you must conduct a search again. That's not the most convenient way to check up on a topic of interest. To make things easier, you can customize Bing News to create a custom news experience.

Adding a Source as a Section in Bing News

You can add a source to Bing News as a new section so that you can easily read news from that source.

1. While viewing the source, swipe up from the bottom of the screen.

2. Tap Add as a Section.

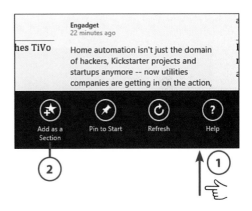

Removing a Section from Bing News

You might want to remove a section from Bing News in order to make it easier to find sections that interest you.

1. Swipe down from the top of the screen and tap the arrow next to Bing News.

2. Tap a section that you want to remove.

3. While the section is displayed, swipe up from the bottom of the screen.

4. Tap Remove as a Section to remove the section from Bing News.

It's Not All Good

No Undo When Deleting Sections

If you delete a section and decide that you made a mistake, you have to add back all the sources from that section manually. There isn't a way to undo a deletion.

Adding Multiple News Sources

In a previous step-by-step exercise, you added a news source while viewing the source. Doing so allows you to check out the source to ensure that you like it before adding it. However, you might already recognize news sources as ones that you want to keep up with, so you can easily add multiple news sources without first opening the source.

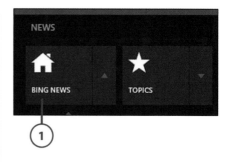

1. Swipe down from the top of the screen and tap Bing News to return to the Bing News home screen.

2. Swipe up from the bottom of the screen and tap Customize.

3. Tap Sources.

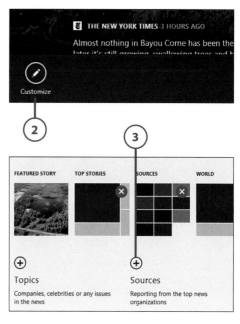

4. Tap a category.

5. Tap the plus sign next to each source you want to add to Bing News. The sign changes to a check mark when the source is added.

Customize Missing

If you don't see the Customize button right away, don't worry. It appears only after Bing News has finished loading all news stories.

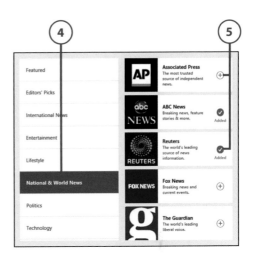

Adding a News Topic

News sources are a great way to read the news, but news presented by news sources is curated by the source. You can add a news topic to Bing News and you will see stories that match a search term you enter for the topic.

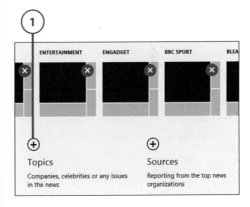

1. From the Customize screen, tap Topics.

2. Enter a topic. You can enter any topic you want.

3. Tap Add to add articles on the topic to Bing News.

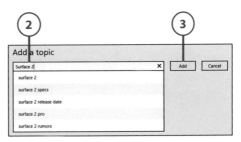

Rearranging Sections in Bing News

You can rearrange the sections in Bing News so that sections that interest you most are easier to get to.

1. From the Customize screen, tap on a section and drag it until it snaps free from its current position.

2. Drag the section to its desired location.

3. Release the section when it's positioned where you want it.

Cannot Move Features Story

The Featured Story cannot be moved. All other sections can be rearranged to your liking.

Quickly Delete a Section

You can quickly delete a section by tapping on the X that appears in the upper-right corner of the section while on the Customize screen.

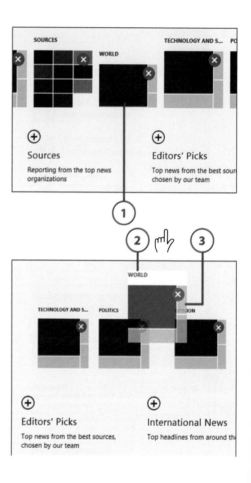

Sharing News

While reading the news, you will certainly find something that you want to share with someone. As with other apps in Windows RT 8.1, the News app enables you to use the Share charm to easily share news with others.

Emailing a News Article

You can send a thumbnail picture and synopsis text of an article to an email contact, along with a link to the full article.

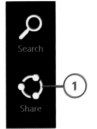

1. While viewing an article that you want to share, swipe in from the right edge of the screen and tap Share.

2. Tap Mail.

3. Enter the email address of the person with whom you want to share the article.

4. Enter a message if you want.

5. Tap Send to share the article.

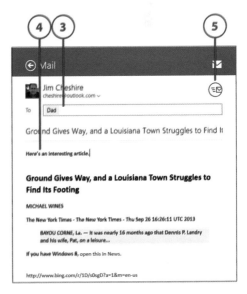

Sharing an Article on Social Networks

If you want to share an article with your social networking friends, you can easily do that without leaving the News app.

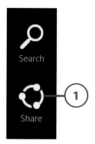

Setting Up Connections

To share on social networks, you first must configure a connection with your social networks in the People app. For more details on that, see "Working with Contacts" in Chapter 8, "Connecting with People."

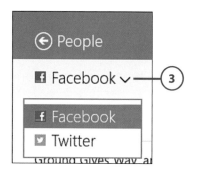

1. While viewing the article that you want to share, swipe in from the right side of the screen and tap Share.

2. Tap People.

3. Tap the arrow and choose your social network if the default network is not where you want to share the article.

4. Enter a message to share on your social network.

5. Tap Send to post your message.

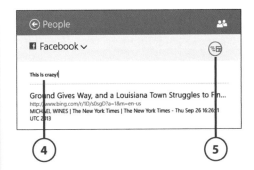

View your files in the cloud with SkyDrive and networked files with HomeGroup.

Upload your files to the cloud.

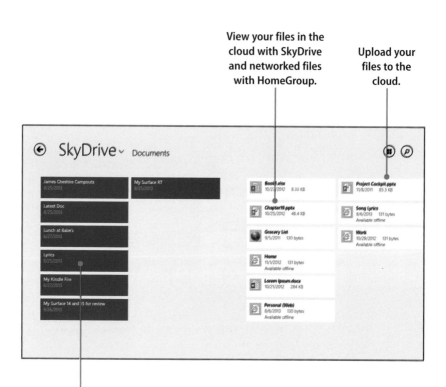

Download files from the cloud to your PC.

12

HomeGroups and SkyDrive

As you might have realized by now, a big component of the Surface 2 (and Windows 8.1 devices in general) is the capability to share files and content with friends and family. Both HomeGroups and SkyDrive make that possible, but in different ways. HomeGroups enable you to see files that others have shared on your home network. SkyDrive enables you to share files with anyone who has Internet access, and you can use SkyDrive to share files between all of your devices as well.

Using HomeGroups

Using HomeGroups is a convenient way to share files with others on your network. You can create a HomeGroup on a Windows 7, Windows 8, or Windows 8.1 PC. You then choose what you want to share on the HomeGroup. When that basic setup is complete, you can join the HomeGroup from your Surface 2 and you'll be able to see any files that have been shared.

Creating HomeGroups

You will need Windows 7 Home Premium, Windows 7 Ultimate, Windows 8, or Windows 8.1 to create a HomeGroup. You cannot create a HomeGroup on your Surface 2 or any other Windows RT 8.1–based device.

I won't go into how you create a HomeGroup in this book, but you can find that information at http://windows.microsoft.com/en-us/windows-8/homegroup-from-start-to-finish.

Joining a HomeGroup

To see the files in a HomeGroup, you first must join the HomeGroup on your Surface 2.

1. From the Start screen, swipe in from the right side of the screen and tap Settings.

2. Tap Change PC Settings.

3. Tap Network.

4. Tap HomeGroup.

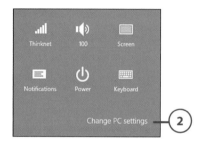

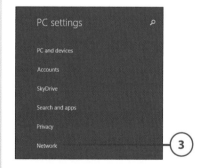

5. Enter the password to join the HomeGroup.

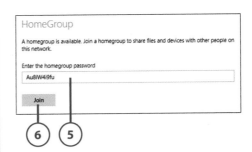

HomeGroup Passwords

The password that's already in the textbox should be correct. However, if you need the password, the person who created a HomeGroup can find out the password from the HomeGroup settings screen on his or her PC.

6. Tap Join.

Leaving a HomeGroup

If you no longer want to be a member of a HomeGroup, you can leave it. When you do, you will no longer be able to see files shared on that HomeGroup.

1. From the Network Settings screen, tap HomeGroup.

2. Tap the Leave button.

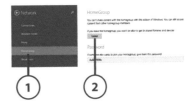

Changing Your Mind

If you change your mind, you can always rejoin a HomeGroup at any time.

Accessing Shared Files

You can access files that are shared in your HomeGroup from any app that enables you to browse for files. For example, you can open a Word document shared on your HomeGroup, or you can open a picture shared on your HomeGroup. You also can save files back to shared folders on your HomeGroup.

Ensuring That Files Are Available

For you to access a file on your HomeGroup, the computer where the file is saved must be powered on. If it's not, you'll be able to see the computer when browsing for files, but Windows RT 8.1 won't be able to connect to it.

In this step-by-step, I use a free app called FotoEditor (available from the Windows Store) to open a picture that is shared on my HomeGroup. The steps used are essentially the same in any app.

1. Within FotoEditor, tap Photos to browse for a photo to edit.

2. Tap the This PC drop-down.

3. Tap Homegroup.

4. Tap the HomeGroup owner's name.

5. Tap the name of the computer where the file is located.

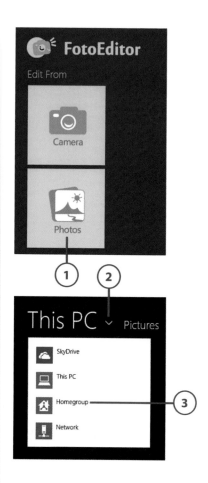

6. Tap the folder that contains the file. (You might need to tap multiple folders to get to the folder containing the file.)

7. Tap the file to select it.

8. Tap Open.

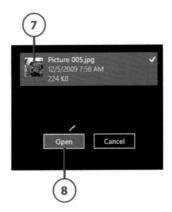

Using SkyDrive

SkyDrive is Microsoft's cloud storage service. By signing up for a Microsoft account, you get 7GB of SkyDrive storage free. You can purchase additional storage for a small fee from SkyDrive.live.com. Your Surface 2 comes with 200GB of SkyDrive at no charge for two years. (That's a $200 value.) Microsoft also gives you additional free storage when you sign up for Office 365.

SkyDrive No More

Microsoft has recently agreed to change the SkyDrive name due to a lawsuit from the British Sky Broadcasting Group. At the time of this writing, the new name has not been announced, nor has the timeline for the name change. However, you can expect that the SkyDrive name will be dropped.

Microsoft Account Required

These steps require a Microsoft account to be used. For more information on using a Microsoft account, see Chapter 2, "Connecting to Networks."

Browsing Files in SkyDrive

You can access your files in SkyDrive using the SkyDrive app included with Windows RT 8.1.

1. From the Start screen, tap the SkyDrive tile to launch the SkyDrive app.

Connect Your Microsoft Account

If you are using a local account, the first time you launch the SkyDrive app, you'll be asked to log in with a Microsoft account to access SkyDrive.

2. Tap a folder to open it.

3. Tap a file to open it.

4. Tap Back to go back to the previous view.

5. Tap Details View to change to Details view.

6. Tap Thumbnails View to switch back to Thumbnail view.

7. Tap Search to search for a file.

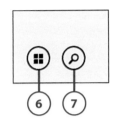

Opening Files with a Specific App

If you have more than one app installed that can open a particular file, you can, from SkyDrive, open a file using the app of your choice.

1. In SkyDrive, swipe down on a file to select it.

2. Tap Open With.

3. Check the box if you always want to open files of this type using the app you select.

4. Tap More Options to see more apps that you can use.

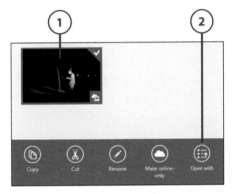

5. Tap an app to open the file using that app.

6. Tap Look for an App in the Store to open the Windows Store and locate an app to use to open your file.

How do you want to open this file?

☑ Use this app for all .png files

Internet Explorer

Notepad

Word (desktop)

Look for an app in the Store

Look for another app on this PC

Creating a New Folder

You can create new folders in SkyDrive from the SkyDrive app. Folders enable you to better organize your SkyDrive content.

1. Navigate to the folder where you want the new folder created.

2. Swipe up from the bottom of the screen and tap New Folder.

3. Enter a name for your new folder.

4. Tap Create.

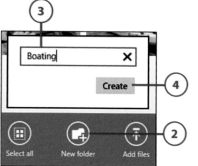

← SkyDrive ˅ Texoma 2010

Boating ✕

Create

Select all   New folder   Add files

Uploading Files to SkyDrive

You can upload files to SkyDrive from within the SkyDrive app, making it easy to share your files with other people or back up your files to the cloud.

1. Navigate to the folder into which you want to upload your files.

2. Swipe up from the bottom of the screen and tap Add Files.

3. Navigate to the folder containing the files you want to upload.

4. Tap each file you want to upload or tap Select All to select all the files in the folder.

Select from Multiple Folders

You can select files in one folder and then navigate to another folder and select files in that folder without your previously selected files being deselected. This makes it easy to upload files from multiple folders at one time.

5. Tap Copy to SkyDrive to upload your files.

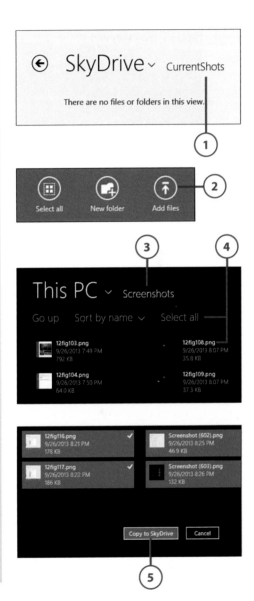

It's Not All Good

Cannot Share Files to SkyDrive

In Windows 8, you could use the Share charm to send files to SkyDrive. That feature has been removed in Windows 8.1 because the SkyDrive app was rewritten from the ground up and the Windows team didn't have the time to add that feature. We can hope to see the feature return in a later version.

Deleting Files from SkyDrive

You can delete files from your SkyDrive to free up disk space or clear up clutter from files that you no longer need. You also can delete an entire folder and the files within that folder in one step.

1. Swipe down on one or more files or folders to select them.

2. Tap Delete.

3. Tap Delete to confirm the deletion.

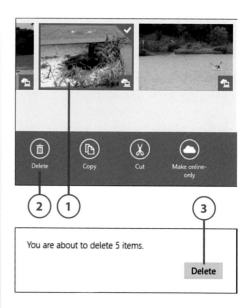

Reviewing SkyDrive Usage

As I said previously, Microsoft provides 7GB of SkyDrive storage at no charge and 200GB free for two years for Surface 2 buyers. That's quite a lot of free storage, but if you copy a lot of pictures, music, or video into your SkyDrive folders, you might find that you need additional storage. Keeping track of your SkyDrive use is simple.

1. From the PC Settings screen, tap SkyDrive.

2. Here you can see how much space you have available out of your total storage allotment. If you are close to running out of storage and can't free up space by deleting files you can tap Buy More Storage to buy additional SkyDrive storage.

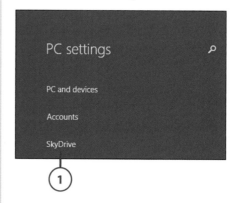

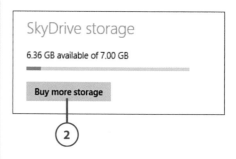

Disabling Automatic Save to SkyDrive

When you save any document in Windows RT 8.1, the default save location is your SkyDrive. You can disable this feature so that the save location defaults to your local PC instead.

1. From the PC Settings screen, tap SkyDrive.

2. Tap the Save Documents to SkyDrive by Default slider to set it to the Off position.

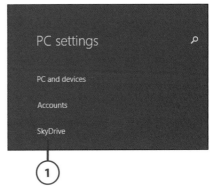

Enabling Access to All SkyDrive Files When Offline

SkyDrive makes your files available only when you're online by default. That means that if you lose your Internet connection, you won't be able to access your files. You can configure SkyDrive so that it makes all of your files available offline.

Changing Offline Status

You can also make individual files or folders available offline. I'll show you how in the next walkthrough.

1. From the SkyDrive app, swipe in from the right side of the screen and tap Settings.

2. Tap Options.

3. Tap the Access All Files Offline slider to change the setting to On.

4. Wait until your files show "Available Offline" when viewing them in Details view before you disconnect from the Internet.

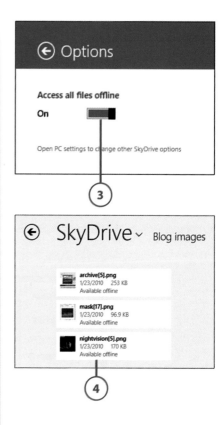

Enabling Access to Selected SkyDrive Files When Offline

You can make selected files or folders available when you're offline. By not making all files available when you're offline, you save memory on your Surface 2.

1. Make sure that Access All files Offline (as shown in the previous walkthrough) is set to Off.

2. If you've previously made files
   or folders available offline, select
   those files or folders, swipe up
   from the bottom of the screen,
   and tap Make Online-Only. (Doing
   this removes the local copy.)

3. Swipe down on the files and
   folders you want to be available
   offline.

4. Tap Make Offline.

5. Wait until the files and folders
   show "Available Offline" before
   disconnecting from the Internet.

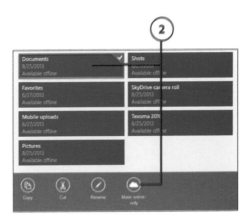

Some Files Always Available Offline By Default

Files that you create or edit on
your Surface 2 will be available
offline by default regardless of
your SkyDrive settings.

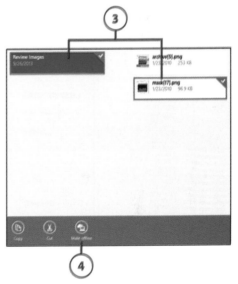

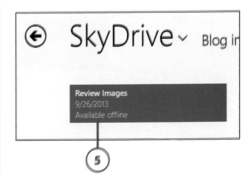

Explore and buy
music from the Xbox
Music Store.

Play music in your music
collection, stream free for
10 hours per month, or use
an Xbox Music Pass.

Use playlists to
play the music
you want to hear.

Discovering and Playing Music

Your Surface 2 comes with Office 2013 so that you can get real work done, but it also comes with apps and features that let you play. You can discover music, listen to an astounding number of songs using Xbox Music Pass, and watch movies and TV shows, all from the comfort of your favorite relaxation place.

This chapter covers the Music app. In Chapter 14, "Watching Video," I show you how you can watch television and movies in the Video app.

Browsing Music

The Music app is your window into Xbox Music, Microsoft's online music service. When you first launch the app, you'll see a link to Collection, Radio, and Explore Catalog. You can use these as a launching point into all the music that Xbox Music has to offer.

Exploring the Catalog

The Music app is an excellent way to explore a particular artist, listen to some of the artist's music, read about the artist, and see all the albums released by the artist.

Xbox Music Pass

These steps show you what you'll experience without an Xbox Music Pass. I show you the enhanced experience available with an Xbox Music Pass in the "Using an Xbox Music Pass" section, later in this chapter.

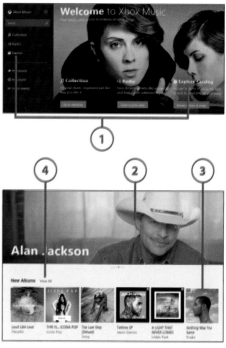

1. From the opening screen in Xbox Music, tap Explore Catalog or tap Explore in the pane on the left.

2. Tap an artist in the scrolling marquee to see albums by that artist.

3. Tap an album tile to see details on the album.

4. Tap View All to see all albums in a category.

5. Drag up to see additional items to explore.

Browsing Albums

I show you how you can browse for albums later in this chapter.

6. After tapping an album tile, tap a song to select it.

7. Tap Play to play a song.

8. Tap Add to Playlist to add the song to a playlist.

9. Tap Play to play an entire album.

10. Tap Add to Playlist to add the album to a playlist.

11. Tap Buy to purchase the album.

12. Tap More to see more options.

13. Tap Explore Artist to see more on the album's artist.

14. Tap Start Radio to create an Xbox Radio station based on the artist.

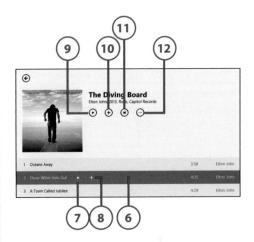

Free Streaming

After you sign into Xbox Music (signing in happens automatically if you sign into your Surface 2 with your Microsoft account), you can stream most music in Xbox Music free for the first six months. After six months, you are limited to 10 hours of free streaming per month. If you want to continue to stream music without a time constraint, you will need to purchase an Xbox Music Pass.

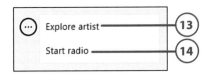

Using Radio

I show you how to use Radio stations in the "Using Radio" section later in this chapter.

It's Not All Good

Commercials and Music

Xbox Music provides for free streaming, but you get ads in the process. If you want to get rid of the ads, you have to purchase an Xbox Music Pass for either $10 a month or $100 for a year.

Exploring an Artist

If you find an artist you like, you can explore the artist to see all the artist's albums available in Xbox Music, albums by that artist that are in your music collection, top songs from the artist, related artists, and more.

1. While viewing an album by the artist you want to explore, tap More.

2. Tap Explore Artist.

3. Tap an album in your collection to see details on the album or play it.

4. Drag up to see latest albums by the artist.

5. Tap an album to see details on the album.

6. Tap View All to see all the artist's albums in Xbox Music.

7. Drag up to see top songs by the artist.

8. Tap a song and tap Play to play the song.

9. Tap Add to Playlist to add the song to a playlist.

10. Drag up to see related artists.

11. Tap a related artist to explore.

12. Drag up to see a biography on the artist.

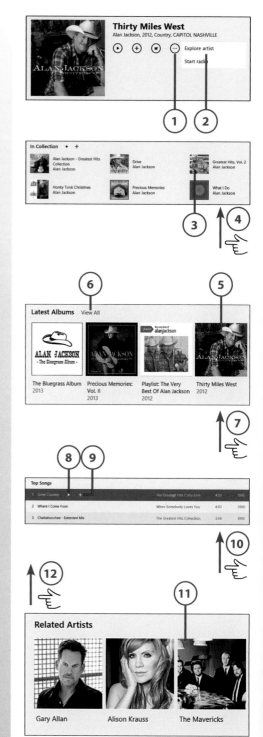

13. Tap Back to go back to the previous screen.

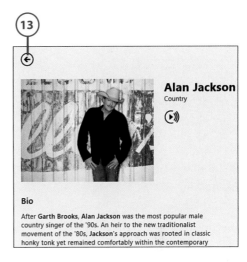

Browsing Albums in the Xbox Music Store

You can browse Xbox Music for albums of a particular genre.

1. Tap Explore to go to the Xbox Music Store.

2. Tap View All next to an album category.

3. Tap the All Genres dropdown.

4. Tap a genre you're interested in exploring.

5. Swipe up and down to view albums.

6. Tap an album to play it, buy it, or add it to a playlist.

Search

You can also search for artists, albums, and songs by tapping in the Search box in the upper-left corner of Xbox Music and entering a search term.

Buying Music

I'm intentionally not showing you how to buy an album at this point. I go into details on how you can buy music in the next section, "Managing Your Music Library."

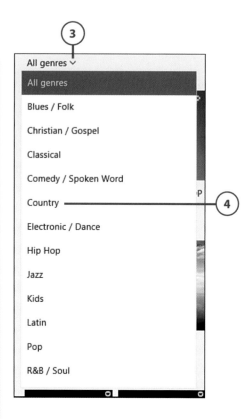

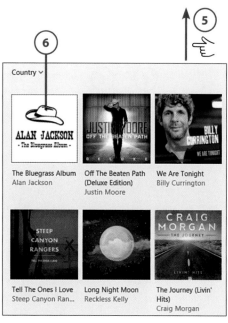

Managing Your Music Library

You probably have some digital music stored on another computer in your house or on an external hard drive or other device. You can add that music to your Music library on your Surface 2 and it will appear in the Music app. You also can purchase music from the Xbox Music Store to add music to your library. Finally, if you have an Xbox Music Pass, you can download many songs in the Xbox Music Store to your library. (I cover using an Xbox Music Pass later in this chapter.)

Adding a Folder to Your Collection

Music looks in the Windows Music library to find music on your PC. You can add additional folders and any music in those folders will be automatically added to your collection in Music.

1. From the Music app, swipe in from the right side of the screen and tap Settings.

2. Tap Preferences.

3. Tap Choose Where We Look for Music on This PC.

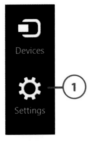

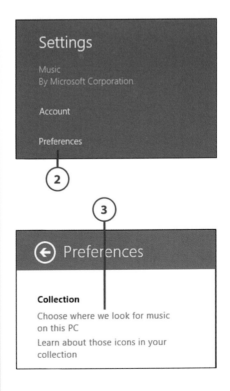

4. Tap Add Folder.

5. Browse to the location you want to add. This can be a local folder, a folder in your HomeGroup, a network folder, or a folder on your SkyDrive.

6. Tap the folder you want to add.

7. Tap Add This Folder to Music

8. Tap OK to confirm that the folder was added.

9. Tap Done.

HomeGroups

If you would like information on joining a HomeGroup and accessing files on a HomeGroup, see Chapter 12, "HomeGroups and SkyDrive."

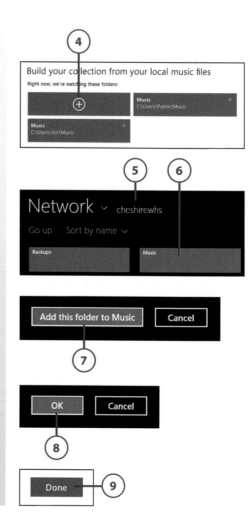

It's Not All Good

Network Folders

Adding a network location to your collection has the benefit of not using any of the memory on your Surface 2. However, there is a disadvantage to using this method: You must be on your network to access your music. It also requires the computer where the music files reside to be turned on for you to access the music files there.

If you have a large music collection, you might be better off using a microSD memory card for your music so that it's available no matter where you take your Surface 2.

Adding Album Art

The Music app can automatically download album art that is displayed when you are browsing and playing your music.

1. From the Settings screen in the Music app, tap Preferences.

2. Tap the Media Info slider to set it to On.

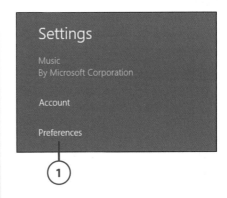

Metadata

In addition to album art, the Music app will also update metadata for your albums. Metadata includes the album name, track name, artist name, and so forth.

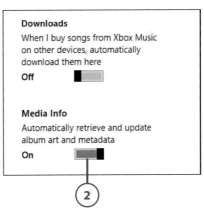

Purchasing an Album

Many online purchasing options exist for music these days, but if you plan on listening to your music on your Surface 2, buying it from the Xbox Music Store is a great choice because it will be automatically added to My Music on your Surface 2.

Music Pass

These steps assume you do not have an Xbox Music Pass.

---

1. Use Search, from Xbox Music, or browse to an album.

2. Tap Buy Album to purchase an album.

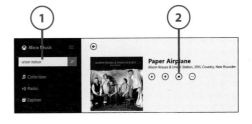

3. Enter the password for your Microsoft account if prompted, and tap OK.

4. Tap Confirm to complete your purchase and add the purchased music to your library.

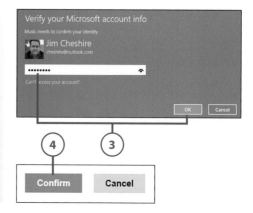

It's Not All Good

Sharing Music

You can't share music that you add to My Music on your Surface 2. Even if you join a HomeGroup on your Surface 2, you cannot share your content with other members of the HomeGroup. If you want to use music from your Surface 2 on another computer, you'll have to move the music to that computer using a USB key or a microSD memory card, or by moving it over the network using Windows Explorer.

If you want to move the files using File Explorer, you can find information on doing so using the Help system included with Windows 8.1 RT.

It's Not All Good

Cannot Upload to Xbox Music

You might be wondering at this point if you can upload music to Xbox Music so that you can play it on other devices via the cloud. Unfortunately, you can't. Xbox Music is not like iTunes Match or Amazon Cloud Player. However, you can upload your music to SkyDrive and point the Music app to your SkyDrive folder.

Automatically Downloading Music

By default, music that you purchase on other devices is added to your cloud library in Xbox Music. You can configure the Music app to automatically download music after you've purchased it from another device.

1. From the Settings panel in Music, tap Preferences.

2. Tap the When I Buy Songs from Xbox Music on Other Devices, Automatically Download Them Here slider to change the setting to the On position.

Download Location
Music that is downloaded by the Music app is placed in the C:\Users\username\Music\Xbox Music\Purchases folder.

Extra Slider
If you have an Xbox Music Pass subscription, you'll see two sliders in the Downloads section. I'll explain the second slider when I go over the details for Xbox Music Pass.

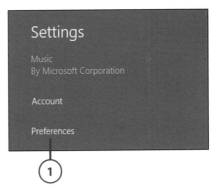

Deleting Music from Your Collection

You can delete music from your music collection. Be careful when doing so because unless the music is backed up somewhere, deleting it from your Surface 2 deletes it permanently. Music that you delete from within the Music app does not get moved to the Windows Recycle Bin.

Purchased Music

If you delete music from your PC that you originally purchased from the Xbox Music Store, you can download that music again from within the Music app.

It's Not All Good

Don't Delete Cloud Music

The Music app will allow you to delete music that's in the cloud. If you don't have another copy of your music and you delete it from the cloud, the only way to get it back is to buy it again. Be very careful when you are deleting music.

1. From within the Music app, tap Collection.

2. Tap All Music and select On This PC to see only music on your PC.

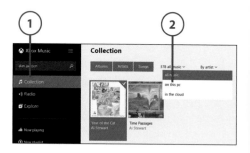

3. To delete an album, swipe left to select it and tap Delete.

4. Tap an album to view the songs on the album.

5. Swipe left on one or more songs to select them.

6. Tap Delete.

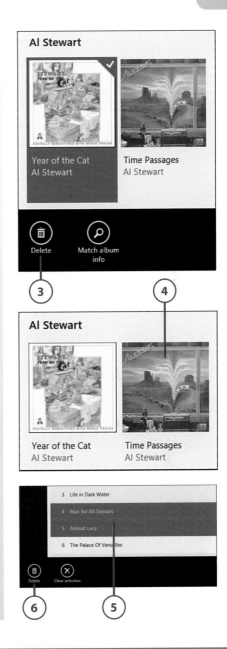

It's Not All Good

Deleting Is Permanent

I've already said this, but it's worth repeating because I don't want you to miss it. If you delete music from the Music app, it deletes the music permanently. Make absolutely sure that you want to delete a music file before you do so.

Matching the Music in Your Collection

If you would like to play your music on all of your PCs, you can let the Music app match your music. When you do, the Music app will check all the music on your PC to see whether there is a matching song in the Xbox Music Store. If there is, the Music app will allow you to play that song on your other PCs, even if that song isn't on the other PC. If the Music app is unable to find a match for your song in the Xbox Music Store, you will not be able to play that song on another device without first copying it to the device.

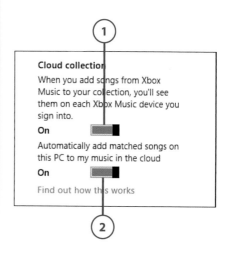

1. From the Preferences panel in the Music app, tap the first slider in Cloud Collection to the On position. This ensures that music added to your Xbox Music collection will be available on other devices.

2. Tap the second slider to change the setting to On. This enables Music Matching.

It's Not All Good

No Such Thing as Cloud-Only Music

I have a fair amount of music, more than 8,000 songs. For that reason, matching my music so it's available in the cloud and then removing it from my Surface 2's memory seemed like a great idea. I figured I would be able to access my music from anywhere as long as I had a Wi-Fi connection. In theory, that's true, but after you remove your music from your local PC, it's no longer considered to be music you own. It will still appear as cloud music in your collection, but playing it will count against your 10-hours-per-month streaming limit unless you have an Xbox Music Pass.

Using an Xbox Music Pass

An Xbox Music Pass is Microsoft's music subscription service. For $9.99 a month (or $99.90 for a year), you can stream or download a large number of songs from the Xbox Music Store. Microsoft has made a huge investment in the Xbox Music Pass experience over the past year, and you can now stream your Xbox Music Pass music on your PC, your Xbox console, your Windows Phone, your Android phone, or your iOS device. These advancements in the Xbox Music Pass offering make it a great value for anyone who loves music.

In this section, I show you how to sign up for an Xbox Music Pass and how you can add Xbox Music Pass music to your library by downloading it. In the section that follows, I explain how you can play Xbox Music Pass music along with other music in your library.

It's Not All Good

No Holy Grail Here

Although it certainly is nice to have an Xbox Music Pass, it's not the Holy Grail for music lovers. There are limitations.

Not all artists and/or record labels allow their music to be played using an Xbox Music Pass; therefore, some songs and albums won't be available. Even worse, record labels can pull songs from Xbox Music Pass whenever they choose, and if they do, you will no longer be able to stream those songs. If you've downloaded a song or album and the record label pulls it, that song or album will simply disappear from your library. It's there one day, gone the next. This has happened to me on numerous occasions.

Xbox Music Pass is still a great feature, and it's one that distinguishes Microsoft's music store from anyone else's. Microsoft will allow you to use the service free for 30 days, so it's worth trying out. The catalog of music has increased tremendously over the past year, so you might find that all the music you want is available with an Xbox Music Pass.

Purchasing an Xbox Music Pass

You can purchase an Xbox Music Pass directly from your Surface 2. (You can also sign up for a trial of the Xbox Music Pass service.)

1. From the Settings panel in the Music app, tap Account.

2. Tap Get Xbox Music Pass.

3. Enter your Microsoft account password.

4. Tap OK.

5. Tap to choose your Xbox Music Pass option.

6. Tap Next.

7. Tap Confirm to confirm your purchase.

8. Tap Done to return to the Music app.

Billing Information

If you have not already provided your billing information for your Microsoft account, you are required to enter your billing name, address, and phone number at this point.

Automatic Renewal

Your Xbox Music Pass automatically renews, so if you signed up for the trial and you don't want to continue using the service when your trial expires, be sure you cancel your subscription before your trial ends. You can cancel at any time and your Xbox Music Pass will still be active through the entire 30-day trial period.

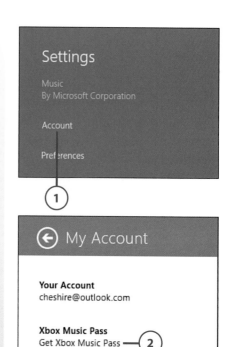

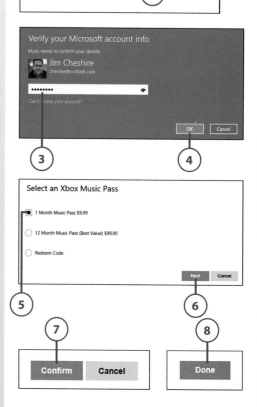

Automatically Downloading Xbox Music Pass Music

If you like to listen to music when you're not connected to Wi-Fi, you can configure the Music app to automatically download your Xbox Music Pass music after you add it to a playlist.

1. From the Preferences screen in Music, swipe down to show the Downloads section.

2. Tap the When I Add Songs from Xbox Music on This Device, Automatically Download Them Here to set the slider to On.

3. If you also want music that you add or buy on other devices to download to your Surface 2, tap the slider to automatically download music added or purchased from other devices to turn it on.

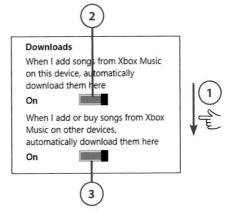

Playlists

I show you how to use playlists in Music in the "Music Playlists" section later in this chapter.

Downloading Xbox Music Pass Music

You can manually download Xbox Music Pass music to your Surface 2 so that you can play it even when you're not connected to the Internet. To manually download music, you will need to disable the automatic download feature described in the previous walkthrough.

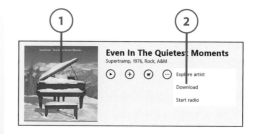

1. Browse or search to locate an album or song.

2. To download an entire album, tap More and then tap Download.

3. To download one or more songs, swipe left on the songs to select them.

4. Tap Download.

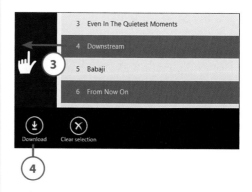

Playing Music on Other Devices

You can play music in your collection that you own on other devices such as an Xbox console. Microsoft used to call this technology Play To, but now it's simply called Play.

It's Not All Good

"Own" Is the Operative Word

Play in Windows 8.1 works great, but it's limited to content that is not copy-protected. That means that you can't use it to play Xbox Music Pass music on another device. If you want to play music on another device, you must own the music and the music must be on your PC in a folder that is configured in the Music app. If the songs are not on your local PC and added to the Music app, you won't be able to play them on another device.

Adding a Play Device

Before you can play your music on another device, you need to make sure that device is available on your Surface 2.

1. From PC Settings, tap PC and Devices.

2. Tap Devices.

3. If your device is listed under Play Devices, you are ready. Otherwise, tap Add a Device.

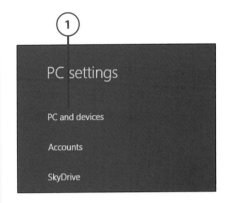

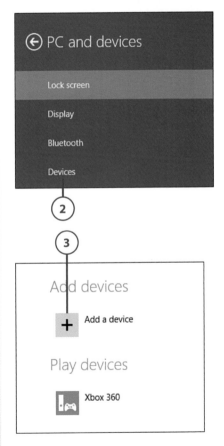

4. Select your device from the list.

5. Wait while your device is configured.

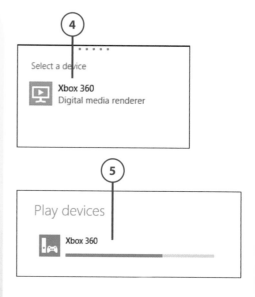

Playing Music on a Play Device

After your device is available on your
Surface 2, you can play your music
on the device.

1. Start playing the music on your
   Surface 2.

2. Swipe in from the right side of the
   screen and tap Devices.

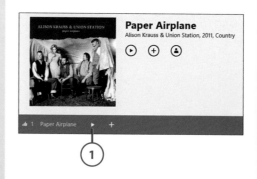

3. Tap Play.

4. Tap your device.

5. Wait for your Surface 2 to connect to the remote device and music will begin playing.

Switch Playback to Your Surface 2

You can switch playback to your Surface 2 by tapping This PC from the Play panel.

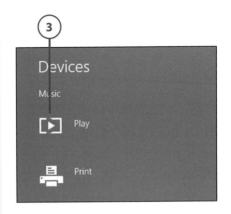

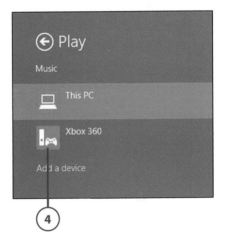

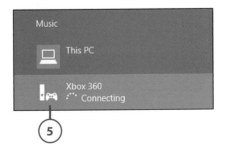

Music Playlists

Music playlists are a great way to play through a series of songs that you choose. For example, if you're having a party, you might want to play a certain type of music for your guests. A playlist makes it possible to do so easily.

Adding Songs to the Now Playing Playlist

The Music app auto-creates a playlist called Now Playing when you start playing any music. Think of the Now Playing playlist as a queue of songs to which you can add songs.

1. Tap a song, an artist, or an album to select it.

2. Tap Add.

3. Tap Now Playing to add the item and start playing.

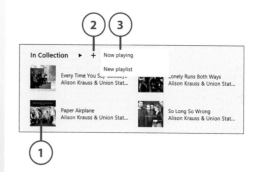

Adding Music
You can add to the Now Playing queue (or any other playlist) wherever you see the Add button.

Creating a Playlist

You can create your own playlists using songs from the Xbox Music Store, your collection, and from Xbox Music Pass.

1. After selecting the song, album, or artist that you want to add to the new playlist, tap Add.

2. Tap New Playlist from the menu.

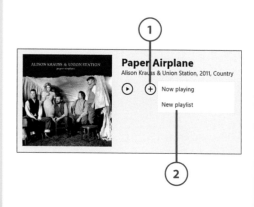

3. Enter a name for your playlist.

4. Tap Save.

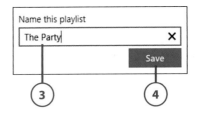

It's Not All Good

Limited Streaming and Advertising

If you don't have an Xbox Music Pass, you are limited to 10 hours per month of streaming and you'll hear ads after a few songs play. That includes playing songs added to a playlist.

Adding Songs to a Playlist

You can add songs to a playlist you've already created. As you've already seen, you can add a single song, an entire album, or all songs by a particular artist.

1. While viewing an album, artist, or song that you want to add to your playlist, tap Add.

2. Tap the name of the playlist to which you would like to add your songs.

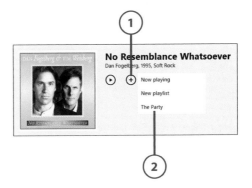

Editing a Playlist

You can edit a playlist by removing songs from it, or by changing the order of songs. Note that deleting a song from a playlist only removes the song from the list. It doesn't actually delete the song from your collection.

1. Tap the playlist you want to edit.

2. To remove a song, swipe left on the song to select it and tap Remove from Playlist.

3. To move a song up in the play order, select it and tap Move Up.

4. To move a song down in the play order, select it and tap Move Down.

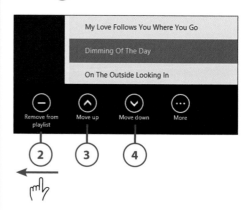

Renaming a Playlist

You can rename a playlist if you want to change the name.

1. Tap the playlist you want to rename.

2. Tap the Rename button.

3. Enter a new name for the playlist.

4. Tap Save.

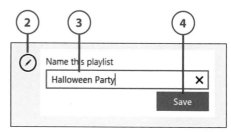

Deleting a Playlist

If you want to delete a playlist entirely, you can do so. Keep in mind that there isn't a way to restore a playlist after you do that. Note that deleting a playlist does not delete the songs in your collection.

1. Tap the playlist that you would like to delete.

2. Tap More.

3. Tap the Delete button.

4. Tap Delete to confirm that you want to delete the playlist.

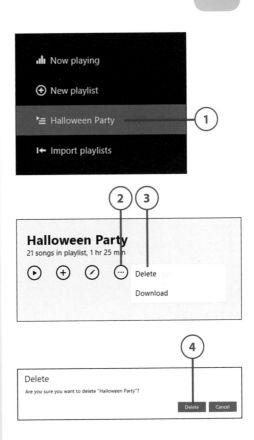

Seeing What's Playing

While you are playing songs on a playlist, you can see the songs that have already played, the song that's currently playing, and what's coming up.

1. Tap Now Playing while playing music.

2. Swipe up to scroll through the songs.

Cannot Change Song Order

Although you can shuffle the songs in the Now Playing playlist, you cannot change the order so that songs are played in a specific order of your choosing.

Shuffling or Repeating Songs in a Playlist

If you want to mix things up, you can shuffle the playback order of songs in your playlist. (This also applies to the Now Playing playlist.) You can also turn on Repeat mode so that playback will repeat until you explicitly stop it.

1. While your playlist is playing, swipe up from the bottom of the screen and tap More.

2. Tap Repeat to turn on repeat mode.

3. Tap Shuffle to turn on shuffle play.

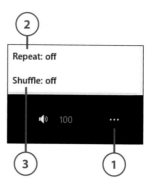

Toggle

Both the Repeat and the Shuffle buttons are toggle buttons. In other words, if the feature is turned on and you tap the button, the feature turns off.

Using Radio

If you have a hard time deciding what to listen to, you can let the Music app choose for you by using Radio. Radio is similar to Pandora; it chooses music that is similar to an artist that you select.

Creating a Radio Station

To use Radio, you must first create a Radio station.

1. Tap Radio.

2. Tap Start a Station.

3. Enter an artist.

4. Tap the artist name from the results or tap the Radio button.

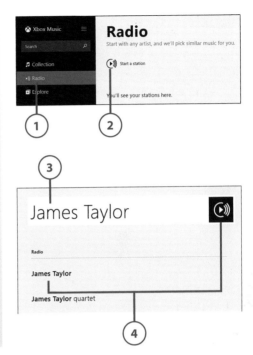

It's Not All Good

Like Pandora, But Not Pandora

In my experience, the number of artists available in Xbox Radio is limited compared to Pandora. I've also found that the music Radio chooses is not at all similar to my selected artist at times. Your use of Radio also counts towards your 10 hours per month of free streaming, so if you want to listen for longer than 10 hours per month, you'll need to purchase an Xbox Music Pass.

Playing a Radio Station

You can play any of your Radio stations from within the Music app.

1. Tap Radio.

2. Tap the Radio station that you want to play.

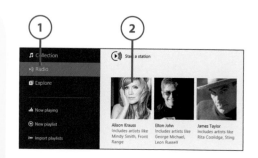

Deleting a Radio Station

If you no longer want to listen to a station, you can delete it.

1. Tap Radio.

2. Swipe left on the station you want to delete to select it.

3. Tap Delete.

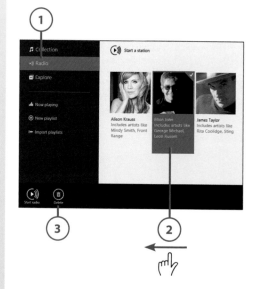

Stream movies
to your Xbox
console.

Rent and
purchase movies
and TV shows.

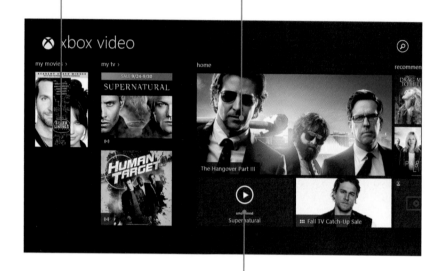

Watch your personal
videos on your
Surface 2.

14

Watching Video

Managing Personal Videos

The Personal Videos section of the Video app contains videos that are in your video library. You can add videos to your video library to add them to Personal Videos. To remove a video from Personal Videos, delete the video from your video library.

Start in Personal Videos

The Video app starts in Personal Videos by default. I show you how to configure the Video app to launch into the Xbox Video Store in the "Setting the Default View" walkthrough later in this chapter.

Adding Videos to Personal Videos

To add videos to Personal Videos, you can point the Video app to one or more folders where your videos are stored.

Playing Videos

I walk you through how to play videos in the "Playing Videos" section later in this chapter.

---

1. From the Start screen, tap the Video app to launch it.

2. Swipe in from the right side of the screen and tap Settings.

3. Tap Preferences.

4. Tap Choose Where We Look for Videos on This PC.

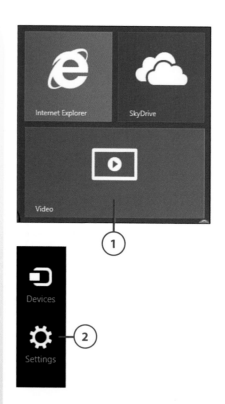

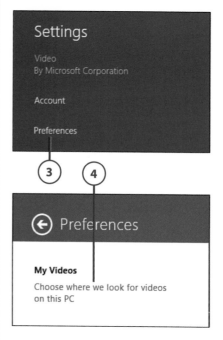

5. Tap Add to add a new folder.

6. Browse to the folder that contains your videos.

7. Tap Add This Folder to Videos.

8. Tap OK.

9. Tap Done.

Updating Might Be Slow

If you add a network folder to Personal Videos, it might take a few minutes before videos start appearing.

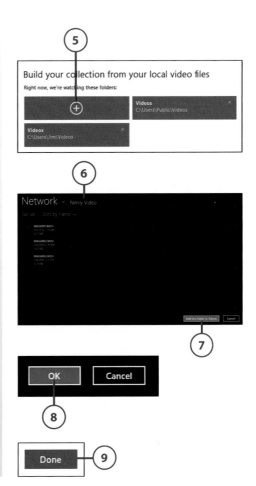

It's Not All Good

Video Over Networks

If the folder you add to the Video app is a network folder on another computer, you might experience choppy performance when playing videos from that folder. If you want to use a network folder for video, make sure that you test playback. If playback isn't as good as you would like, you can copy the video files to a local drive for better performance.

Deleting Videos from Personal Videos

You can remove videos from Personal Videos.

1. From the Video app, swipe down on the video you want to delete.

2. Tap Delete to delete the video.

3. Tap Delete to confirm that you want to delete the video.

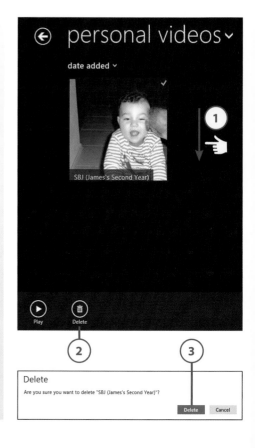

It's Not All Good

Deleting Videos

When you delete a video from Personal Videos, it also deletes the video from your video library. In other words, you aren't just deleting the video from Personal Videos. Deleting a video from the Video app actually deletes the video file itself. If you are deleting a video that is located on a network drive, it deletes the video permanently. However, if the video is on a local drive, it will be moved to the Recycle Bin.

Setting the Default View

As mentioned earlier, when you launch the Video app, it opens in Personal Videos by default. You can change the default view so that it opens in the Xbox Video Store instead.

1. From the Video app, swipe in from the right side of the screen and tap Settings.

2. Tap Preferences.

3. Tap Open My Personal Videos When I Start the App to change the setting to Off.

Exploring, Buying, and Renting Videos

In addition to watching your own videos, you can watch movies and television shows from the Xbox Video Store. You can purchase or rent videos.

Browsing Movies

Finding something to watch is sometimes a challenge, not because of a limitation on content in the store, but simply because so much good content is available. There are some features of the Xbox Video Store that make it easy to find a video to fit your current mood.

This section describes how to browse the Xbox Video Store for movies. In a later section, I show you how to browse for TV shows.

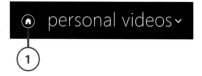

1. If you aren't already in the Xbox Video Store, tap Home to go to the store.

2. Tap a tile to see more details on a movie.

3. Swipe left to see additional categories of movies.

4. Tap a category to see more movies.

5. Swipe left or right to see more movies.

6. Tap the category header to see more categories.

7. Tap All Genres and tap a genre to filter movies based on genre.

8. Tap All Studios to filter based on the studio that produced the movie.

Filtering

Featured movies do not offer the ability to filter on genre or studio.

9. Tap a movie's tile to see details on the movie.

10. Tap a cast member to search for movies associated with a particular actor, director, and so forth.

11. Swipe left to see related movies.

12. Tap Play Trailer to watch the movie trailer for the movie.

13. While the trailer is playing, tap the video for playback controls.

14. Tap Pause to pause the video.

15. Tap Details to go back to the movie details.

16. Tap Back to return to the list of movies.

Search

You can search the Xbox Video Store by tapping the magnifying glass in the upper-right corner of any screen.

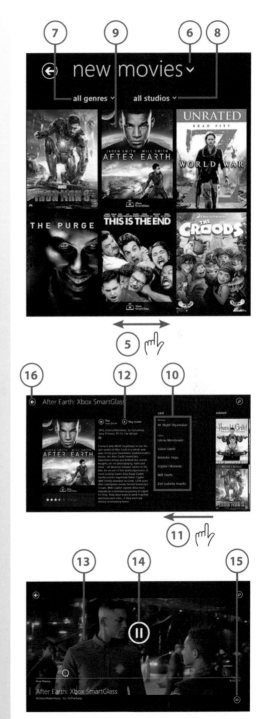

Renting Movies

You can rent movies for 14 days or 24 hours from the time you start watching your rental. Options are available for both streaming and downloading, and many movies enable you to choose between standard and high-definition versions.

1. After selecting a movie, tap Rent to rent the movie.

2. Enter your Microsoft account password and tap OK.

3. Select the rental option you want.

Rental Options

Not all rental options are available for all movies and not all movies can be rented. New movies typically don't offer the option of renting.

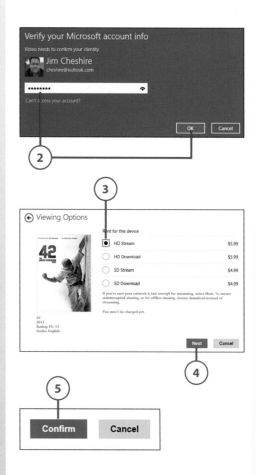

4. Tap Next.

5. Tap Confirm to confirm your rental purchase.

Payment Options

You can tap Change Payment Options if you want to use a new credit card for your purchase.

Renting Movies

Movies that you rent and choose to download are added to My Movies after you download them. You are given the opportunity to download the movie after your rental is complete.

It's Not All Good

Streaming and Downloading

Many movies require you to choose between streaming and downloading when you rent them. For those movies that require you to choose, you will only be able to play the movie using the option you select. If you choose to stream the movie, you won't be able to download it, and vice versa. This is important to keep in mind because if you select the streaming option, you must be connected to the Internet the entire time you are watching the movie.

Buying Movies

If you want to add a movie to your music library without any time limits on watching it, you can purchase the movie. Most movies you purchase can be watched on your Surface 2 or on your Xbox console.

1. After tapping a movie you want to purchase, tap Buy.

2. Enter your Microsoft account password and tap OK.

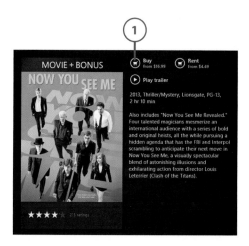

3. Tap a purchase option.

4. Tap Next.

5. Tap Confirm to complete your purchase.

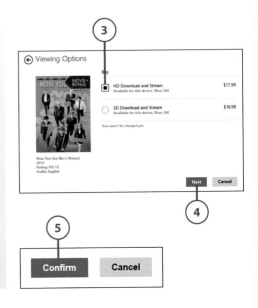

It's Not All Good

Copy Protection

When you buy a movie, you are actually just buying a license to play it whenever you want on the devices I listed. (You can play rented videos only on the device on which you rented them.) You don't have the right to burn it to a DVD or watch it on another device because copy protection will prevent it. This might surprise you because most music you buy can be freely used on any device and can also be burned onto a CD for listening in your car or on your stereo. Unfortunately, the movie companies and television studios haven't yet been persuaded to drop the copy protection from videos, so some stiff restrictions are still in place even after you buy a video.

Browsing the Television Store

In addition to movies, the Xbox Video Store provides access to a large number of television shows that you can buy. You can buy single episodes, an entire season that has already aired, or a season pass for a current season so you can keep up with the show as it airs.

1. From the Xbox Video Store, swipe left to the TV show categories.

2. Tap a TV show category.

3. Tap the category header to see additional categories.

4. Tap All Genres to filter your results by genre.

5. Tap All Networks to filter your results by network.

6. Swipe left to see additional TV shows.

7. Tap a show's tile to see more about the show.

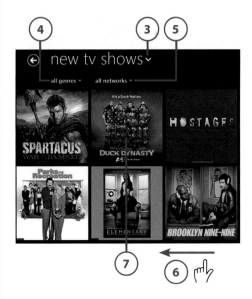

8. Tap the Season dropdown to select a different season.

9. Swipe up in the episode list to see additional episodes.

10. Tap an episode to see details on the episode.

11. Tap outside of the episode details window to return to the list of episodes.

12. Tap Back to return to the list of TV shows.

Sharing Videos

You can share movies and TV shows with an email recipient or with your social networks. Simply swipe in from the right of the screen and tap Share.

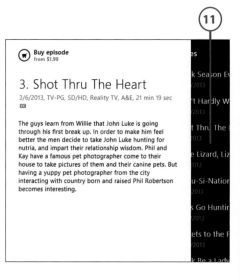

Buying TV Shows

Television shows cannot be rented, but you can purchase an entire series of a television show or one or more single episodes.

1. Tap the tile for a show you would like to purchase.

2. Select a season.

3. To purchase the entire season, tap Buy Season Pass.

4. Tap an episode you're interested in purchasing. (You can swipe up to see additional episodes.)

5. To purchase an episode, tap Buy Episode.

Buy episode
from $1.99

4. Lost at Sea

10/23/2012, TV-PG, SD/HD, Drama, CBS, 41 min 10 sec

When a helicopter crew is adrift at sea and later discovered on shore, the NCIS team must determine the cause of the crash and locate the missing pilot. Meanwhile, Tony and McGee channel their inner "Maverick" and "Iceman," a la "Top Gun," and Ziva challenges them to a dare. Diane Neal returns to guest star as CGIS Agent Abigail Borin.

6. Enter your Microsoft account password and tap OK.

7. Select the viewing option you would like to purchase.

8. Tap Next.

9. Tap Confirm to complete your purchase.

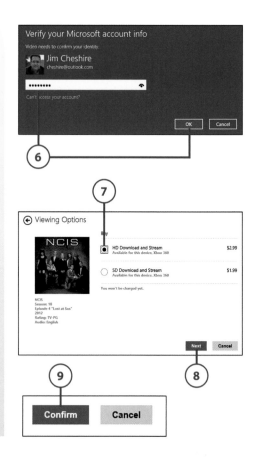

It's Not All Good

It's All or Nothing

When you buy a season pass, you must pay for the entire season (typically about $15 for SD and $25 for HD) up front. Many video stores enable you to pay for episodes as they are made available and cancel a season pass to stop being billed for episodes. The Xbox Television Store doesn't offer this option.

I'll often buy season passes when I want to get caught up on a show that I've just started watching because it allows me to easily buy all episodes up to the current episode in one step. If you want to do this with Xbox Television Store purchases, you'll need to purchase each episode individually instead. The end result is the same, but it's a bit of a hassle.

Playing Videos

Your Surface 2 has a high-resolution screen that is excellent for watching video. However, you can also play some videos on your Xbox console so that you can watch them on your home entertainment system.

Playing Videos on Your Surface 2

Videos can be streamed or downloaded to your Surface 2. If you're going to stream videos, you'll need to be connected to the Internet throughout the playback of the video.

Stream and Download

It's up to the rights owner of a video as to whether you can download a video. The Xbox Video Store lets you know what rights are available to you when you buy or rent a video.

Notice that the images you see in this walkthrough show a video that allows for both streaming and downloading; therefore, I can tap Download to download a video for offline watching.

1. From the Video app, tap on the video you would like to play.

2. Tap Play. (If you tapped a television series in step 1, you'll need to tap an episode first.)

3. While a video is playing, tap the video to access playback controls.

4. Drag the scrubber handle to quickly move to a particular part of the video.

5. Tap Back to return to the Video app home screen.

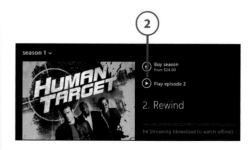

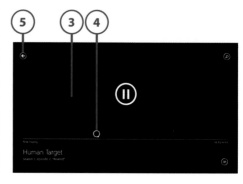

Playing Videos on Your Xbox Console

You can use your Xbox console to watch videos that you've purchased using your Surface 2 tablet. (Note that this applies only to Xbox Video Store purchases that specifically say they can be played on an Xbox console.) You can also play unprotected videos that you've copied into Personal Videos.

1. Start playing your video in the Video app on your Surface 2.

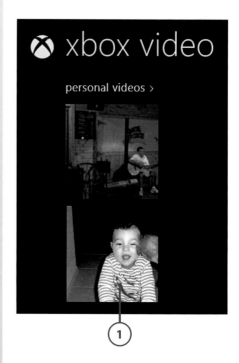

2. Swipe in from the right side of the screen and tap Devices.

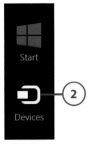

Xbox SmartGlass Not Required

Windows RT required that you first install the Xbox SmartGlass app before you were able to play videos on an Xbox console. Windows 8.1 RT removes that requirement.

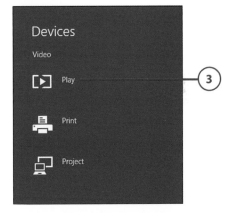

3. Tap Play.

4. Tap your Xbox console.

5. From the Play panel, tap This PC to transfer playback to your Surface 2.

If you start watching a movie rental on your Surface 2 and you later decide that you want to watch that video on your Xbox console, you'll have to rent the movie again to watch it on your Xbox console. Unfortunately, there isn't an option to switch devices for rented movies at this time.

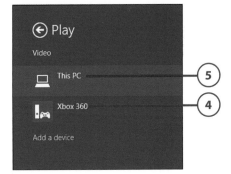

It's Not All Good

Project to a TV Doesn't Work

You might have noticed a Project item on the Devices panel. This option allows you to use a standard known as Miracast to send a video signal to a television using an intermediary device that also supports Miracast. Unfortunately, the Surface 2 does not support using Miracast, so you cannot project a video to a television using this feature.

Edit your pictures
using powerful
editing tools.

Share your pictures with
friends and family.

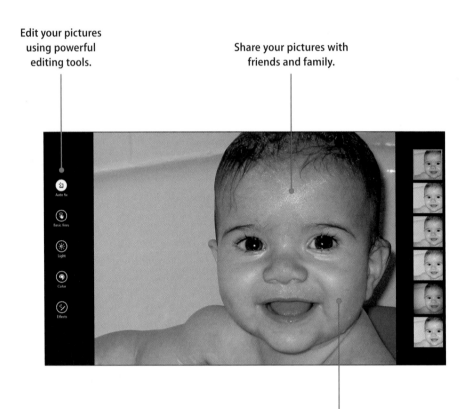

Take and view your
pictures on your
Surface 2.

In this chapter…

Pictures

Adding Pictures to the Photos App

The Photos app is the repository for pictures on your Surface 2 device, on your SkyDrive, and on other computers on your network. In addition to viewing pictures, the Photos app includes basic editing functionality.

Importing Pictures into the Pictures Library

If you have files on a removable drive, a microSD memory card, or a digital camera that can be connected to your Surface 2 using USB, you can import pictures from the device into your Surface 2.

Importing from Other Devices

If you have another storage device such as a CompactFlash card, an SD card, and so forth, you can import photos from them as long as you have a USB card reader that you can attach to your Surface 2.

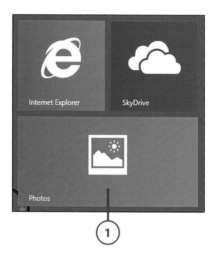

1. From the Start screen, tap Photos to start the Photos app.

2. With your device connected to your Surface 2, swipe up from the bottom of the screen and tap Import.

My Device

In this walkthrough, my device is an SD memory card inserted into an SD card reader and inserted into the USB port on my Surface 2. This is one of the great things about the Surface 2; plug almost anything into the USB ports and it just works.

3. Tap the device that contains the pictures you want to import.

4. Swipe down to select any pictures you want to import.

5. To select all pictures, tap Select All. You can then swipe down on those pictures that you don't want to import to deselect them.

6. To deselect all pictures, tap Clear Selection.

7. Tap Import to import the pictures.

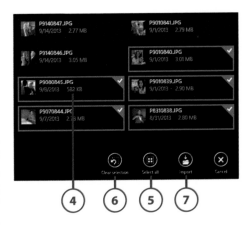

Folder Created on Import

When you import pictures, the Photos app will create a folder named using the current date and will import all the pictures into that folder.

Importing Videos

You can also import videos into the Photos app. Videos will play inside of the Photos app.

Viewing Pictures and Video

After you've added some pictures to your Pictures library, you can view them in the Photos app. You also can watch a slide show of images and set a picture as your lock screen image.

Browsing Pictures

You can browse through all the pictures in your Pictures library and pictures from your SkyDrive.

1. From the Photos app, tap the folder that contains the pictures you want to view.

2. Swipe left and right to see additional pictures.

3. Tap the down arrow and tap SkyDrive to see pictures in your SkyDrive.

4. Tap a picture to see the picture full screen.

5. Reverse pinch to zoom in on a picture.

6. Drag to move the picture while zoomed in.

7. Pinch to zoom out on a picture.

8. Tap the screen and tap Back to go back to the previous screen.

Going Back

You can continue to tap Back to go all the way back to the home screen of the Photos app.

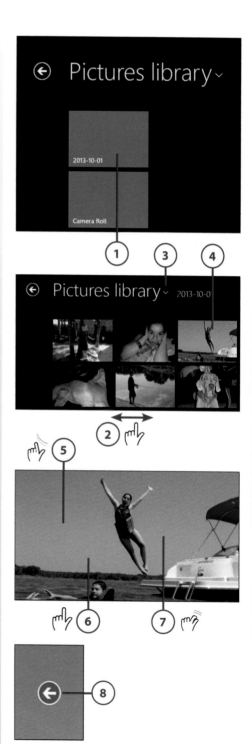

Watching a Slide Show

You can view a slide show of pictures. When you are viewing a slide show, the Photos app transitions through all the pictures in the folders that are visible when you start the slide show. Each picture is displayed for four seconds.

1. In the Photos app, tap a folder that contains the pictures you want to view in your slide show.

2. Tap any picture in the folder to view it in fullscreen mode.

3. Swipe up from the bottom of the screen and tap Slide Show to start the slide show.

Stopping a Slide Show

You can stop a slide show simply by tapping the screen or switching away from the Photos app.

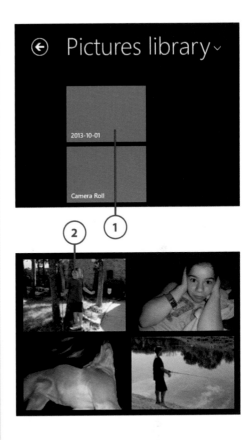

It's Not All Good

No Slide Show Settings

When viewing a slide show, you cannot control the transition or the length of time that pictures are displayed. Your pictures will always fade from one to the next, and each picture will always be displayed for four seconds.

Deleting Pictures

You can delete pictures from the Photos app, but only those pictures that are in your Pictures library.

1. Browse to the folder that contains the picture or pictures that you want to delete.

2. Swipe down on one or more pictures to select them. (You can also tap Select All to select all pictures.)

3. Tap Delete.

4. Tap Delete to confirm the deletion.

It's Not All Good

Deletion Fails

By default, Windows 8.1 RT does not prompt you when you delete a file. However, if you configure Windows 8.1 RT to prompt you before recycling files, the Photos app will display an error when you attempt to delete files. Unfortunately, this error is not intuitively presented.

In the next walkthrough, I'll show you how to deal with this issue.

Deleting Pictures When the Recycle Bin Is Configured to Prompt

If you open the Windows Recycle Bin and click on Properties, you see a checkbox that allows you to configure the Recycle Bin to prompt on deletion. (This was the default behavior in Windows 7 and earlier.) If you enable this option, deleting files from the Photos app becomes a bit more complicated.

1. Select the pictures that you want to delete and tap Delete.

2. Tap Delete to confirm that you want to delete the files.

3. Tap Some Items Couldn't Be Recycled in the upper-right corner of the screen.

4. Tap Some Items Couldn't Be Recycled again.

5. Tap Yes to delete the pictures.

6. Tap Back to return to your pictures.

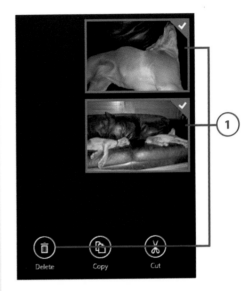

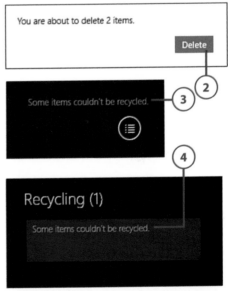

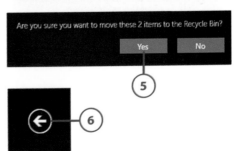

Using a Picture in Your Lock Screen

You can change the background image for your lock screen so that it displays one of your favorite pictures.

1. While viewing the picture you want to use as your lock screen background image, swipe up from the bottom of the screen and tap Set As.

2. Tap Lock Screen.

No Cropping

Windows 8.1 RT uses the full picture as your lock screen background. There is no option to crop the image or reposition it. If you want to use a cropped image for your background, you'll need to crop the image first and then set it as your lock screen picture.

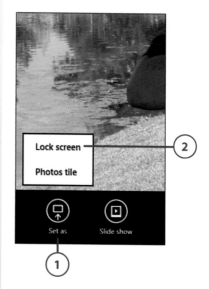

Setting the Pictures App Tile Image

By default, the Photos app's tile shuffles through pictures from the Photos app. However, you can choose to have it display one picture on the tile.

1. While viewing the picture that you want to use as the tile's background, swipe up from the bottom of the screen and tap Set As.

2. Tap Photos Tile.

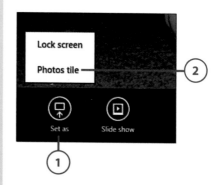

Shuffling Pictures on the App Tile

If you've set a picture as the background picture for the Photos app's tile and you want to switch back to the default setting where pictures are shuffled, you can do that from the Options pane.

1. While in the Photos app, swipe in from the right side of the screen and tap the Settings charm.

2. Tap Options.

3. Tap the Shuffle Photos on the Photos Tile to turn on photo shuffling.

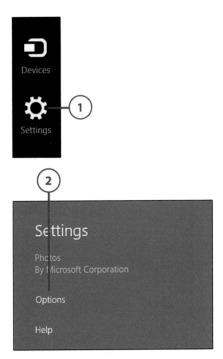

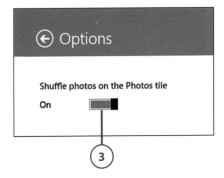

Sharing Pictures

One way that you'll undoubtedly share pictures on your Surface 2 is by handing the device to someone else so that he or she can look at the pictures on the screen. However, if you want to share pictures with someone who's not nearby, you can use the Share charm to share pictures through email.

Sharing a Picture with Email

You can share pictures using email with the option to either send the picture as an attachment or using SkyDrive. When a picture is sent using SkyDrive, a link to the picture is sent and the recipient of the email can download the picture from SkyDrive.

1. Select one or more pictures that you want to share.

2. Swipe in from the right side of the screen and tap the Share charm.

3. Tap Mail.

4. Enter one or more email addresses.

5. Enter a subject for your email.

6. Enter a message for your email if you want.

7. Tap Send to send the email.

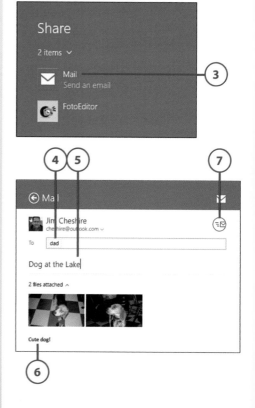

Editing Pictures

The Photos app has basic photo editing features. In addition to cropping pictures and rotating pictures, you can also adjust color, contrast, brightness; add effects; fix red eye; and much more.

Rotating and Cropping Pictures

The most basic editing operations are rotating and cropping pictures.

1. Tap a picture that you want to rotate or crop.

2. Swipe up from the bottom of the screen.

3. To rotate the picture 90 degrees clockwise, tap Rotate. Each tap of Rotate will rotate the picture another 90 degrees.

4. To crop a picture, tap Crop.

5. Tap and drag inside of the cropping frame to reposition the picture.

6. Drag the handles on the cropping frame to resize the area to be cropped.

7. Tap Aspect Ratio and tap a desired aspect ratio to size the cropping frame accordingly.

8. Tap Apply to apply the crop.

9. Tap Save a Copy to save the cropped picture as a new picture file.

10. Tap Update Original to overwrite the original file with the cropped image.

11. Tap Undo to undo the cropping and return to the crop screen where you can adjust the crop.

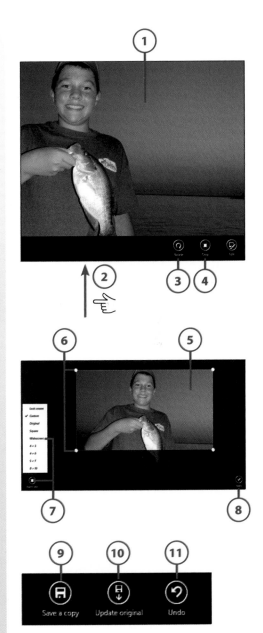

Saving Edits

After you complete any of the walkthroughs in this section, you can save your edits to a new picture or overwrite the original using the same steps I outlined in steps 9 through 11 in the "Rotating and Cropping Pictures" walkthrough.

Automatically Fixing Image Problems

You can use the Photo app's Auto Fix feature to automatically fix problems with a picture. You can choose from one of six presets to fix an image or to convert a color image to black and white with a single tap.

1. Tap a picture you want to edit.

2. Swipe up from the bottom of the screen and tap Edit.

3. Tap Auto Fix.

4. Tap one of the six presets on the right edge of the picture.

Removing Red Eye

You can easily remove red eye from a picture with a single tap.

1. Tap a picture with a red eye problem.

2. Swipe up from the bottom of the screen and tap Edit.

3. Tap Basic Fixes.

4. Tap Red Eye.

5. Tap on the red eye to remove it.

Zooming Helps

By reverse pinching to zoom in on a picture, you can make it easier to tap someone's red eyes or to make other adjustments.

Retouching a Photo

Retouching is a great way to remove blemishes, splotchy skin, and other qualities of a picture that you want to touch up.

1. From the Editing screen, tap Basic Fixes.

2. Tap Retouch.

3. Tap on an area that you want to retouch.

4. Tap one or more times if necessary to complete the touch up.

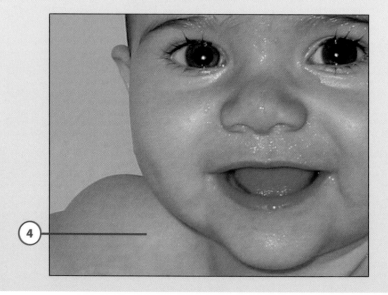

Adjusting Lighting

You can adjust the lighting of your picture. This includes brightness, contrast, highlights, and shadows.

1. From the Editing screen, tap Light.

2. Tap and hold on Brightness, Contrast, Highlights, or Shadows depending on what you want to adjust.

3. Drag the dial counterclockwise to decrease the value and clockwise to increase the value.

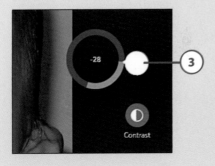

Adjusting Color

You can adjust color temperature (how warm or cold the pictures looks), color tint, and color saturation.

1. In the Editing screen, tap Color.

2. Tap and hold on Temperature, Tint, or Saturation depending on what you want to adjust.

3. Drag the dial counterclockwise to decrease the setting and clockwise to increase the setting.

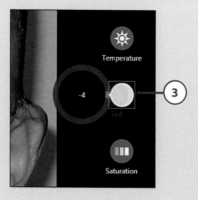

Enhancing a Color

You might want to enhance one or more colors in a picture so that they stand out more. (You can also tone down a particular color.) The Photos app can help you do this easily.

1. From the Editing screen, tap Color.

2. Tap and hold on Color Enhance.

3. Drag the color droplet to the color you would like to enhance and release your finger to select that color.

4. Drag the dial counterclockwise to decrease saturation for the selected color across the entire image.

5. Drag the dial clockwise to increase saturation for the selected color across the entire image.

6. Drag the color droplet to a new color if you want to adjust one or more additional colors.

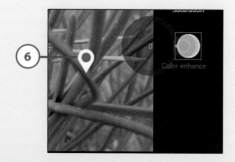

Applying a Vignette Effect

A vignette effect makes the edges of a photo either lighter or darker than the rest of the picture. It's a commonly used effect to draw attention to something in the center of an image.

1. From the Editing screen, tap Effects.

2. Tap and hold on Vignette.

3. Drag the dial counterclockwise to apply a darkening to the edges of the picture.

4. Drag the dial clockwise to apply a lightening to the edges of the picture.

Using Selective Focus

Another way that you can emphasize the focal point of a picture is by using selective focus. This allows you to have one part of the picture in crystal clear focus while the rest of the picture is blurred to a certain degree.

1. While in the Editing screen, tap Effects.

2. Tap Selective Focus.

3. Drag the ellipse to encompass the portion of the image you want to be in focus.

4. Use the sizing handles to resize and reshape the ellipse.

5. Tap Strength and tap a blurring strength to control how blurry the rest of the image is.

6. Tap Preview to remove the ellipse temporarily so that you can see the effect more clearly.

7. Tap Preview again to restore the ellipse for further adjustments.

8. Tap Apply to apply the effect.

Using the Camera App

Your Surface 2 has two cameras that you can use to take pictures and video. Pictures and video taken with the Camera app are added to your Pictures library in the Photos app.

Taking Pictures

You can take pictures with either the front-facing camera or the rear-facing camera. The front-facing camera is typically used for videoconferencing. The rear-facing camera is better suited for taking pictures that you might normally take with a point-and-shoot camera.

1. From the Start screen, tap the Camera tile to launch the Camera app.

2. Swipe up from the bottom of the screen and tap Change Camera to toggle between the front-facing and rear-facing camera.

3. Tap Timer to enable a timer that will count down prior to a photo being taken. (The first tap enables a 3-second timer and the second tap changes it to a 10-second timer.)

4. Tap anywhere on the screen or tap the camera button to take a picture.

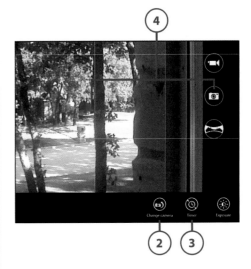

Changing Picture Exposure

You can change the exposure for pictures that you take with your Surface 2.

1. While viewing an image in the desired camera, swipe up from the bottom of the screen and tap Exposure.

2. Drag the slider up to increase exposure and down to decrease exposure.

Exposure Settings

When you first tap Exposure, the slider appears to be set to maximum exposure. However, the actual setting is at the half-way point on the Exposure slider unless you change it.

Adding Location Information to Pictures

You can have location information added to your pictures. When you launch the Camera app for the first time, you'll be asked whether it can use your location info. You can also decide at any time to allow or disallow location information in your pictures.

1. From the Camera app, swipe in from the right side of the screen and tap Settings.

2. Tap Options.

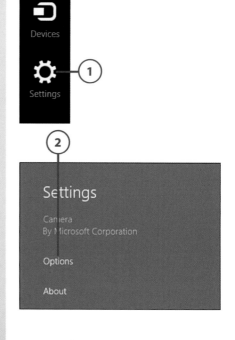

3. Set the Location Info slider to On to automatically add location information to your pictures.

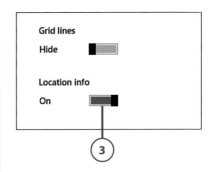

Location Info and Social Networks

Many people turn off location info in pictures because they are afraid that bad people can use that information to track them or their children using pictures uploaded to social networks. In fact, all the popular social networking sites remove all location information from pictures that you upload.

Changing Photo Aspect Ratio

You can change the aspect ratio of the pictures you take. Changes to this setting apply to all pictures you take after you change the setting.

1. From the Options screen in Camera, tap Photo Aspect Ratio.

2. Tap the desired aspect ratio.

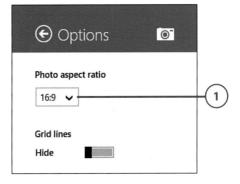

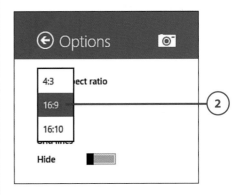

Showing Grid Lines

Keeping your Surface 2 level when taking pictures can sometimes be difficult. Although you can certainly straighten pictures in your favorite photo-editing app after taking it, ensuring your camera is straight when you take the picture makes much more sense. Grid lines can help you do that.

1. From the Options screen in Camera, tap the Grid Lines slider to change the setting to Show.

2. Use the Grid Lines to help keep the camera level when taking a picture or video.

3. Tap the Grid Lines slider again to turn off grid lines if you want to.

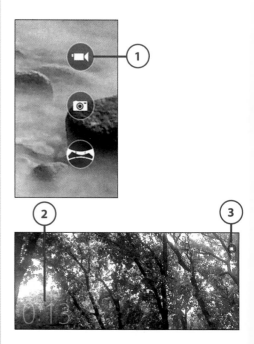

Taking Video

In addition to taking still pictures, you can shoot video with your Surface 2. Videos are also saved to your Pictures library.

1. Tap Video to start recording a video.

2. While recording a video, the total recording time appears in the lower-left corner.

3. Tap Stop to stop recording and save your video to the Camera Roll.

Taking Panoramic Pictures

You can take panoramic pictures that you can view in the Photos app. Panoramas allow you to capture up to a 360-degree view of a scene.

1. Tap Panorama to start taking a panoramic shot.

2. Tilt your Surface 2 up and down and left and right slowly to take the pictures necessary to build the panorama. Your Surface 2 will automatically take pictures as you move the device.

3. To restart your panorama, tap Undo.

4. When you are satisfied with the panorama, tap the check to save it.

5. Wait while the panorama images are stitched together to build the panorama.

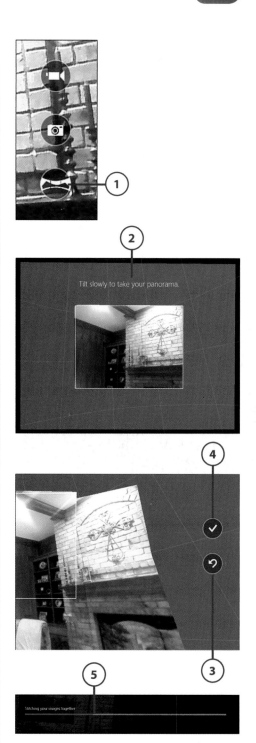

It's Not All Good

Windows 8.1 and Windows 8.1 RT Only

Panoramas are pretty cool, but they can only be viewed in the Photos app in Windows 8.1 and Windows 8.1 RT. That means that although you can share your panoramas with friends and family, they can only be viewed by people who have Windows 8.1 or Windows 8.1 RT.

Viewing the Camera Roll

Pictures, videos, and panoramas that you take with the Camera app are saved to the Camera Roll. You can access the Camera Roll from the Photos app, but you can also access it directly from the Camera app.

Viewing Pictures and Videos

Pictures and videos are stored in the Camera Roll and can be conveniently viewed with one touch from the Camera app.

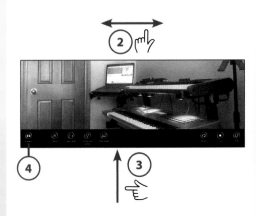

1. While in the Camera app, swipe up from the bottom of the screen and tap Camera Roll.

2. Swipe left and right to browse through the pictures and videos in the Camera Roll.

3. While viewing a picture, swipe up from the bottom of the screen to interact with the picture.

4. Tap Camera to return to the Camera app.

Interacting with Pictures in Camera Roll

When you swipe up from the bottom of the screen in Camera Roll, you will have the options available to you from the Photos app. For more information on using those features, see the appropriate sections earlier in this chapter.

Viewing Panoramas

Viewing panoramas is a bit different than viewing pictures or videos because they are 3D-like image files that allow you to pan throughout the scene.

1. Tap a panorama in the Camera Roll.

Identifying Panoramas in Camera Roll

Panoramas show four directional arrows inside of a circle when viewing thumbnails in the Camera Roll.

2. The Photos app automatically pans across your panorama. Tap the circle in the middle of the screen to stop the automatic pan.

3. Drag to pan around in your panorama.

4. Swipe up from the bottom of the screen, tap Tilt to View, and tilt your Surface 2 to pan around the panorama by tilting the device.

5. Tap Tilt to View to turn off Tilt to View.

6. Tap Back to return to the Camera Roll.

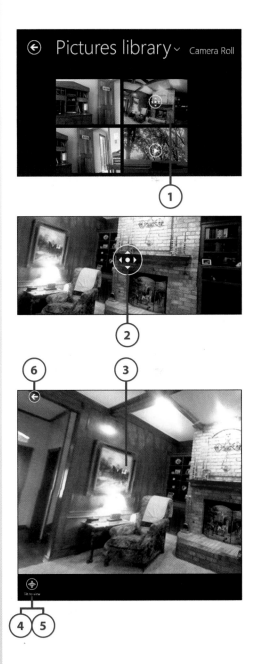

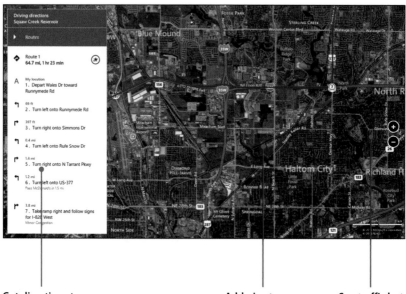

Get directions to
addresses and
other locations.

Add pins to your
favorite locations.

See traffic hot
spots and details
on delays.

Using Maps

The Maps app enables you to use the Bing Maps service to explore maps, search for places and addresses, and find directions. You can view road maps with minimal clutter as well as aerial maps that provide a satellite view of an area. In many cases, you can also view an angled aerial view that provides a three-dimensional perspective of the map.

Exploring Maps

The Maps app provides maps of practically the entire world, and satellite imagery is available for many areas. Many of its tools enable you to easily explore any area you want.

Viewing and Zooming

While you are viewing the map, you can easily move around and zoom in and out using touch.

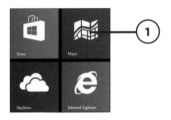

1. From the Start screen, tap Maps to launch the Maps app.

2. If prompted, tap Allow to let the Maps app use your location or Block to prevent the Maps app from using your location.

3. Tap and slide to move around on the map.

4. Reverse-pinch to zoom in on the map.

5. Pinch to zoom out on the map.

6. Double-tap to zoom in and center the map on the point where you double-tapped.

Map Scale

A map scale is displayed in the lower-right corner of the map. Use this to determine distances while viewing the map.

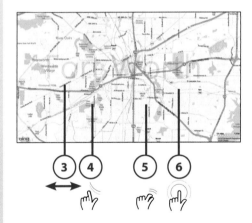

It's Not All Good

Location Services

Many apps you use might use location services to provide you with a better experience. The Maps app uses location services so that it can show you your current location on the map, and so it can provide a better experience when you are getting directions.

Every Wi-Fi access point transmits a unique identifier called a MAC address. There are companies that drive around the country collecting these MAC addresses and the approximate GPS coordinates of each one. Your Surface 2 uses services provided by these companies to get your approximate location based on the MAC addresses that your tablet picks up.

Using Zoom Controls

For more precise control over zooming, you can use zoom controls in the Maps app. Zoom controls are off by default, so before you can use them, you'll need to turn them on.

1. While viewing a map, swipe in from the right side of the screen and tap the Settings charm.

2. Tap Options.

3. Tap Always Show Zoom Controls on the Map to turn on the setting.

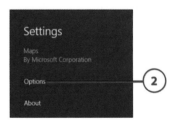

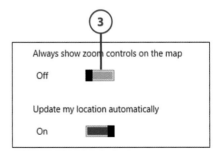

4. Tap the + sign to zoom in on the map.

5. Tap the – sign to zoom out on the map.

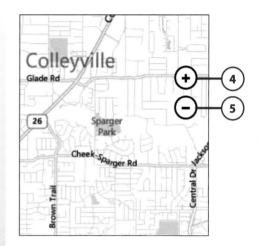

Viewing Your Location

If you've allowed the Maps app to use your location, when you launch the app, it will center the map on your current location. When you drag to move the map elsewhere, you can return the map to your current location.

1. While viewing the map, swipe up from the bottom of the screen.

2. Tap My Location to center your current location on the map.

Changing the Units of Measurement

By default, the Maps app shows distances using miles as the unit. If you prefer, you can switch the Maps app to use kilometers instead.

1. While in the Maps app, swipe in from the right side of the screen and tap the Settings charm.

2. Tap Options.

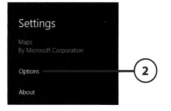

3. Tap Kilometers to switch to using kilometers for distance measurement.

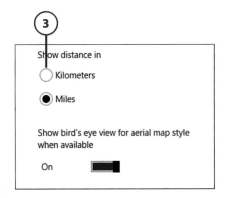

Changing the Map Style

The Maps app shows maps using the Road style by default. This style of map is similar to paper maps and uses a solid-colored background and displays roads using different colors based on the size of the road. You can switch to Aerial style, which uses a satellite image for the map with colored roads drawn on top of the image.

1. While viewing the map, swipe up from the bottom of the screen and tap Map Style.

2. Tap Aerial View to switch to Aerial view.

3. To switch back to Road view, tap Road View.

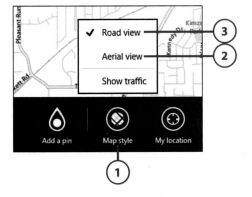

Using Bird's Eye View

Many larger metropolitan areas offer an angled, 3-D perspective view called Bird's Eye view when the map is in Aerial view, provided the feature is enabled (which it is by default).

No Bird's Eye View in Road View

Bird's Eye view is available only when the Aerial View map style is enabled.

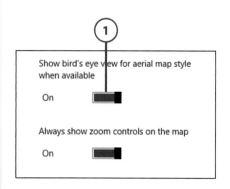

1. From the Options pane, tap Show Bird's Eye View for Aerial Map Style When Available if necessary to turn on the feature.

2. Reverse-pinch to zoom in. Angled view activates automatically when you reach a zoom level where 1 inch is equal to 200 yards.

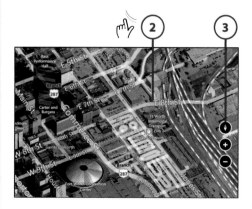

3. Tap the compass rose to change your view. Each press of the button rotates the map 90 degrees.

4. The fourth press of the compass rose button turns off angled view. Tap the square button to re-enable angled view.

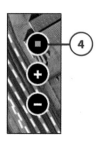

Showing Traffic

The Maps app can show you traffic congestion from Microsoft's Bing service. Maps uses colors overlaid on roads to indicate the speed of traffic. Areas where traffic is very slow are shown in red, slow traffic is orange, somewhat slow traffic is yellow, and fast traffic is green. If a road doesn't show any of these colors, traffic data for that road isn't available.

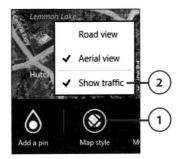

1. While viewing a map, swipe up from the bottom of the screen and tap Map Style.

2. Tap Show Traffic.

3. To see details on a traffic incident, tap the triangle icon.

4. Tap the map to dismiss the details popup.

Searching Maps

In addition to browsing through a map, you can search the Maps app for an address or a place of interest.

Searching for a Place

You can search for a business or a place using the Maps app. For example, you can use the Maps app to find museums by searching for "museum."

1. Swipe up from the bottom of the screen and tap Search.

2. Enter a place name or a search term and press Enter.

Use Search History

You can easily find a place or address you've previously searched for by tapping the search term in the search history that is listed directly under the search box.

3. To view a search result on the map, tap the result.

4. Tap Directions to get directions to the selected place.

5. Tap Nearby to see nearby attractions.

6. Tap Website to open the location's website in Internet Explorer.

7. Tap Call to call the location using Skype or another installed telecommunications app.

8. Tap Add Favorite to add the place to your favorites.

9. To clear your search results from the map, swipe up from the bottom of the screen and tap Clear Map.

Finding an Address

You can use this same search technique to find an address on the map.

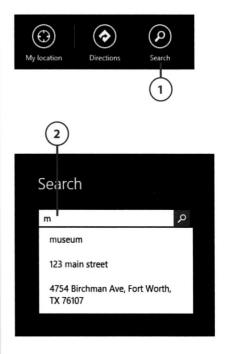

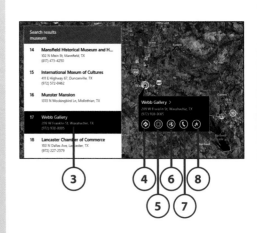

Adding Pins

You can drop a pin on a visible place on the map. You use pins to save a location on the map for future reference. As you'll see later, you can also use pins to get directions to a visible location on the map.

1. While viewing the map, swipe up from the bottom of the screen.

2. Tap and hold on Add a Pin and drag it to the map, releasing it when it is on the location where you want the pin added.

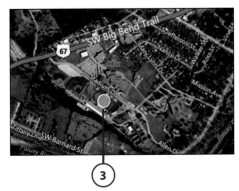

3. Tap a pin to display information on the pin.

4. Tap Directions to get directions to the location where the pin is located.

5. Tap Nearby to see locations of interest nearby.

6. Tap Add Favorite to add the location to your favorites.

7. Tap Remove to remove the pin.

8. To remove all pins from the map, swipe up from the bottom of the screen and tap Clear Map.

Getting Directions

The Maps app can generate directions so that you can easily find an address or a place on the map. This feature works best when you've allowed the Maps app to use your current location.

Allowing Maps to Use Your Updated Location

You can always swipe up from the bottom of the screen and tap My Location to update your location. However, you can also allow Maps to update your location automatically. (If you are allowing Maps to use your location, this feature is on by default.)

1. From the Options panel, slide up to reveal the Update My Location Automatically slider.

2. Tap the slider to change the setting to On to allow the Maps app to automatically update your location.

⊛ Options

Show temperature in

◯ Celsius

◉ Fahrenheit

Show distance in

◯ Kilometers

◉ Miles

Show bird's eye view for aerial map style when available

On ▭

Always show zoom controls on the map

On ▭

Update my location automatically

On ▭

Getting Directions

You've already seen how you can get directions to a pinned location or to a place you've searched for. You can also get directions from your location to an address or from one place to another place using the Directions feature of Maps.

1. Swipe up from the bottom of the screen and tap Directions.

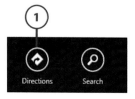

Directions   Search

2. By default, the starting point is your current location. Tap inside the A box and enter a new address to use a different starting location.

3. Enter a destination place name or address in the B box. You can also tap the crosshairs to use your current location for a destination. If you do, you'll need to enter a starting point in the A box.

4. Tap the bus or the pedestrian symbol to get directions for public transit or walking directions.

5. Tap Options to set an option to avoid highways and toll roads.

6. Tap the arrow or press Enter on the keyboard to generate the directions.

7. To choose a different route, tap Routes and tap an alternate route.

8. Tap Add Favorite to add the route to your favorites.

9. To see a zoomed-in view of a particular turn on the route, tap the turn in the directions.

10. Slide up to see additional turns on the route.

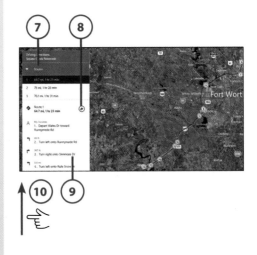

Recalling Favorite Locations and Favorite Routes

Throughout the walkthroughs in this chapter, you've seen several places where you can add a location or a route to your favorites. You can easily recall these favorite locations and routes.

1. Swipe down from the top of the screen.

2. Tap Favorites.

3. Tap a favorite location or a favorite route to load it into Maps.

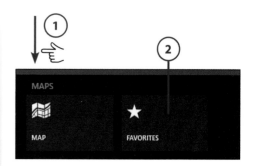

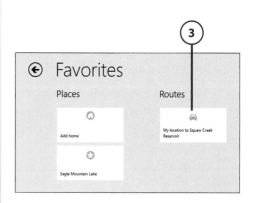

Editing Favorites

When you add a favorite, it might not use the name you would like. Many of my favorites are lakes, and when I add them by dropping a pin, they are often named using the ZIP code for the lake. Editing the name so it reflects something descriptive to you is simple to do.

1. Swipe down from the top of the screen and tap Favorites.

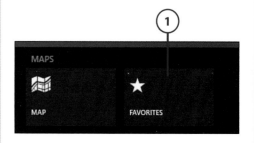

2. Drag down on the favorite you want to edit.

3. Tap Edit.

4. Enter a name for the favorite.

5. Tap Always Show On Map to choose whether a pin is always displayed on the map where the favorite is located.

6. Tap Set as Home to set the favorite as your home. (You would typically only do this if the favorite is located at your home.)

7. Enter any notes you want to edit for the favorite.

Editing Favorites

If you tap a favorite so that it's displayed on the map, you'll also see an Edit button on the favorite's popup. You can edit the favorite using this method if you aren't sure where a particular favorite that is shown on the Favorites screen is located.

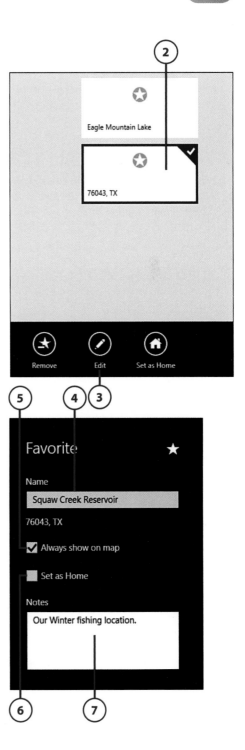

Sharing Maps

You can share maps with others using email. Sharing a map provides others with an image of the map you are sharing, and if you are viewing directions when you share a map, you can share the directions along with screenshots of the map.

Sharing with Other Windows 8.1 Users

When you share a map or directions, users of Windows 8.1 who receive your shared map will be able to open the shared map inside the Maps app.

Sharing Maps with Email

Sharing maps with email is a great way to send someone directions to a particular location. Recipients of the email can open the shared map in Bing Maps in a browser or in the Maps app (if they are using Windows 8.1), or see details in the email message that you send.

1. While viewing the map you want to share, swipe in from the right side of the screen and tap the Share charm.

2. Tap Mail.

3. Enter a recipient email address.

4. Modify the Subject if you want to.

5. Enter a message.

6. Tap Send to send the message.

It's Not All Good

No People Sharing

Notice that the People app shows up when you tap the Share charm; however, you cannot share maps with the People app. If you try, you're told to try another app, such as Mail.

Proof your document with spell check, a dictionary, a thesaurus, and more.

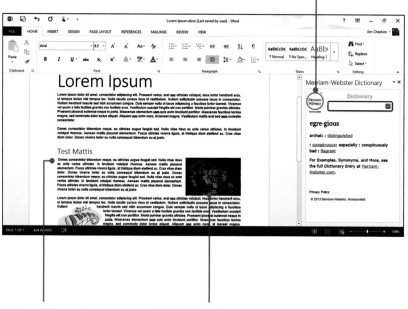

Enter and format text, including using styles for advanced formatting.

Add pictures for a more engaging document.

In this chapter...

→ Creating, Opening, and Saving Documents
→ Formatting Text
→ Adding Pictures
→ Proofing Documents
→ Sharing Documents
→ Printing Documents
→ Tips and Tricks

Creating Documents with Microsoft Word 2013

Windows 8.1 RT includes Microsoft Word 2013, a powerful word processor with all the features necessary to create complex documents. Complete coverage of Microsoft Word would require an entire book, but this chapter provides you with the skills you need to start creating and editing documents. I end this chapter with a few tips and tricks that will make using Microsoft Word more enjoyable and productive.

Creating, Opening, and Saving Documents

Like other Microsoft Office 2013 applications, Word is cloud-enabled by default, which means that not only can you save your documents to your SkyDrive, but you can also create documents using templates that Microsoft makes available in the cloud.

Creating a New Blank Document

A blank document is based off of Word's default template. The default template contains a collection of basic styles that you can use to format your document.

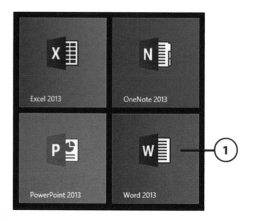

Styles

For more information on using styles to format your document, see "Formatting Text," later in this chapter.

1. From the Start screen, tap Word 2013 to launch Word.

Desktop Apps

Office 2013 apps are desktop apps. When you launch one of them, it launches in the Windows 8.1 RT desktop.

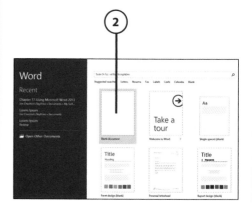

2. Tap the Blank Document template to create a new document. Notice that there are several other template styles you can select. You learn more about them in the next section.

Creating a Document from a Template

When you create a blank document, you start with a clean slate. In some cases, you might want to create a document based on a template instead. Document templates can supply boilerplate content, styles, and other tools to make it easier to create documents.

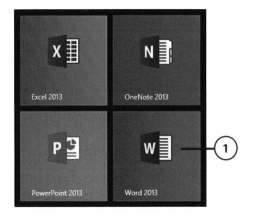

1. From the Start screen, tap Word 2013 to launch Word.

2. Tap a template to create a new document based on the template.

3. To see more templates, tap a suggested search, or enter a search term and tap the Search button.

4. To filter your search results, tap a category from the list.

5. Tap a template.

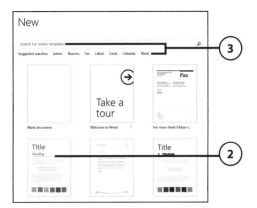

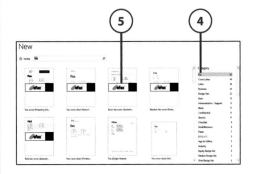

6. Tap Create to create a document based on the template you selected.

Saving Documents to Your Tablet

You can save a document to your tablet so that you can access it even when you don't have Internet access.

1. When ready to save your document, tap File.

2. Tap Save As.

3. Tap Computer.

4. Tap Browse.

5. Navigate to the folder where you want to save the document.

6. Enter a name for the document.

7. Tap Save.

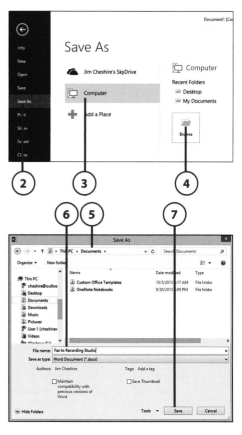

Quick Save

After you save a document for the first time, you can quickly save revisions to that document by tapping Save instead of Save As. You also can tap the blue diskette icon on the Quick Access toolbar at the top of the Word window.

For more information on the Quick Access toolbar, see "Tips and Tricks," later in this chapter.

Saving Documents to SkyDrive

Saving a document to SkyDrive is a convenient way to ensure that the document will be available to you on any PC that you use.

1. Tap File.

2. Tap Save As.

3. Tap your SkyDrive account.

4. Tap Browse.

5. Navigate to the folder where you want to save the file.

6. Tap Save.

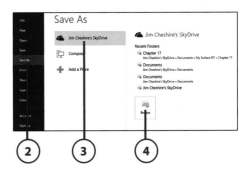

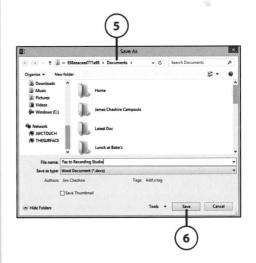

Opening Documents on Your Tablet

When you're ready to continue working on a document you previously saved to your tablet, you will first need to open the document in Word.

1. Tap File.

2. If your document appears in Recent Documents, tap it to open it; otherwise, tap Computer.

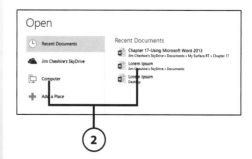

Tap Open

If a document is already open in Word when you tap File, you'll have to tap Open to see the recent document list.

3. Tap Browse.

4. Browse to the folder containing your document, and tap your document.

5. Tap Open.

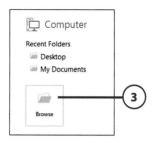

Open Documents When Starting Word

When you start Word, you are automatically taken to the Open screen so that you can open a new document.

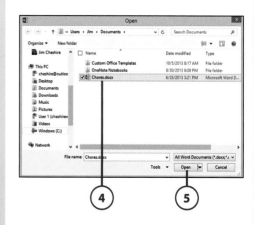

Opening Documents on SkyDrive

If you're connected to the Internet, you can open documents directly from your SkyDrive.

1. From the Open screen, tap your SkyDrive account.

2. Tap Browse.

3. Navigate to the folder containing your document, and tap the document.

4. Tap Open.

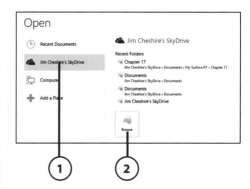

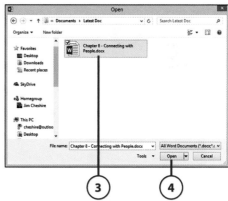

Managing Recent Documents

Word maintains a list of recent documents so that you can quickly open a document that you've worked on previously. You can remove documents from this list or clear the list if you want. You also can pin documents to the list so that they remain on the list even after you've cleared it.

1. From the Open screen, tap Recent Documents.

2. Tap and hold on a document.

3. Tap Remove from List to remove the document from the list.

4. Tap Pin to List to pin the document so that it remains on the list even after the list is cleared.

5. Tap Clear Unpinned Documents to remove all unpinned documents from the list.

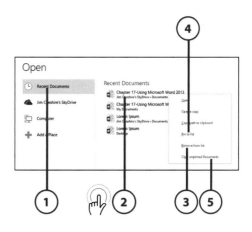

Switching Microsoft Accounts

Word's connection to SkyDrive is tied to your Microsoft account. If you would like to connect to the SkyDrive of a different Microsoft account, you'll need to switch the Microsoft account used in Word.

1. In Word, tap the current Microsoft account in the top-right corner.

2. Tap Switch Account.

3. Enter your Microsoft account email address.

4. Tap Next.

5. Enter your password.

6. Tap Sign In.

Quickly Switching Accounts

If you've previously switched to a different Microsoft account, when you tap Switch Account, you'll see a list of the Microsoft accounts you've used previously. You can switch to one of the other accounts by tapping the account.

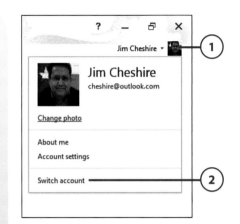

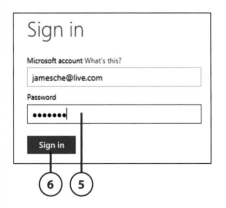

Formatting Text

Adding text to a document is simple and intuitive, but to create the kind of compelling documents you likely want, you must know how to format your text. In this section, I show you how you can format text directly and using styles.

Formatting Existing Text

You can change the formatting of anything from a single letter up to an entire document by selecting it and then applying the desired formatting.

1. Tap to place the insertion point at the beginning of the text you want to format.

2. Drag the selection indicator to select the text you want to format.

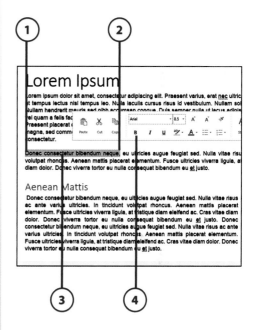

Use Zoom for Easier Selection

You will find it easier to select text using touch if you reverse-pinch on your document to zoom in.

---

3. Tap the selected text.

4. Tap a formatting option on the pop-up toolbar to format your text.

Formatting New Text

If you enable a particular style of formatting, any text you enter will take on that formatting until you explicitly change the formatting settings. For example, if you enable bold formatting, any text you enter will be bolded until you explicitly disable bold formatting.

1. With no text selected, tap Home to display the Home ribbon.

2. Tap to select the desired formatting from the formatting options on the Home ribbon.

3. Add text to your document and it will use the formatting you've selected.

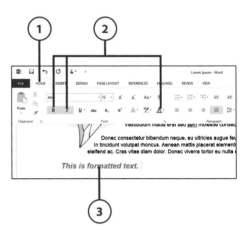

Formatting Text Using Styles

I've shown you how you can directly format text; however, you also can indirectly format text using styles. The benefit of using styles is that you can easily reformat an entire document by editing the style. When a style is edited, any text formatted using that style is automatically reformatted.

1. Select the text you want to format.

2. Tap Home to open the Home ribbon.

3. Tap the Styles drop-down.

4. Tap a style to apply the style.

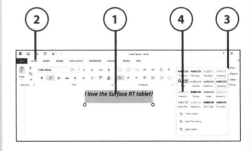

STYLES

There are two types of styles in Word: character styles and paragraph styles. Character styles can be applied to only parts of a paragraph. Paragraph styles, which show a small paragraph character next to the name in the Styles drop-down, apply to an entire paragraph. Therefore, a paragraph can contain several different character styles, but only one paragraph style can be applied to a paragraph.

It's important to realize that even if a paragraph is formatted with a paragraph style, character formatting remains intact. For example, if a word in a paragraph is formatted in the color red and you then apply the No Spacing paragraph style to the paragraph, the word will still be red because the color applied to it is character formatting and not part of the paragraph style.

Using styles is an advanced feature of Word, and I don't cover the feature in its entirety in this book. For a full explanation of using styles and other advanced Word features, read *Office 2013 In Depth* from Que Publishing.

Editing Styles

As I said earlier, you can reformat parts of your document that are formatted with a style by editing the style. When you edit your style, any content that is formatted with that style updates automatically.

1. Tap the Home tab to display the Home ribbon.

2. Tap the Styles button to display the Styles panel.

3. Tap and hold on the style you want to edit.

4. Tap Modify.

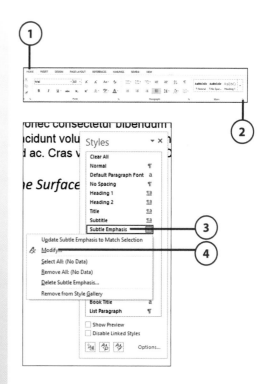

5. Make any desired modifications to the style.

6. To modify other style properties, tap Format and select a property.

7. Tap OK to apply your change.

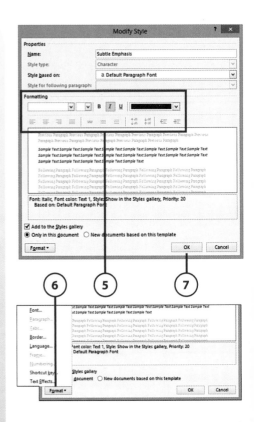

Creating a New Style

If you can't find a style that fits your needs, you can create your own style. Your new style can be made available only in the current document or to any document you use from now on.

1. Format text the way that you want your new style to look.

2. Tap the Home tab to display the Home ribbon.

3. Tap the Styles drop-down.

4. Tap Create a Style.

5. Enter a name for your new style.

6. Tap Modify if you would like to change any properties of the style.

7. Tap OK to create the style.

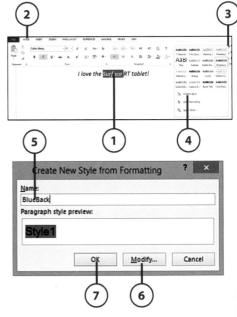

Style Preview

The style preview might not show exactly what the style will look like. For example, in the figure shown here, the preview doesn't show the white text for my new style because the white text is direct character formatting. Even so, when you apply the style, the white text will be applied.

Adding Pictures

Nothing drives a point home in a document better than pictures. (Just think of what this book would be like without the figures!) Word 2013 makes it easy to add pictures to your documents. You can also format pictures and change the way that they are laid out and how text flows around them.

Adding Pictures from Your Tablet or Removable Media

If you have pictures on your tablet that you want to add to your Word document, you can do so. If you have pictures on a removable drive or on a memory card (such as pictures on your digital camera), you can add those directly from the removable media. Copying them to your tablet first is not necessary.

1. Tap to place the insertion point where you want your picture to be added.

2. Tap Insert to display the Insert ribbon.

3. Tap Pictures.

4. Browse to the folder where your picture is located, and tap the picture to select it.

5. Tap Insert.

Formatting Pictures

Your picture probably doesn't look exactly the way you want it to look at this stage. I show you how to format and position the picture later in this section.

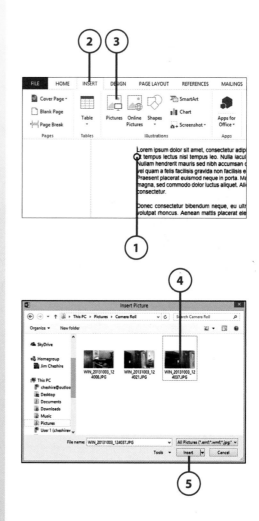

Adding Pictures from the Cloud

You can add pictures from Office.com, Bing, your SkyDrive, or Flickr. After you insert the picture, you don't need to be connected to the Internet to view it in your Word document. Word will actually save the image as part of the document.

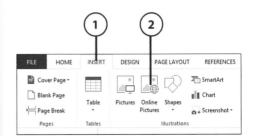

1. With the insertion point at the place where you want the picture inserted, tap Insert to show the Insert ribbon.

2. Tap Online Pictures.

3. To add a picture from Office.com or from Bing, enter a search term and tap Search.

4. To add a picture from Flickr, tap See More.

5. To add a picture from your SkyDrive, tap Browse.

6. Tap a picture to select it.

7. To see a larger preview, tap the magnifying glass.

8. Tap Insert to insert the picture into your document.

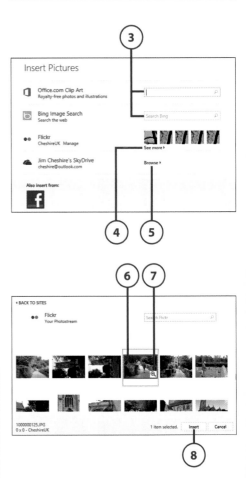

Inserting Facebook Pictures

You can also insert pictures from Facebook by tapping the Facebook icon and entering your Facebook username and password.

Formatting Pictures

It's likely that your picture is large and not formatted exactly the way you might want it to be. You can resize your picture and format it right within Word.

1. Tap the picture to select it.

2. Drag a sizing circle to resize the picture. Dragging a corner will resize the picture while keeping proportions.

3. Drag the rotation handle to rotate the picture.

4. Tap Format to show the Format ribbon where you can perform additional formatting, such as adding a border, applying a style, or positioning it on the page.

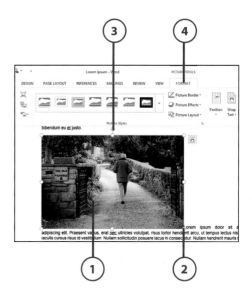

Changing Picture Layout

By default, your picture will be inserted inline with text. This might not be what you want because it can cause a large amount of white space surrounding your picture. You can easily change a picture's layout so that it flows better with your document.

1. Tap the picture.

2. Tap the Layout Options button.

3. Tap a layout option. When you select an option, the picture's layout is changed automatically.

4. If you selected a text wrapping layout, tap and drag the picture to position it where you want it to be.

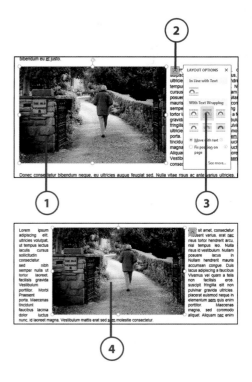

Proofing Documents

Word checks your spelling while you type, but its proofing tools don't stop there. You also have access to a dictionary and a thesaurus right within Word.

Correcting Misspelled Words

As you type, Word checks your spelling. Any word that it believes you've misspelled is underlined in red. You can correct a misspelled word quickly and easily.

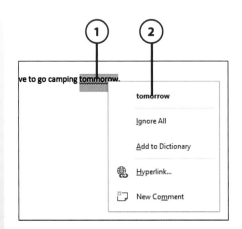

1. Tap and hold on a word that Word has underlined with a red, squiggly line.

2. Tap the correctly spelled word from the context menu to replace the misspelled word with the correctly spelled word.

Adding Words to the Dictionary

Some words that Word marks as misspelled might be spelled correctly. This happens often with names and other proper nouns. In these cases, you can choose to add the word to the dictionary so that it's no longer marked as misspelled.

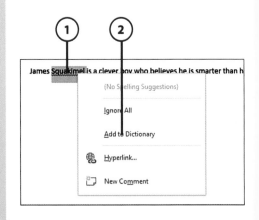

1. Tap and hold on a word that you want to add to the dictionary.

2. Tap Add to Dictionary.

Using the Dictionary

So far, you've seen how to use the spelling dictionary, but that doesn't help you if you want to look up a particular word in the dictionary. Word provides several dictionaries in the Office Store that you can download and use in Word.

1. Tap Review to display the Review ribbon.

2. Tap the Dictionaries button.

3. Tap Download to download a dictionary. (If you've already downloaded a dictionary, this step is skipped.)

4. Enter a word that you want to look up in the dictionary.

5. Tap Search.

Easier Lookups

If you select a word before tapping the Dictionary button, a search for that word is automatically entered for you.

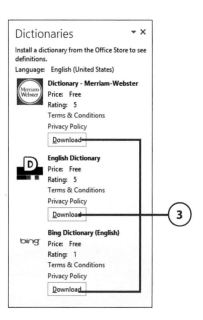

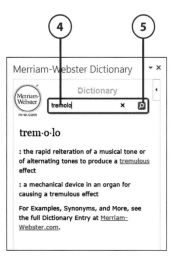

Using the Thesaurus

Word can also help you find synonyms and antonyms for words in your document. (You must download a dictionary using the steps in "Using the Dictionary" before you can use a thesaurus.)

1. Select the word you want to look up in the thesaurus.

2. Tap Review to display the Review ribbon.

3. Tap the Thesaurus button.

4. Tap a word in the thesaurus to replace the selected word.

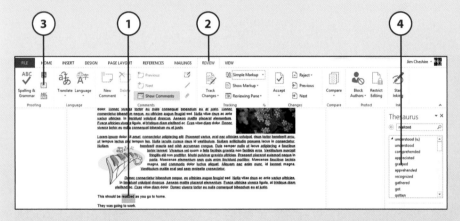

Searching the Thesaurus
Just as with the dictionary, you can search for words in the thesaurus by entering the word in the search box and tapping Search.

Sharing Documents

Sharing documents isn't a new concept, but Word 2013 makes it easier than ever to share not only through email, but also using Facebook or Twitter. Word documents are shared using the Word Web app, a cloud-based version of Microsoft Word.

Sharing from the Desktop
Because Word runs from the desktop, you can't use the Share charm to share a Word document. Instead, Word provides its own interface for sharing.

Sharing Documents Using Email

When you share a document using email, you can choose whether to require that those viewing your document log in using a Microsoft account before accessing the document. You also can choose whether others can view or edit the document.

1. Tap File.

2. Tap Share.

3. Tap Invite People.

4. If you haven't yet saved the document to your SkyDrive, tap Save to Cloud and save the document to SkyDrive.

5. Enter an email address or the name of one of your contacts.

6. Tap Address Book to select a contact from your contact list.

7. Tap Can Edit, and select Can View in the drop-down if you don't want the person with whom you're sharing the document to be able to edit it.

8. Enter a message.

9. Tap Require User to Sign In Before Accessing Document if you want to require that users sign in using a Microsoft account before accessing the document. This is especially useful when allowing editing so that you can see who last saved the document.

10. Tap Share.

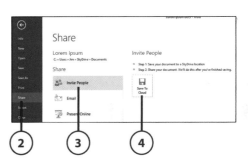

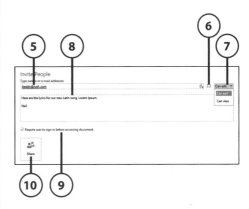

What Happens on the Other End?

When someone receives an email sharing a document, she can click the link to the document and open the document in Word Web App. Word Web App doesn't require that the user have Microsoft Word installed on her computer.

Sharing Using Social Networking

You can share a document using Facebook or Twitter. Sharing over social networks also uses the Word Web App.

Must Be a Cloud Document

Word allows you to choose Invite People even if the open document is not in the cloud. However, if your document is not in the cloud, you won't even see the option to share with your social networks. Before you share using a social network, be sure to save your document to SkyDrive.

1. From the Share screen in Word, tap Post to Social Networks.

2. Check Facebook to share the document on Facebook.

3. Check Twitter to share the document on Twitter.

4. Tap Can View, and change it to Can Edit if you want the document to be editable.

5. Enter a message.

6. Tap Post.

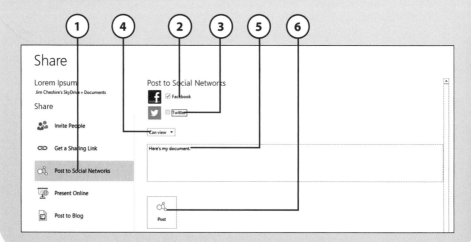

>>>Go Further

UNSHARING

Although Word does enable you to unshare documents, doing so doesn't seem to have any effect on other users accessing the document. Even after unsharing a document and waiting for more than an hour, I was still able to open a shared document and make edits to it.

Printing Documents

Word provides many options for printing your documents. You can print an entire document or specific pages of a document.

Printing an Entire Document

You can print an entire document to any installed printer, but you also can print to the Microsoft XPS Document Writer to create a portable document that users who don't have Word can read.

Reading XPS Documents on a Mac

If you have a Mac and you want to read an XPS document, download NiXPS View from www.nixps.com.

1. Tap File.

2. Tap Print.

3. Enter the number of copies to print.

4. Select a printer.

5. Tap Page, and select Print All Pages.

6. Tap the Print button.

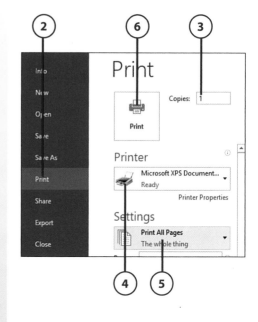

Printing Specific Pages

You can print specific pages or combinations of pages.

1. From the Print screen, enter the number of copies to print.

2. Select a printer.

3. In the Pages box, enter the pages to print. Multiple pages should be separated by commas, and ranges of pages should use a dash.

4. Tap the Print button.

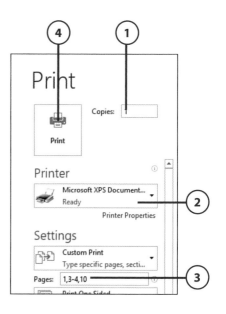

Tips and Tricks

I've just scratched the surface of what you can do in Word 2013. Here are some other features that will make your use of Word more enjoyable.

Using the Quick Access Toolbar

The Quick Access toolbar appears above the ribbon in the upper left of the Word window. By default, the Quick Access toolbar contains a Save button, an Undo button, a Redo button, and the Input Mode button. However, you can customize the Quick Access toolbar so that it contains the buttons you use often.

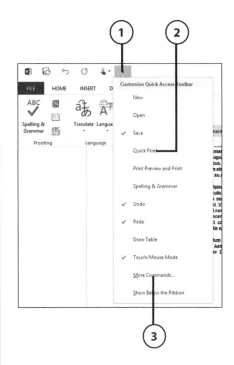

1. Tap the Customize Quick Access Toolbar button.

2. Tap a command to add it to the Quick Access toolbar.

3. To see more commands, tap More Commands.

4. Tap a command from the list.

5. Tap Add to add the command to the Quick Access toolbar.

Locating Commands

You can filter the list of commands by tapping the Choose Commands From drop-down and selecting a tab name where the command is located.

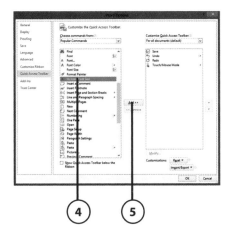

Adjusting Input Mode

Word provides two different input modes: Touch mode (the default in Windows 8.1 RT) and Mouse mode. Touch mode provides increased spacing between menu commands and larger buttons so that you can easily use touch in Word. Mouse mode is better suited to using a mouse. You can choose the input mode that best fits how you use Word.

1. Tap the Input Mode button on Word's Quick Access Toolbar.

2. Tap Mouse to switch to Mouse input mode.

3. Tap Touch to switch to Touch input mode.

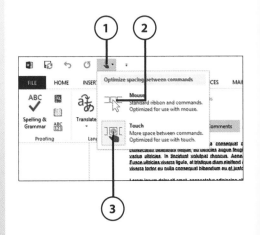

It's Not All Good

Fat Fingers

Even if you turn on Touch input mode, you'll likely encounter frustration with the size of some user interface elements. For example, if you want to dismiss a pane that appears on the left or right side of the Word interface, you simply have to tap the X in the upper-right corner of the panel. However, the X is so small that it's almost impossible to activate using touch. One way to resolve this is to purchase a stylus for use with your tablet.

Using the Format Painter

The Format Painter is a powerful tool that makes it easy to copy formatting from one part of your document to another.

1. Select a word that contains the formatting you want to copy.

2. Tap Home to display the Home ribbon.

3. Tap Format Painter.

4. Tap or select one or more words that you want to be formatted like the original word.

Keep track of important
information.

Use formulas to do
math for you.

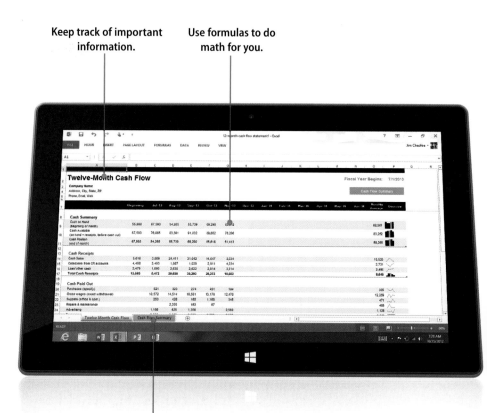

Organize your
data in sheets.

Crunching Numbers with Microsoft Excel 2013

Computers are great at math, and Microsoft Excel 2013 makes it easy for you to take advantage of that. Excel can track your personal budget and expenses, compute your expense reports, and even track your weight loss. It's a versatile application that many PC users have never used because they find it intimidating. As you'll see in this chapter, there's no need to fear Excel.

Creating, Opening, and Saving Workbooks

Excel files are called *workbooks*. When you first launch Excel, you'll have an opportunity to create a new workbook. Like Microsoft Word, Excel uses templates so that you can have rich functionality without having to create a workbook from scratch.

Creating a Workbook

When you create a new workbook, you have the option of choosing a template or creating a blank workbook that you can customize however you want.

1. From the Start screen, tap Excel 2013 to launch Excel.

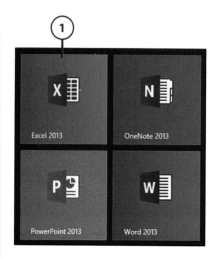

Desktop App

Excel is a desktop app, so when you launch it, you'll automatically be taken to the desktop.

2. Tap a suggested search to find other templates.

First Launch

When you first start Excel, you're taken to the New screen. You can return to the New screen by tapping File and then tapping New.

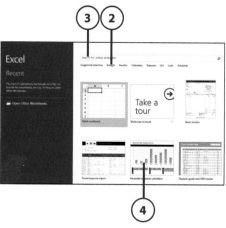

3. Enter a search term to search for online templates.

4. Tap a template to create a workbook based on that template.

5. Tap Create to create your workbook. (You will only see the Create prompt if you choose a cloud-based template.)

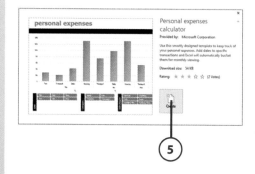

Opening a Workbook

You can open workbooks from your PC or from the cloud. Excel also provides a list of recently opened workbooks so that you can reopen a workbook.

1. From within Excel, tap File.

2. Tap Open.

3. Tap a recent workbook to reopen that workbook.

4. Tap your SkyDrive account to open a workbook saved on your SkyDrive.

5. Tap Computer to open a workbook that is on your PC.

6. Browse to the workbook you want to open, and tap to select it.

7. Tap Open.

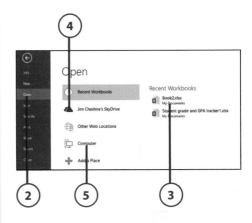

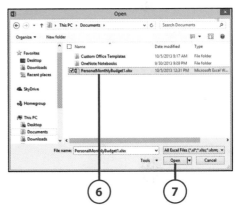

Saving a Workbook

You can save your workbook to your local PC, or you can save it to your SkyDrive account. By saving it to your SkyDrive account, you can access it from other PCs and devices.

1. From within Excel, tap File.

2. Tap Save As.

Quickly Saving

If you've already saved your workbook at least once, you can easily
save it to the same location and
filename by tapping Save instead
of Save As.

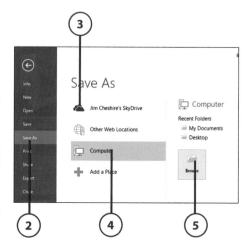

3. Tap your SkyDrive account to save
the workbook to SkyDrive.

4. Tap Computer to save your workbook to your local PC.

5. Tap a recent folder, or tap Browse.

6. Browse to the location where you
want to save your workbook.

7. Enter a filename for the workbook.

8. Tap Save to save the workbook.

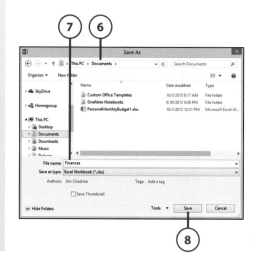

Entering Data

Excel data is typically a mixture of text and numbers. Text typically is used to
describe the numerical data. For example, a grid of numbers will usually have
column and/or row labels that use text.

Excel enables you to format data as needed and also contains some nice features for quickly adding data.

Adding Data

Data in Excel is entered into a cell located on a grid made up of rows and columns. Rows are identified using a number beginning with row 1, and columns are identified using a letter starting from the letter A. Therefore, the cell in the upper-left corner of your workbook is cell A1. The cell immediately to the right of that cell is cell B1. The cell immediately below cell A1 is cell A2.

1. Tap the cell where you want to add your data.

2. Enter your data using the keyboard.

3. Tap Enter.

4. Press your keyboard's arrow keys, or tap a cell to move to a new cell and enter additional data.

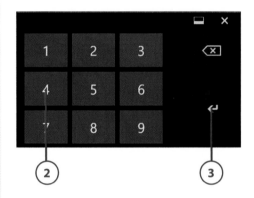

Resizing a Column

By default, columns in your workbook are all the same width. As you enter data into your workbook, you might find that you want to adjust the width of a column to accommodate more data or to make your workbook more legible.

1. Tap the column header for the column you want to resize.

2. Drag the slider to the right to increase the column's width or to the left to decrease the column's width.

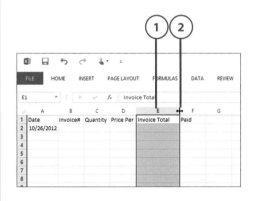

Changing Data Formatting

Excel uses a general format for all workbook data by default. You can change the format of one or more cells to be more appropriate for the type of data that is used in the cell. For example, if you are displaying dollar amounts, you might want a dollar sign to be added, and you might want negative values to show in red. This is easily accomplished by changing the data formatting.

1. Tap on the cell that contains the value you want to format.

Formatting Multiple Cells

You can format multiple cells by dragging the selection handles to enclose all the cells you want to format. You also can tap a header to select an entire column or row and format all data in that column or row.

2. Tap Home to display the Home ribbon.

3. Tap the format drop-down and select a format for the data.

4. For more formats, tap More Number Formats.

5. Tap a category.

6. Tap a format.

7. Tap OK to apply the formatting.

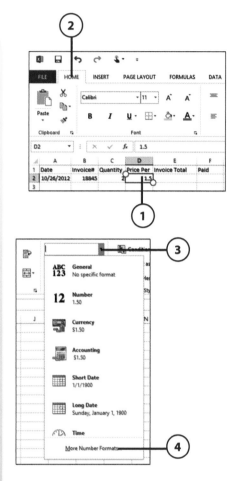

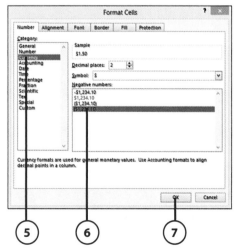

Adding Data with AutoFill

Some data that you enter will follow a predictable pattern. For example, if you are entering invoices into a spreadsheet, the invoice number might be an incremented number. If you are entering a weight loss journal, you might have a column with days of the week. In such cases, you can use Excel's AutoFill feature to automatically enter data for you.

1. Enter one or more values to define a pattern.

Defining Patterns

The amount of data you must enter to establish a pattern depends on many factors. If you want to use AutoFill with dates or days of the week, for example, you often only need to enter one value before you use AutoFill. If you want to use AutoFill for a more obscure pattern, you might need to enter three or more values for Excel to figure out the pattern in your data.

2. Tap the first value to select it.

3. Tap the value again to display the context menu.

4. Tap AutoFill.

5. Tap and drag the AutoFill icon down or across, depending on which direction you want AutoFill to populate your cells.

6. Release your finger, and AutoFill will fill the selection based on your pattern.

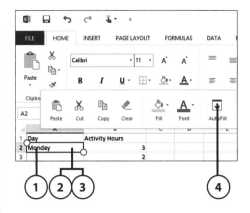

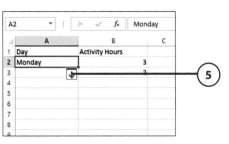

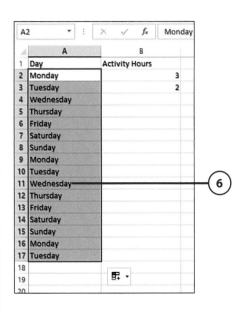

Creating Formulas and Functions

The true power of Excel lies in formulas and functions. Excel can do rudimentary mathematics, such as adding numbers and so on, but it can also perform complex mathematics.

Directly Entering a Formula

You can enter formulas directly into the formula bar. Formulas you enter always start with an equal sign.

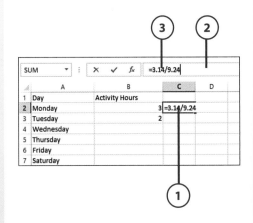

1. Tap a cell where you want the result of the formula to be displayed.

2. Tap inside the formula bar.

3. Enter **=3.14/9.24**. (This is an example formula that divides 3.14 by 9.24.)

4. Tap Enter to insert the result of the formula into the selected cell.

Cell Selections
When you tap Enter, Excel automatically moves to the next cell so that you can continue entering data into your workbook.

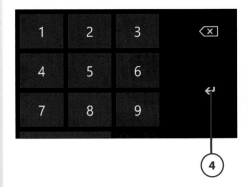

Using the Insert Function Dialog

Complex formulas are called *functions*. Functions take two or more values and return a result based on a calculation. Excel makes using functions easy using the Insert Function dialog.

1. Tap the cell where you want to insert the result of your function.

2. Tap the Insert Function button.

3. Tap the desired function. If you aren't sure which function to use, enter a description of what you want to do and tap Go to search.

4. Tap OK.

5. Enter any arguments the function requires. (Your options will differ based on which function you selected.)

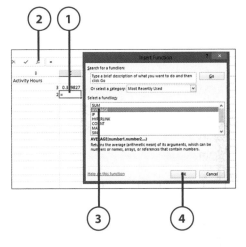

Use Cell Values

If you want your function to use values in a particular cell in your workbook, you can enter the cell location (for example, C2 as shown in the figure) and your function will use the value contained in that cell. If you use this method, changing the value in the cell you use in your function automatically changes the value in the cell displaying the function's result.

Note that Excel displays the function result in the dialog as you are entering your arguments.

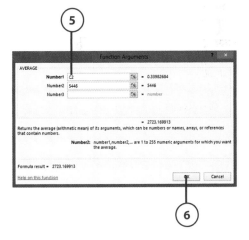

6. Tap OK to insert the function's result into the selected cell.

Creating Formulas from Selections

In many cases, you might want to add a formula that uses a selection of cells to calculate a result. For example, you might want to display the sum of a list of numbers in a column.

1. Select the cells you want to use in your formula.

2. Tap the Quick Analysis button.

3. Tap the type of analysis you want your formula to perform.

4. Tap a function to perform and the result of the formula is entered automatically next to the selection.

More Excel

Formulas in Excel are extremely powerful, and I've only touched the Surface 2 of what they can do. For more information on using formulas in Excel, read *Microsoft Excel 2013 In Depth* from Que Publishing.

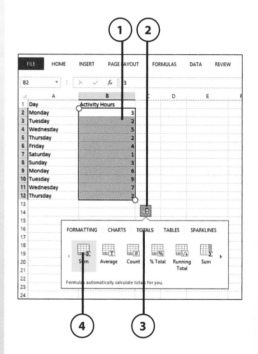

Tips and Tricks

In addition to what you've already learned, there are some other features of Excel that can make using it more productive.

Freezing Panes

If you are working with a workbook that is wider or taller than your screen, you might find it convenient to freeze panes. When you freeze panes, part of the workbook (such as header columns or row labels) remains frozen while you scroll.

1. Tap on the cell where you want to freeze panes. Any rows above or columns to the left of the selected cell will be frozen.

2. Tap View to display the View ribbon.

3. Tap Freeze Panes.

4. Tap Freeze Panes.

Freezing Without Selecting

You can tap Freeze Top Row to freeze the top row of your workbook or Freeze First Column to freeze the first column of your workbook, regardless of what is currently selected.

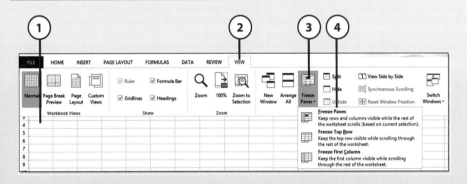

5. To unfreeze previously frozen panes, tap Unfreeze Panes.

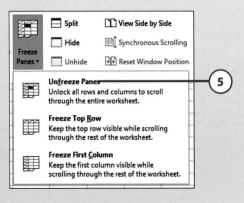

Creating Sheets

Workbooks are made up of sheets.
Each sheet is represented by a tab at
the bottom of the screen. If you have
multiple sets of data you want to
keep track of in your workbook, you
can create a new sheet.

1. Tap + to add a new sheet.

2. Tap and hold the new sheet to
   display the context menu.

3. Tap Rename.

4. Enter a descriptive name for your
   new sheet.

Switching Sheets

You can switch between the
sheets in your workbook by tapping on a sheet's tab.

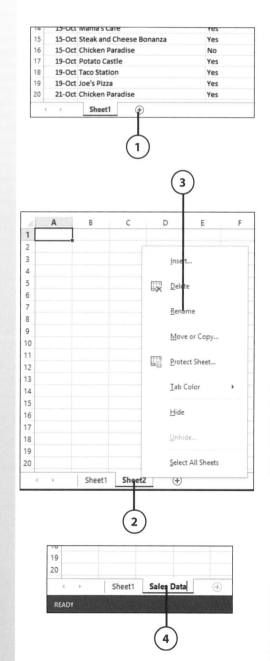

Filtering Data

Filtering enables you to filter data based on column values. For example, if your workbook contains sales data for different vendors, you can filter on particular vendors so that you see only data for the vendors you choose.

1. Tap Home to display the Home ribbon.

2. Tap Filter.

3. Tap Filter.

4. To filter your data, tap the drop-down on a column header.

5. Uncheck Select All to deselect all values.

6. Check the values by which you want to filter the data.

7. Tap OK.

8. Excel displays a blue row number and a filter icon on the column being filtered.

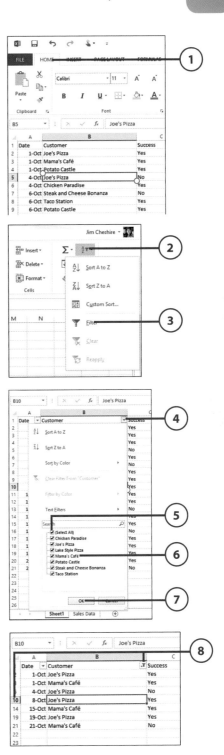

Format slides
using themes.

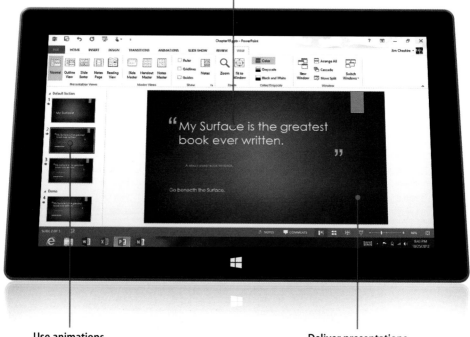

Use animations
and transitions in
presentations.

Deliver presentations
on the monitor of
your choice.

Presenting with Microsoft PowerPoint 2013

Microsoft PowerPoint 2013 enables you to create engaging and informative onscreen presentations. Just as with the other Office applications you've seen up to this point, PowerPoint uses templates to give you a head start in being creative. It also shares the capability to save to and open from the cloud as well as your tablet.

Creating, Opening, and Saving Presentations

When you launch PowerPoint for the first time, you have the option of starting with a blank presentation or choosing a template that applies certain styles and colors. When you've finished working on a presentation, you can save it to your tablet or your SkyDrive so that you can access it on your other devices.

Creating a Presentation

Just as with the other Office applications you've seen, PowerPoint provides access to thousands of templates for jump-starting your presentation.

1. From the Start screen, tap PowerPoint 2013 to launch PowerPoint.

2. Tap a suggested search to locate a particular type of template.

3. Enter a search term, and tap Search if you don't see a template that suits you.

4. Tap a template to choose it.

5. Tap the arrow to see more images of other slide types with the selected template applied.

6. Tap a variation of the template to choose a different color scheme.

7. Tap Create to create your presentation.

Change Your Mind

You're not locked into the template or variation that you choose now. You can easily change it at any time. I'll show you how later in this chapter.

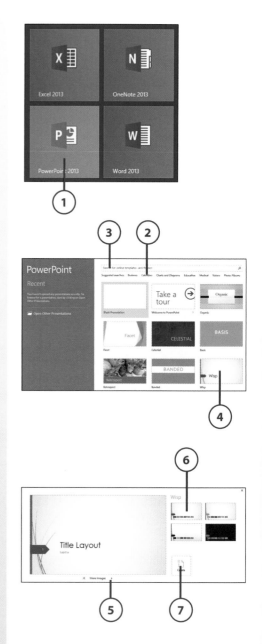

Saving a Presentation

When you are ready to stop working on a presentation, you can save it to your tablet or your SkyDrive.

1. From within PowerPoint, tap File.

2. Tap Save As.

3. Tap your SkyDrive account to save to your SkyDrive.

4. Tap Computer to save to your tablet.

5. Tap a recent folder, or tap Browse.

6. Browse to the location where you want to save your presentation.

7. Enter a name for your presentation.

8. Tap Save to save the presentation.

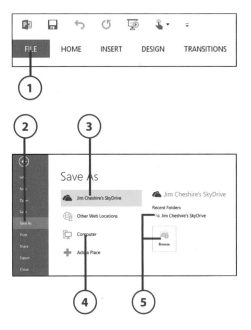

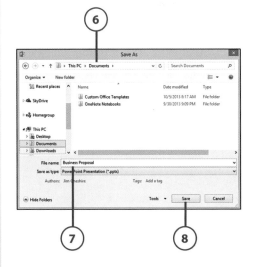

Opening a Presentation

You can open presentations stored on your tablet or your SkyDrive.

1. After launching PowerPoint, tap a recent file from the list to open that file.

2. Tap Open Other Presentations to browse for a presentation.

3. Tap your SkyDrive account to open a presentation from your SkyDrive.

4. Tap Computer to open a presentation from your tablet.

5. Tap a recent folder, or tap Browse to browse to a folder.

6. Browse to the folder containing your presentation.

7. Tap your presentation to select it.

8. Tap Open to open the presentation.

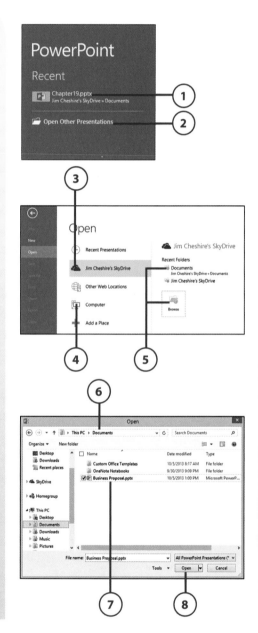

Creating Slides and Content

PowerPoint presentations consist of a series of slides. Slides can contain text, graphics, and other elements used to illustrate a particular point. PowerPoint has specialized tools for creating and laying out slides.

Creating a New Slide

When you create a new slide, it takes on the appearance and attributes applied by the theme you are using. There are numerous types of slides based upon what type of content you want the slide to convey. For example, there are slide layouts appropriate for title slides, slides that provide general content, slides that are great for a side-by-side comparison, and so forth.

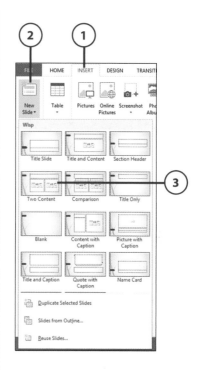

1. After creating or opening your presentation, tap Insert to display the Insert ribbon.

2. Tap New Slide.

3. Tap the slide type you want to insert. A thumbnail of each is provided to make it easier to decide.

Deleting a Slide

If you want to delete a slide you've added, you do so from the thumbnails pane.

1. Tap and hold on the slide you want to delete.

2. Release to display the context menu, and tap Delete to delete the slide.

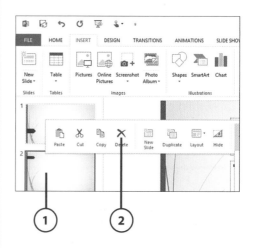

Changing Slide Layout

When you create a new slide, you choose an appropriate layout. If you decide to change the layout, you can. Any text or other content you have already added to the slide will be preserved.

1. Tap the slide for which you want to modify the layout.

2. Tap Home to display the Home ribbon.

3. Tap Layout.

4. Tap the desired layout to change the slide's layout.

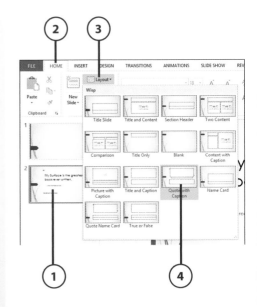

Adding Text to a Slide

Text is added to PowerPoint slides in text boxes that are outlined with a dotted line. Each layout of a slide has different text boxes for entering text.

1. Tap the area where you want to add your text.

2. Enter the desired text.

3. Format the text using the formatting options available on the Home ribbon.

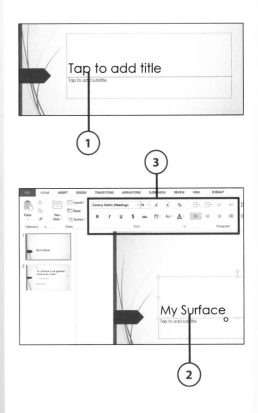

Adding Shapes to a Slide

Shapes are often used in PowerPoint slides because they offer more visual appeal than plain text. Shapes can also contain text overlaid on top of the shape.

1. Tap the slide onto which you want to insert your shape.

2. Tap Insert to display the Insert ribbon.

3. Tap Shapes.

4. Tap the Shape you want to insert.

5. To add text to the shape, tap and hold on the shape.

6. Release to reveal the context menu, and tap Edit Text.

7. Type the text you want to appear in the shape.

Quickly Add Text

You can start typing immediately after adding a shape to add text to the shape. However, you'll need to use the steps provided here if you want to edit the text after adding it.

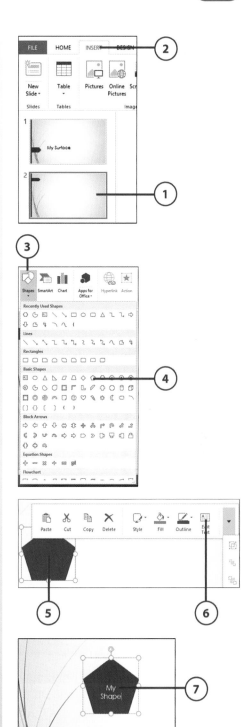

Aligning Objects

If you add two or more shapes or other objects to a slide, you'll likely want to align the objects so that they are more visually appealing. For example, you might want the tops of all of your shapes to line up on your slide.

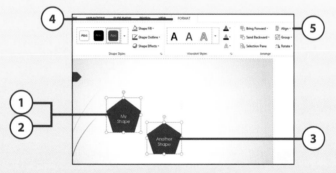

1. Tap the first shape you want to align.

2. Tap the shape again and hold your finger on it.

3. Tap any additional shapes you want to align to select them.

4. Tap Format to display the format ribbon.

5. Tap Align.

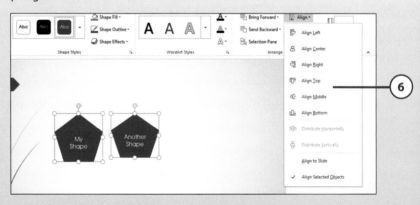

6. Tap an alignment option to align the objects.

Drag to Align

If you are trying to align one object with another one, you can drag the object until you see a dotted line drawn along the point where you want to align the objects. This is a convenient way to align two objects, but if you have more than two objects to align, the Format ribbon is the best choice.

Using Themes

Themes in PowerPoint not only provide an attractive (usually) color scheme for your slides, but they also provide other visual elements that can make your presentation more effective.

Applying a Theme

If you created your presentation using any template other than the blank presentation template, you already have a theme in place. However, you can apply a different theme at any time to change the appearance of your slides.

1. Tap Design to display the Design ribbon.

2. Tap a theme to apply the theme to your presentation.

3. Tap the drop-down to see additional themes.

4. Tap a theme from the dialog to apply the theme.

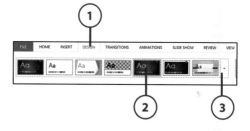

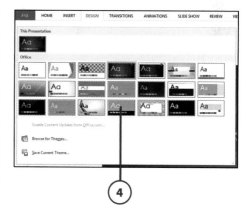

Modifying a Theme

You can change the variation of a theme to change the color scheme. You also can modify other parts of a theme to make it suit your needs.

1. Tap Design to display the Design ribbon.

2. Tap a theme variant to change the color scheme.

3. Tap the drop-down to display other properties that you can change.

4. Tap a category from the drop-down.

5. Tap an option for the category to modify the template.

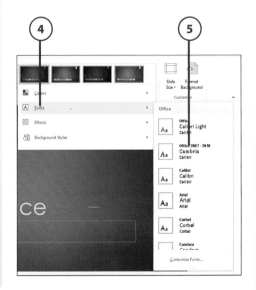

Using Animations and Transitions

Animations and transitions can make a presentation more interesting. Transitions are applied when a presentation changes from one slide to another. Animations are used to control how objects on a slide appear and disappear.

Applying a Transition

You can apply different transitions to different slides. It's not required that a slide have a transition applied to it. If you don't apply a transition, the slide will instantly appear onscreen when you switch to it during a presentation.

1. Tap the slide for which you want to apply the transition.

2. Tap Transitions to display the Transitions ribbon.

3. Tap a transition to select it.

4. Tap the Transitions drop-down to see more transitions.

5. Tap a transition from the dialog to apply the transition.

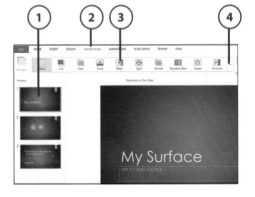

What Does It Look Like?

After you apply a transition, you'll see it played for you in the main PowerPoint window. (You can tap the Preview button on the Transitions ribbon to replay the preview.) If you don't like the transition, you can choose others until you are satisfied.

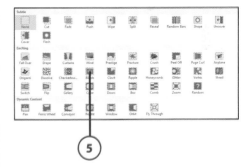

Customizing a Transition

PowerPoint provides several options for customizing a transition. Transition-specific options are available, and you can also add a sound to your transition and control the duration of it.

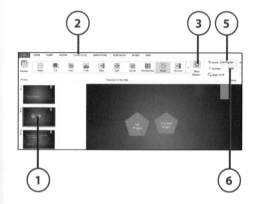

1. Tap to select the slide to which the transition has been applied.

2. Tap Transitions to display the Transitions ribbon.

3. Tap Effect Options to display options for the transition.

4. Tap an effect option to apply it. (Options vary based on the effect you've chosen.)

5. Tap Sound and select a sound to associate a sound with the transition.

6. Tap Duration and enter a new value to change the duration of the transition.

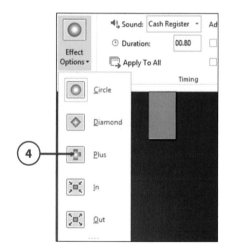

Adding an Animation

You use animations to control how objects appear and disappear from a slide. By default, objects appear as soon as the slide appears, but you can alter that behavior using animations.

More Than One

You can apply as many animations as you want to an object. PowerPoint plays back all the animations that you apply in the order you applied them.

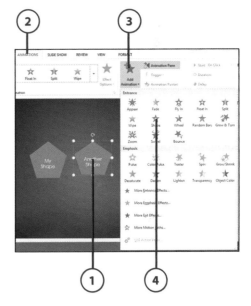

1. Tap the object to which you want to apply the animation.

2. Tap Animations to display the Animations ribbon.

3. Tap Add Animation.

4. Tap an animation from the dialog.

Choosing Animations

Some animations are well suited for playing when an object appears (an object's entrance), and others are better for playing when an object disappears (the object's exit). To find the appropriate animation, tap on More Entrance Effects or More Exit Effects to see more effects.

Configuring an Animation Trigger

By default, animations play when you click on a slide. You can change an animation's trigger so that it plays automatically at a certain point.

1. Tap the object to which the animation is applied.

2. Tap the Start drop-down.

3. Tap With Previous to automatically play the animation simultaneously with the animation immediately preceding it.

4. Tap After Previous to automatically play the animation after the preceding animation finishes playing.

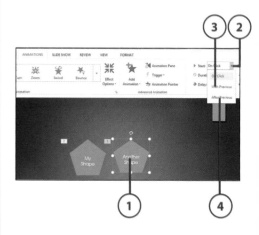

More Information

I've obviously just touched on the functionality available in PowerPoint 2013 here. If you want additional information, read *PowerPoint 2013 Absolute Beginner's Guide* by Que Publishing.

Presenting with PowerPoint

When you've finished creating your PowerPoint presentation, you can present it to others. When you are presenting a presentation, slides are presented in the order in which they appear in the thumbnail panel.

Changing Slide Order

If the slides in the thumbnail panel aren't in the desired order, you can rearrange them before presenting your presentation.

1. Tap View to display the View ribbon.

2. Tap Slide Sorter.

3. Tap and drag slides to the desired location.

4. Tap Normal to switch back to Normal view.

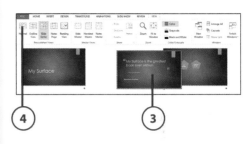

Entering Slide Show Mode

To present your presentation, you must enter Slide Show mode. If you have another monitor connected to your tablet, you can choose which monitor to use for your slide show.

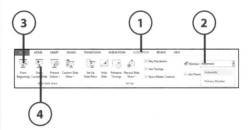

1. Tap Slide Show to display the Slide Show ribbon.

2. If you have another monitor connected, tap Monitor and select the monitor to use for your slide show.

3. Tap From Beginning to start your slide show from the first slide.

4. Tap From Current Slide to start the slide show from the currently selected slide.

5. While in Slide Show mode, tap the screen, and tap Next to move to the next slide or play the next animation.

6. Tap End Slide Show to end the slide show and return to Normal view.

Advancing Slides

While in Slide Show mode, you can advance slides and animations using a mouse button as well.

Tips and Tricks

There are a couple of other features of PowerPoint that you'll find convenient to use in your presentations.

Using Sections

If you have a lot of slides in your presentation, using sections that place slides into groups is a great way to organize your slides.

1. Tap the slide you want to be the first slide in a new section.

2. Tap Home to display the Home ribbon.

3. Tap Section.

4. Tap Add Section.

5. Tap Section again.

6. Tap Rename Section.

7. Enter a name for your new section.

8. Tap Rename.

Section Names

Section names are displayed in the thumbnail panel and in the Slide Sorter.

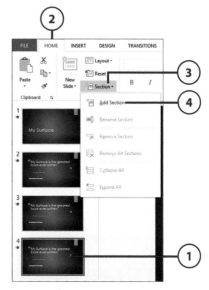

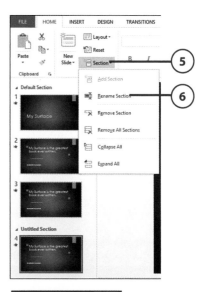

Using Headers and Footers

If you have information you want to display at the top or bottom of every slide, you can set a header or a footer. This feature is commonly used to display copyright or other such information.

1. Tap Insert to display the Insert ribbon.

2. Tap Header & Footer.

3. Check Date and Time to display the date and time at the top of each slide.

4. Tap Update Automatically if you want the date to automatically be updated based on the current date.

5. Tap the drop-down and choose a display format for the date and time.

6. Tap Fixed and enter a value to display a fixed value on each slide.

7. Check Slide Number to display the slide number on each slide.

8. Check Footer and enter a value to display at the bottom of each slide.

9. Check Don't Show on Title Slide if you don't want the header and footer displayed on the title slide.

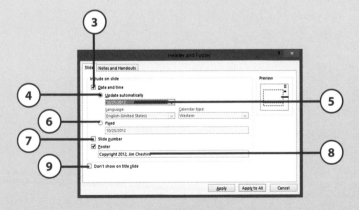

Create multiple notebooks for organizing notes.

Organize notebooks with sections and pages.

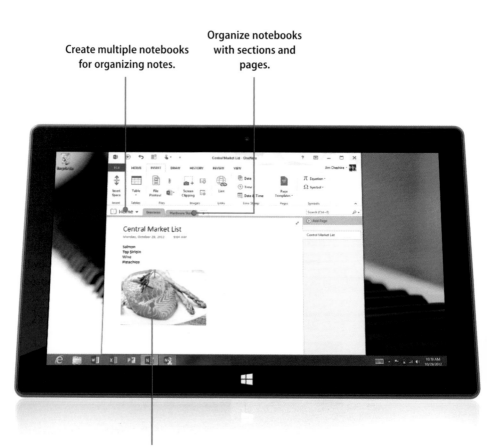

Insert multimedia and text into notes.

Organizing Notes with Microsoft OneNote 2013

OneNote 2013 is Microsoft's app for taking notes on your Surface 2. Note-taking apps are nothing new, but OneNote adds some significant features that make it a great choice.

Notes in OneNote are kept in notebooks. Each notebook can have one or more sections, and each section can have one or more pages. Your notebooks are synchronized across your devices using your Microsoft account.

More on OneNote 2013
This chapter covers the basics of OneNote 2013. For full coverage of OneNote 2013, read *My OneNote 2013* from Que Publishing.

Creating and Organizing Sections

Notebooks in OneNote are organized into sections. Sections are displayed as tabs along the top of the OneNote app, and you can move among sections by tapping its tab.

Auto-Save

As you move through this section of the book, you might wonder how to save a OneNote notebook. In fact, your OneNote notebooks are saved automatically, so you never have to worry about manually saving your work.

Creating a Section

You can create as many sections as you need in any particular notebook.

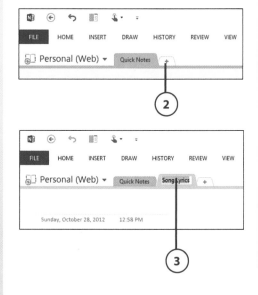

1. From the Start screen, tap OneNote 2013 to launch OneNote.

2. Tap the + tab to create a new section.

3. Enter a name for the new section, and press Enter on your keyboard.

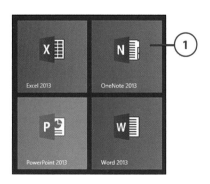

Adding Notes

In the next section, "Creating and Editing Pages," I discuss pages and how you can add notes and content to your notebook sections.

Changing a Section's Color

Sections are color coded. When you create a new section, OneNote assigns a random color for it. You can change the color to something that suits you.

1. Tap and hold on the section's tab, and then release to display the context menu.

2. Tap Section Color.

3. Tap a color from the list.

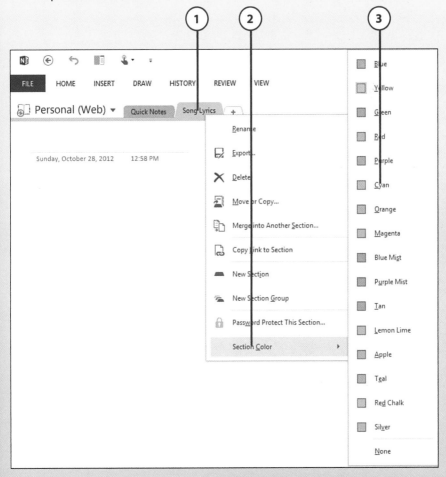

No Color
One of the options in the color menu is None. If you select None, your section will be colored light gray.

Renaming a Section

You might want to rename a section to reflect a more appropriate name. You can rename a section at any time.

1. Tap and hold on the section's tab, and release to display the context menu.

2. Tap Rename.

3. Enter the new name and press Enter to commit it.

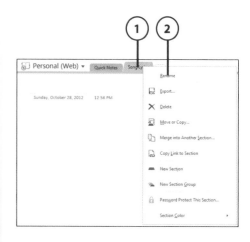

Merging Sections

You might find that you have notes in multiple sections that should be combined into a single section. You can easily merge content from two or more sections into a single section.

1. Tap and hold on a section that you want to merge into another section, and release to display the context menu.

2. Tap Merge into Another Section.

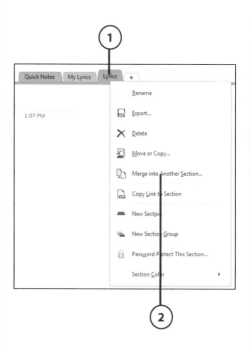

3. Tap the section into which you want to merge the section. If necessary, you can search for a section by entering text that appears in the section's title.

4. Tap Merge to merge the section into the selected section.

5. Tap Merge Sections in the dialog.

6. Tap Delete if you want to delete the original section.

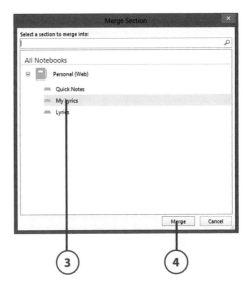

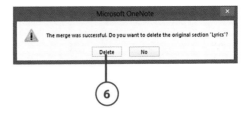

Moving or Copying a Section

Section tabs appear in the order in which the sections were created. If you want to better organize your sections, you can move or copy one or more sections. When you copy a section, a new section is created and the original section remains.

1. Tab and hold on the section you want to move, and release to display the context menu.

2. Tap Move or Copy.

3. Tap the section name after which you want your section to appear.

4. Tap Move to move the section, or Copy to copy the section to the location you selected.

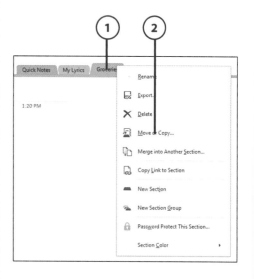

Moving with Mouse or Track Pad

If you're using a mouse or a track pad with your Surface 2, you can also drag and drop section tabs to move sections.

Moving Between Notebooks

If you've created more than one notebook, you'll have the option to also move a section to another notebook.

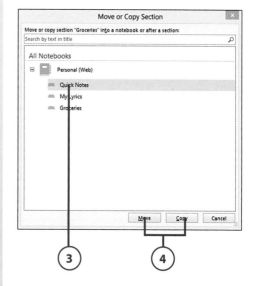

Deleting a Section

If you no longer need a section, you can delete it.

1. Tap and hold on the section you want to delete. Release to display the context menu.

2. Tap Delete.

3. Tap Yes to delete the section.

Deleting Isn't Permanent

When you delete a section, the section is moved into the notebook's Recycle Bin. Later in this chapter, I show you how to use the Recycle Bin to recover deleted items.

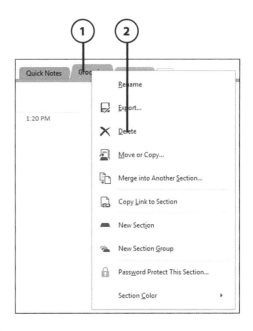

Creating and Editing Pages

Notes in a section are contained in one or more pages. Pages appear as tabs within a section along the right edge of the OneNote app. In the previous section, I created a notebook section called Lyrics that can be used to store lyrics to songs. In this scenario, each song can be stored into its own page.

Creating a Page

When you create a new section, a blank page called Untitled Page is created for you. However, you can add additional pages as you need them.

1. Tap the section to which you want to add a new page.

2. Tap Add Page to create a new page.

3. Enter a title on the page to name the page.

Adding Text to a Page

You can add text to a page and then move that text freely so that it's positioned exactly where you want it.

1. Tap the desired section.

2. Tap a page, or create a new page for your note.

3. Tap anywhere on the page to place the cursor at that point.

4. Enter text for your note.

5. Tap and hold on the bar above your text, and drag it to position it elsewhere on the page.

6. To add additional text, tap within the box and enter additional text.

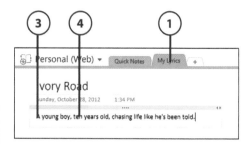

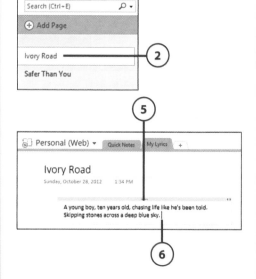

Adding Pictures on Your Tablet to a Page

In addition to text, your notes can contain pictures that are stored on your tablet.

1. Tap on a page where you want to insert a picture.

2. Tap Insert to display the Insert ribbon.

3. Tap Pictures.

4. Browse to the picture you want to insert, and tap it to select it.

5. Tap Insert.

6. Drag the sizing handles to resize the picture if necessary.

7. Drag the directional arrows to position the picture on your page.

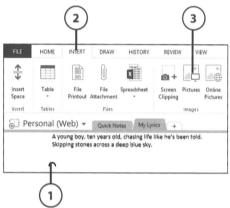

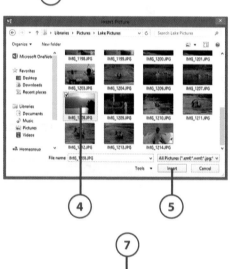

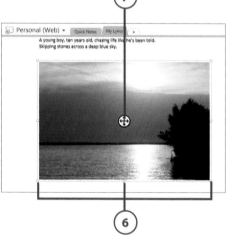

Adding Pictures from the Cloud to a Page

In addition to adding pictures from your tablet, you can add pictures from the cloud to your page.

1. Tap on your page where you want the picture inserted.

2. Tap Insert to display the Insert ribbon.

3. Tap Online Pictures.

4. Tap Office.com Clip Art or Bing Image Search and enter a search term to search for a picture.

5. Tap Flickr or your SkyDrive to insert a picture from either of these cloud services.

6. Tap a picture to select it.

7. Tap Insert to add the picture to your page.

8. Drag the sizing handles if necessary to resize your picture.

9. Drag the directional arrows to reposition the picture.

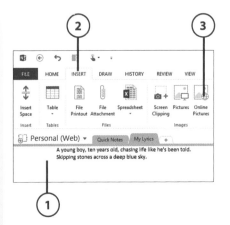

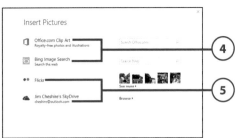

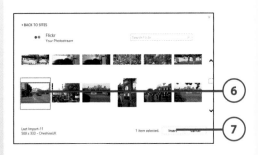

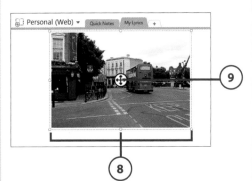

Renaming a Page

You can change the name of a page. Doing so changes the name that you see on the tab and the name on the page itself. In fact, when you choose to rename a page, you do it by changing the header on the page.

1. Tap and hold on the page you want to rename, and then release to display the context menu.

2. Tap Rename.

3. Enter a new name for your page.

Another Way to Rename

You can also rename a page by simply navigating to the page and changing the text that appears on the page's header.

Moving or Copying a Page

You might want to move or copy a page to another section in the current notebook or to another notebook altogether. When you move a page, the page is removed from its original location and added to the new location. When you copy a page, the page is added to the new location and the original copy remains.

1. Tap and hold on the page you want to move, and release to display the context menu.
2. Tap Move or Copy.
3. Tap the location where you want to move or copy the page.
4. Tap Move to move the page or Copy to copy the page.

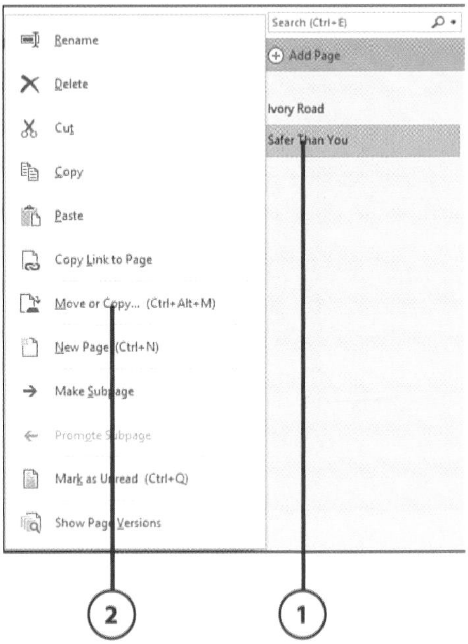

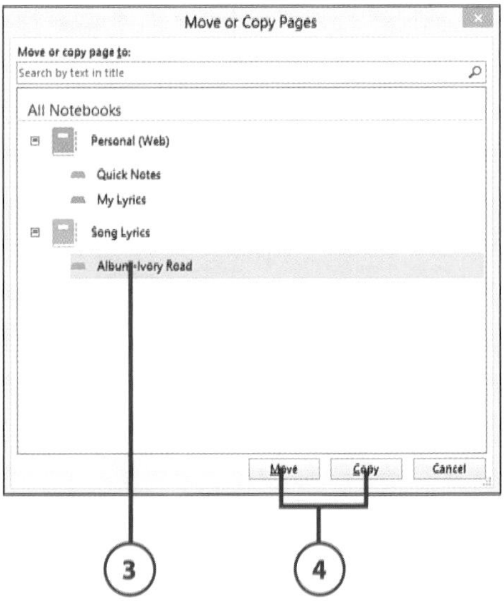

Deleting a Page

If you no longer need the information on a page, you can delete the page.

1. Tap and hold on the page you want to delete, and release to display the context menu.

2. Tap Delete.

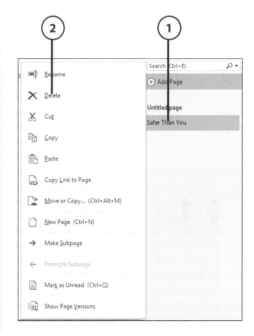

Deleting Isn't Permanent

When you delete a page, it actually gets moved to the notebook's Recycle Bin. I show you how to use the Recycle Bin later in this chapter.

Creating and Organizing Notebooks

So far you've been using the Personal notebook that OneNote creates for you automatically. You can create additional notebooks so that you can better organize your notes. Notebooks can be stored on your tablet or in your SkyDrive so that you can access them from any Internet-connected computer.

Not Limited to Windows

OneNote isn't just available on Windows devices. You can get OneNote on your iPhone, iPad, Mac, and Android devices. Notebooks on your SkyDrive are available on any of these devices.

Creating a Notebook

Notebooks are a great way to keep your notes organized. I keep one notebook for work notes, one notebook for home notes (for things like shopping lists and so forth), and numerous other notebooks for various hobbies. You can create as many notebooks as you need to keep your notes organized.

1. From within OneNote, tap File.

2. Tap New.

3. Tap your SkyDrive account to create the notebook in your SkyDrive.

4. Tap Computer to create the notebook on your tablet.

5. Enter a notebook name.

6. Tap Create Notebook.

7. Tap Not Now when asked whether you want to share the notebook. I show you how to share a notebook a little later in this chapter.

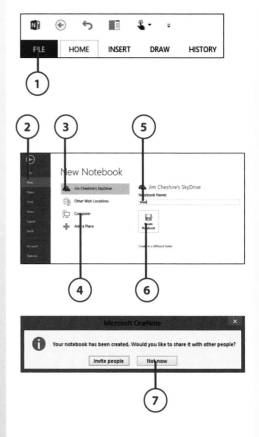

More Places for Notebooks

You can also create notebooks on Office 365 SharePoint locations, but I don't cover that in this book. For details on using OneNote and Office 365, read *My OneNote 2013* from Que Publishing.

Switching and Opening Notebooks

You can switch between your open notebooks and open other notebooks stored on your tablet or your SkyDrive.

1. Tap the name of the currently open notebook.

2. Tap another open notebook to switch to that notebook.

3. Tap Open Other Notebooks to access other notebooks you might have but aren't currently listed.

4. Tap a notebook on your SkyDrive to open it.

5. Tap a recently opened notebook to open it.

6. Tap Computer to see notebooks stored on your tablet.

7. Tap a folder on your tablet to browse notebooks in that folder.

8. Tap Browse to browse for a notebook in a different folder.

9. Browse to the location of your notebook, and tap it to select it.

10. Tap Open.

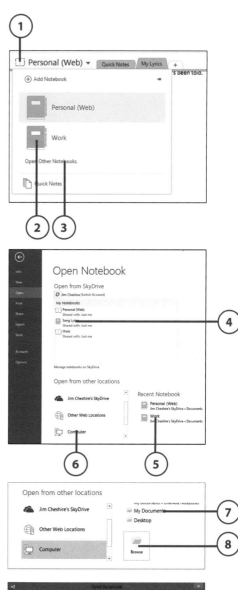

Moving and Sharing a Notebook

You can move a notebook from your tablet to your SkyDrive. When a notebook is on your SkyDrive, you can share it with other people.

1. Open a notebook that's stored on your tablet, and then tap File.

2. Tap the Settings button for the notebook you want to share.

3. Tap Share or Move.

Another Way to Share

You can also share a notebook by tapping the Share on Web or Network link.

4. If you want to use a different name for your notebook when it's moved to SkyDrive, enter a new name.

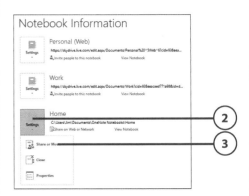

5. Tap Move Notebook.

6. Tap OK.

7. Enter the email address for one or more people with whom you want to share the Notebook.

8. Tap the Can Edit drop-down and select Can View if you don't want others to be able to edit your notebook.

9. Enter a message.

10. Tap Require User to Sign In Before Accessing Document if you want users to sign in with a Microsoft account before accessing the notebook. This is useful if you want to keep track of who is accessing the notebook.

11. Tap Share to share the notebook.

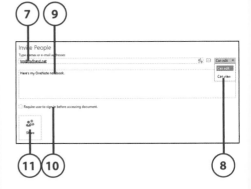

Using the Recycle Bin

When you delete pages or sections from a notebook, they aren't permanently deleted—they are moved to the notebook's Recycle Bin. You can then choose to restore them.

1. Delete a section or page from a notebook.

2. Tap History to display the History ribbon.

3. Tap Notebook Recycle Bin.

4. Tap and hold on a section or page you want to restore, and release to display the context menu.

5. Tap Move or Copy.

6. Tap the location where you want to restore the item.

7. Tap Move.

8. Tap Notebook Recycle Bin again to see your restored item.

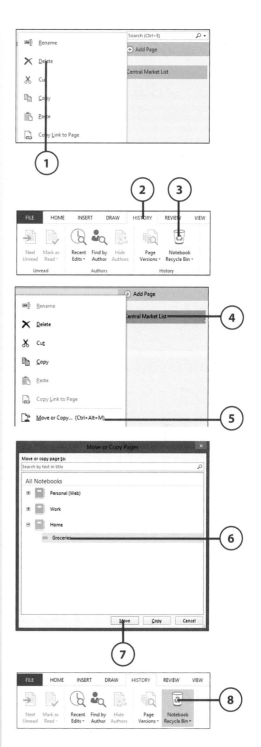

It's Not All Good

Items Deleted After 60 Days

Items in a notebook's Recycle Bin are automatically deleted after 60 days. When they are automatically deleted, there is no way you can recover them.

Using Send to OneNote

OneNote is designed to enable you to add almost anything to a note, and Send to OneNote makes it easy to add screen clippings or content from other apps, or jot down a quick note as you're using your tablet.

Send to OneNote Launched Automatically

Send to OneNote is launched automatically when you start OneNote.

Capturing a Screen Clipping

If you need to add a screen shot of what you are viewing on your tablet to a note, you can do so using Send to OneNote.

1. While viewing something that you want to add to a note, tap the Send to OneNote tool on the taskbar.

2. Tap Screen Clipping.

3. Drag across the screen to select the region that you want to add to your note. Release your finger when the desired region is selected.

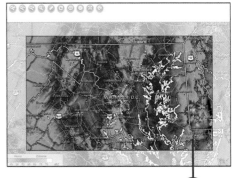

It's Not All Good

Limited Use in Windows 8.1 RT

Send to OneNote's screen clipping feature works only in Desktop apps, so on Windows 8.1 RT, you can only use it with Office documents, File Explorer, Windows desktop utilities such as Control Panel, and desktop Internet Explorer.

4. Tap the section or page where you want the item to be added.

5. Tap Send to Selected Location.

Manipulating Screen Clippings

After you add a screen clipping to a page, you can manipulate it just as you would any other picture.

Copying to the Clipboard

You can tap Copy to Clipboard to copy the selected screen region to the Windows Clipboard instead of moving it directly into a notebook. You can then paste the image wherever you like.

Sending Content to OneNote

You can send content from other Office apps or desktop Internet Explorer to OneNote using Send to OneNote.

1. Open an Office document or browse to a website in desktop Internet Explorer.

2. Tap Send to OneNote on the taskbar.

3. Tap Send to OneNote.

4. Tap the section or page where you want to add the content.

Same as Printing

When you send content to OneNote using Send to OneNote, what you see in your OneNote notebook is the same as what you would see if you were to print the content to a printer.

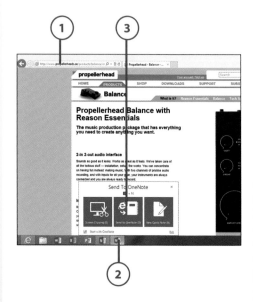

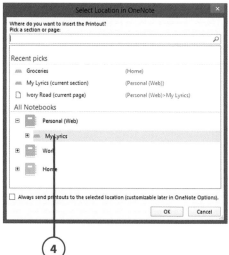

Adding a QuickNote

If you want to jot down a quick note while using your tablet, the New Quick Note feature of Send to OneNote is convenient.

1. Tap Send to OneNote on the taskbar.

2. Tap New Quick Note.

3. Enter your note.

4. Tap the X to close the Quick Note dialog.

Location of Quick Notes

Quick Notes are added to the Quick Notes section of the Personal notebook.

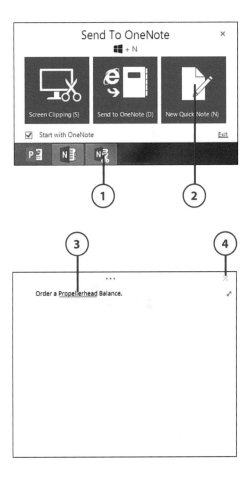

Use rules to automatically move email for you.

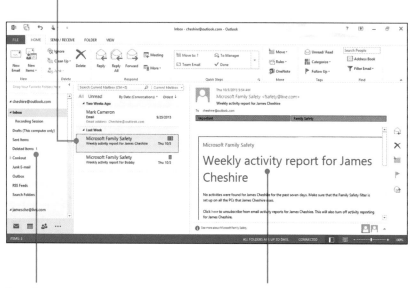

Organize your email in folders and categories for easier access.

Read and send emails in a rich environment.

In this chapter…

- → Adding an Email Account in Outlook 2013
- → Reading and Sending Email
- → Managing and Organizing Email
- → Configuring Windows 8.1 RT to Use Outlook 2013

21

Using Email and Staying Organized with Microsoft Outlook 2013

Adding an Email Account in Outlook 2013

Outlook 2013 is Microsoft's flagship email application and it's the email program of choice for many businesses. For that reason, Microsoft now makes it available in Windows 8.1 RT.

Outlook 2013

This chapter only scratches the surface of all that is possible in Outlook 2013. For complete coverage of how you can use Outlook 2013 to manage email, calendars, and more, read *Office 2013 In Depth* by Que Publishing.

Starting Outlook for the First Time

When you first launch Outlook 2013, you'll be walked through a wizard that makes setting up your first email account easy.

1. From the Start screen, type **Outlook** to search for Outlook 2013.

2. Tap Outlook 2013 to launch Outlook 2013 on the Windows desktop.

3. Tap Next to move to the next step in the wizard.

4. Select Yes to configure an email account.

5. Tap Next.

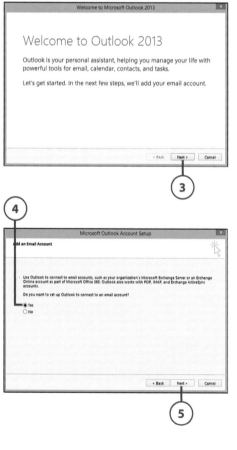

6. Enter your name.

7. Enter your email address.

8. Enter your password.

9. Re-enter your password.

10. Tap Next.

11. Tap Finish to complete the account setup.

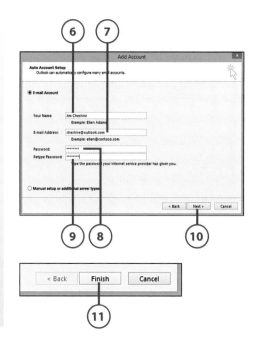

It's Not All Good

Outlook Can't Add Some Accounts

When you go through the wizard to add your first email account, Outlook uses the information you enter to attempt to discover the correct settings for the email account. This works in most cases, but it doesn't always. If your email account can't be successfully set up using the wizard, see "Manually Adding an IMAP or POP Email Account" later in this chapter.

Adding a New Email Account

You can add new email accounts after setting up your first account. You can add an Outlook.com account, an IMAP account, a POP3 account, or an Exchange account.

1. In Outlook, tap File.

2. From the Info tab, tap Account Settings.

3. Tap Account Settings again.

4. In the Account Settings dialog, tap New.

5. Enter your name.

6. Enter your email address.

7. Enter your password.

8. Re-enter your password.

9. Tap Next.

10. Tap Finish to complete adding your account.

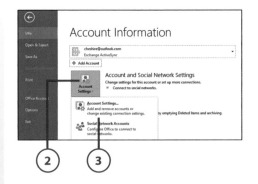

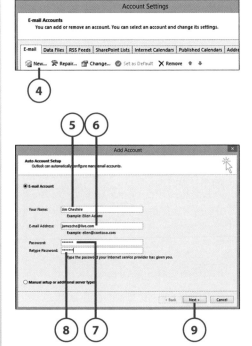

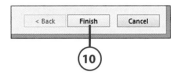

Manually Adding an IMAP or POP Email Account

Some IMAP and POP email accounts can't be added automatically. In such cases, you can manually add the email account.

1. From the Account Settings dialog (see "Adding a New Email Account"), tap New.

2. Tap Manual Setup or Additional Server Types.

3. Tap Next.

4. Tap POP or IMAP.

5. Tap Next.

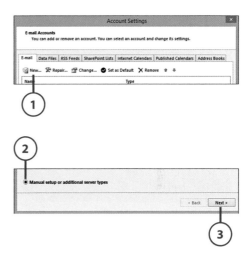

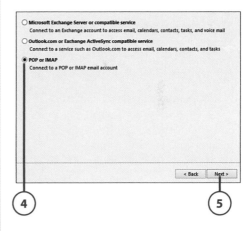

6. Enter your name.

7. Enter your email address.

8. Tap Account Type and select either POP3 or IMAP depending on your account type.

9. Enter your incoming mail server address.

10. Enter your outgoing mail server address.

11. Enter your username.

12. Enter your password.

13. Check Remember Password to allow Outlook to remember your password.

14. Tap More Settings.

15. Tap the Outgoing Server tab.

16. If your outgoing server requires authentication (and most do), tap the My Outgoing Server (SMTP) Requires Authentication option.

17. If your outgoing server does not use the same username and password used by your incoming server, tap Log On Using and enter your username and password.

18. Tap OK.

19. Tap Next.

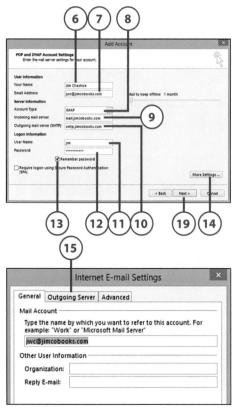

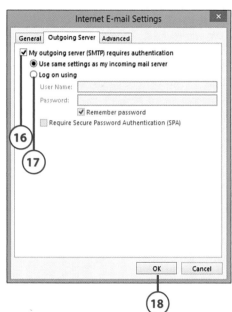

20. Tap Close.

21. Tap Finish to add the new email account.

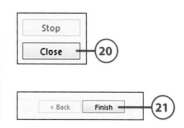

It's Not All Good

Sending Test Message Might Fail

When Outlook connects to your outgoing mail server, it uses a specific *port*. (You can think of a port as a channel number.) The standard port for outgoing mail is port 25, but many Internet service providers will block you from using port 25. When that happens, Outlook experiences a failure when it tries to send the test message to your new email account.

You can resolve this problem by changing the port for your outgoing email server. I show you how to do that in the "Changing the Outgoing Server Port" walkthrough.

Changing the Outgoing Server Port

If you are unable to send email in Outlook, it's likely that your Internet service provider is blocking the port that Outlook uses to connect to your outgoing email server. You can resolve this problem by changing the port number.

1. From the Account Settings screen, tap the email account that is not working.

2. Tap Change.

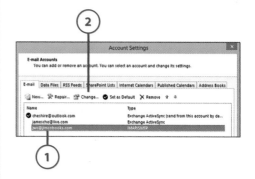

3. Tap More Settings.

4. Tap Advanced.

5. Enter **587** in the Outgoing Server (SMTP) textbox.

6. Tap OK.

7. Tap Next.

8. Tap Close.

9. Tap Finish to complete the email account setup.

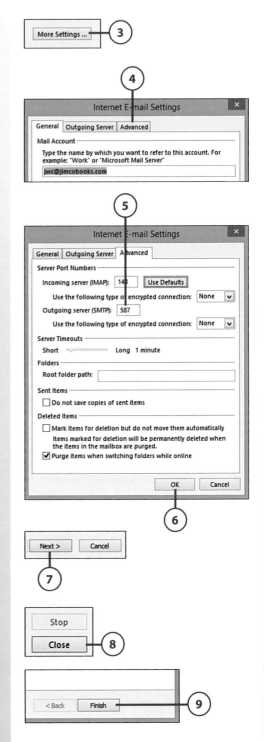

Reading and Sending Email

You can read and send emails in Outlook using pictures and rich text. Outlook actually uses the same functionality you find in Microsoft Word for displaying and editing email messages.

Microsoft Word

For details on how you can use Microsoft Word, see Chapter 17, "Creating Documents with Microsoft Word 2013."

Reading an Email Message

You can read email messages from any of the accounts you've added to Microsoft Outlook.

1. Tap the folder that contains the messages you want to read.

2. Tap the email message you want to read.

3. Slide up to see more of an email message.

4. Tap a link in a message to navigate to the link.

5. To show embedded pictures, tap Click Here to Download Pictures.

6. Tap Download Pictures.

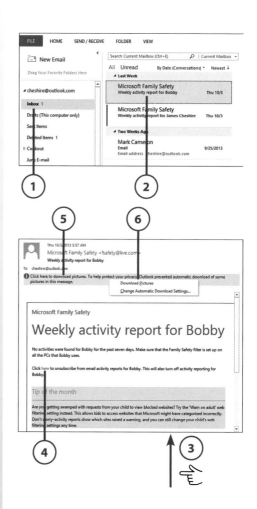

Replying to an Email

You can reply to an email and send your response to just the sender or to everyone who received the message.

1. While reading an email, tap Reply.

2. Tap Reply to send a response only to the sender of the mail.

3. Tap Reply All to send a reply to everyone who received the message.

4. Enter your message.

5. Tap Send to send the email.

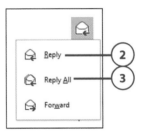

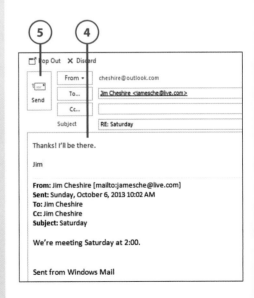

Sending a New Email

You can create a new email message using the same editing features you find in Microsoft Word 2013.

1. Tap the email account you want to use to send the message.

2. Tap New Email.

3. Enter the email address for one or more people to whom the message should be sent. (Separate multiple email addresses with a semicolon.)

4. Enter one or more email addresses in the Cc textbox to copy other recipients.

5. Enter a subject for your email message.

6. Enter your message.

7. To format text, select the text.

8. Tap Format Text.

9. Format the text the way you want using the Format Text options.

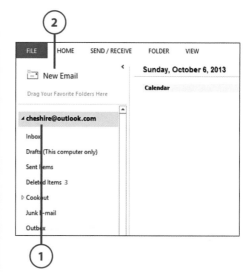

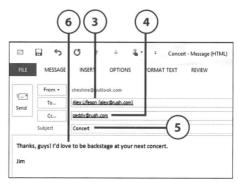

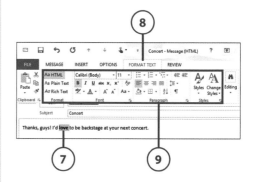

10. To change the email account used to send the message, tap From and select a new email account.

11. Tap Send to send the message.

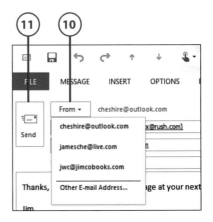

Managing and Organizing Email

Outlook 2013 has many features designed to help you manage and organize your email messages.

Moving Messages

You can organize messages by moving them into a folder.

1. While viewing the message that you want to move, tap Move.

2. Tap Other Folder to move the message to another folder.

3. Tap Always Move Messages in This Conversation to move the current message and to automatically move future messages in the conversation.

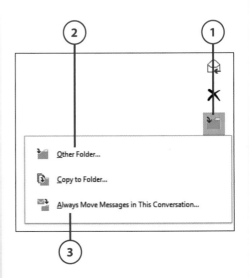

4. Tap a folder into which you would like the message to be moved.

5. To create a new folder, tap New.

6. Type a name for your new folder.

7. Tap a folder where you want the new folder to be created. (The new folder will be a subfolder of the selected folder.)

8. Tap OK.

9. Tap OK to move the message.

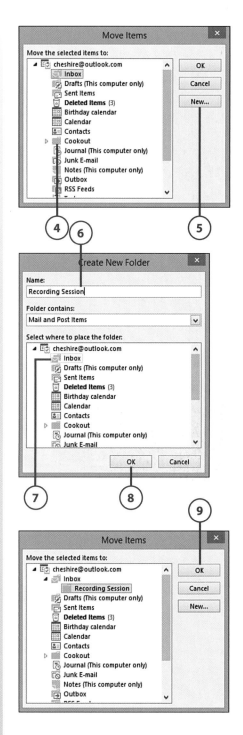

Ignoring Conversations

You might find that you are included in an email conversation that isn't of any interest to you. In such cases, you can easily ignore the conversation. When you do, messages in that conversation are automatically moved to the trash as they arrive.

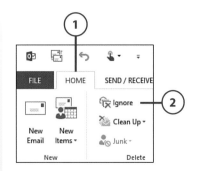

1. While viewing a message in the conversation you want to ignore, tap Home.

2. Tap Ignore.

Categorizing Email Messages

Moving messages to folders is a good way to categorize emails, but there are times when you would like to categorize messages without moving them. You can assign a color-coded category to messages.

Assign Multiple Categories

You can assign multiple categories to a message.

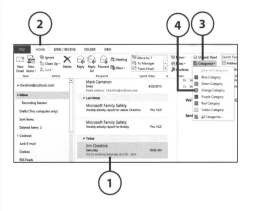

1. Tap the message that you want to categorize.

2. Tap Home.

3. Tap Categorize.

4. Tap a color category to assign that category to the message.

5. Enter a name for the category.

6. Tap Color and select another color if you want.

7. Tap Yes to create the category and assign the message to the category.

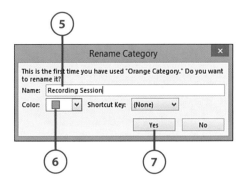

Adding Messages to Categories

You will only see the prompt to rename a category when you use a category for the first time. Thereafter, selecting a category from the Categorize menu assigns the category to the message without a prompt.

It's Not All Good

Shortcut Keys

You can assign a shortcut key to a category so that you can easily add a message to the category by selecting the message and pressing your shortcut key on the keyboard. Unfortunately, shortcut keys use the function keys (F1–F12) on your keyboard, and the keyboard on the Surface 2 doesn't include function keys.

Removing a Category from a Message

If you want to remove a category applied to a message, you can do so.

1. Tap the message for which you want to remove a category.

2. Tap Home.

3. Tap Categorize.

4. Tap the category you want to remove from the message.

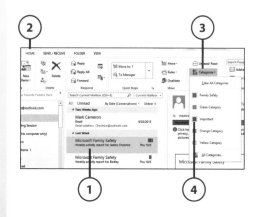

Filtering Messages by Category

If you have a lot of messages, you might find filtering your view by category convenient.

1. From the Home ribbon, tap Filter Email.

2. Tap Categorized.

3. Tap a category to see only emails in that category.

Removing Filters

You can remove a category filter by selecting Any Category for the filter.

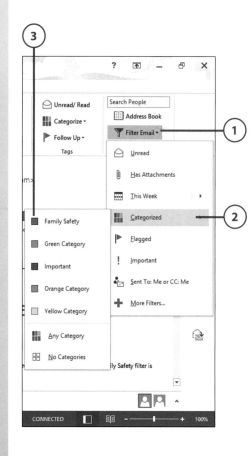

Configuring Windows 8.1 RT to Use Outlook 2013

If you prefer to use Outlook 2013 instead of Windows 8.1 RT's Mail app, you can configure your Surface 2 to do that.

Configuring the Default Mail App

When you use email in Windows 8.1 RT, the default email app is used. You can change the default email app so that Outlook is used instead of the Mail app.

1. From the PC Settings screen, tap Search and Apps.

2. Tap Defaults.

3. Tap the Mail icon in the Email section.

4. Tap Outlook (Desktop).

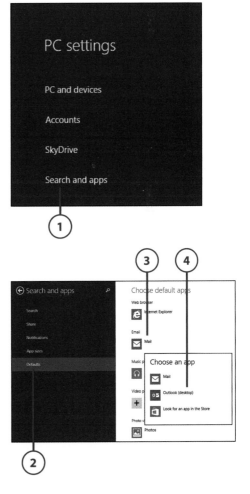

It's Not All Good

Cannot Use Outlook with Share Charm

You cannot use Outlook with the Share charm in Windows 8.1 RT. The Share charm only works with Modern UI apps, so the Mail app is currently your only choice when sharing content using the Share charm.

Changing the Email App Used for Mail Hyperlinks

One of the methods used to launch email is hyperlinks in mail messages and web pages. Setting the default email app will not impact which email application is used when clicking these links. You have to make a change to which app handles email links using a different method.

1. From the Defaults screen in Search and Apps, slide up to move to the bottom of the screen.

2. Tap Choose Default Apps By Protocol.

3. Slide up to the MAILTO protocol.

4. Tap Mail.

5. Tap Outlook (Desktop) to switch to Outlook.

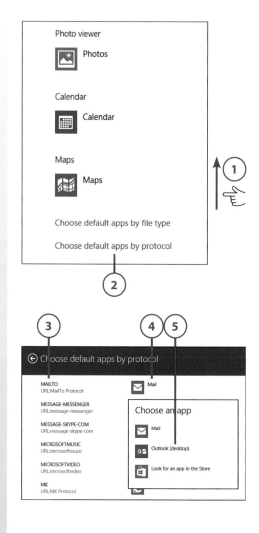

Enhance your Surface 2
tablet with apps from
the Windows Store.

Find and install
the latest apps.

Update your apps
to fix bugs and
add features.

Enhancing Windows with Apps

The Surface 2 tablet is a powerful tablet with enormous capabilities straight out of the box, but by adding additional apps from the Windows Store, you can make it even more powerful. Thousands of apps are available in the app store, and more apps are being added all the time.

Browsing the Windows Store

The Windows Store is the source of apps for your Surface 2. Apps are categorized for easier browsing, but you can also search for apps using the Search charm.

Browsing Categories

Apps in the Windows Store are categorized for easy browsing. You can browse apps by category when you're looking for a particular type of app.

1. From the Start screen, tap the Store tile.

2. In the Store, swipe down from the top of the screen and tap a category.

3. Slide left to see additional apps in the selected category.

4. Tap a subcategory to see additional apps.

5. Swipe down from the top of the screen and tap a different category to change categories.

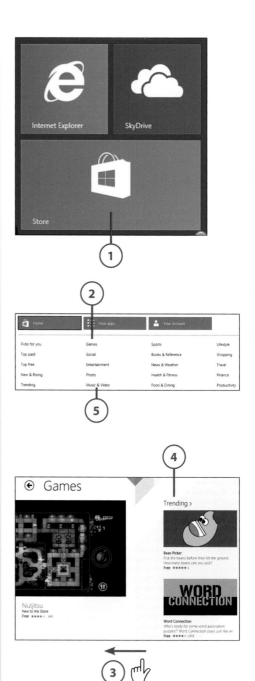

Exploring Apps

Plenty of information is available to help you decide whether you want to purchase an app. You can view screenshots, reviews of the app from other users, and more.

1. Tap an app in the Windows Store that you're interested in.

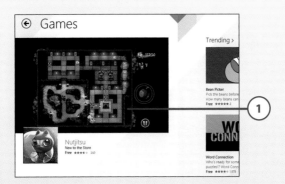

2. Tap Show More in the Overview section to see more information.

3. Tap a screenshot to see additional screenshots.

4. Slide left to see reviews on the app.

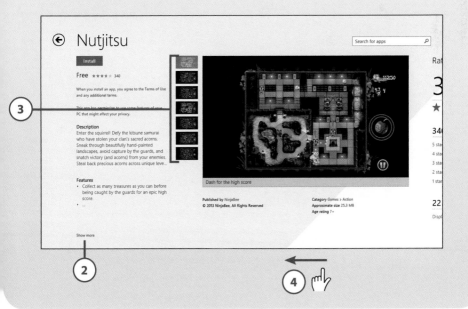

5. Tap Yes or No to vote on whether a review is helpful.

6. Tap a flag and tap an option to report a review as being inappropriate due to spam or content issues.

7. Tap Ratings and Reviews to drill further into the app's reviews.

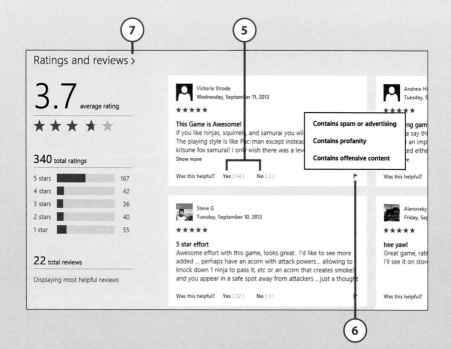

Ratings and reviews ›

3.7 average rating

★ ★ ★ ★ ☆

340 total ratings

5 stars	▬▬▬▬	167
4 stars	▬	42
3 stars	▬	36
2 stars	▬	40
1 star	▬▬	55

22 total reviews

Displaying most helpful reviews

Victoria Strode
Wednesday, September 11, 2013
★ ★ ★ ★ ★

This Game is Awesome!
If you like ninjas, squirrels, and samurai you will
The playing style is like Pac-man except instead
kitsune fox samurai! I only wish there was a lev
Show more
Was this helpful?   Yes (24)   No (2)

Steve G
Tuesday, September 10, 2013
★ ★ ★ ★ ★

5 star effort
Awesome effort with this game, looks great... I'd like to see more
added ... perhaps have an acorn with attack powers... allowing to
knock down 1 ninja to pass it, etc or an acorn that creates smoke!
and you appear in a safe spot away from attackers .. just a thought
Was this helpful?   Yes (22)   No (3)

Andrew H
Tuesday, S
★ ★ ★ ★ ★

ng gam
a say th
an imp
ed eith
e
Was this helpful?

Contains spam or advertising

Contains profanity

Contains offensive content

Alanovsky
Friday, Sep
★ ★ ★ ★ ★

hee yaw!
Great game, rate
I'll see it on stor

Was this helpful?

8. Tap Newest to change the sort order of reviews.

9. Tap All Reviews to filter reviews by rating.

10. Tap Back to return to the app's details.

11. Slide left to see details on the app, related apps, and more.

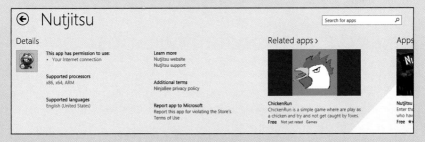

Searching for Apps

When you need to find a specific app or a specific type of app, searching for apps is often your best choice.

1. In the Windows Store, tap in the Search box and enter a search term.

2. Tap a search result to see details on a suggested result.

3. Tap the magnifying glass or press Enter on your keyboard to search for apps.

4. Use the drop-downs to filter and sort the search results.

5. Tap an app to view more details on the app or to install it.

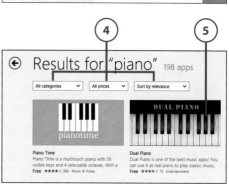

Installing and Uninstalling Apps

When you have found an app that you want to use, you'll need to install it on your Surface 2. If you later decide you don't want the app, you can remove it from your Surface 2 by uninstalling it. Finally, you can easily locate apps that you've purchased and reinstall them on your Surface 2.

Installing Apps

Many apps are free, whereas other apps require you to pay for them. However, many of these paid apps offer trial versions so that you can try the app and decide whether it's worth purchasing. You can install any of these apps onto your Surface 2 tablet immediately via the Windows Store.

Piano Library
Piano Library is a great utility for referencing, learning to play piano chords, scales, learning
$1.99 (free trial) ★★★★★ 1   Music & Video

1. Locate an app that you want to install, and tap it to view the details on the app.

2. Tap Buy to purchase the app. You'll be able to confirm your choice before the purchase is finalized.

3. Tap Try to install a trial version of the app.

Free Apps

Free apps have an Install button instead of a Buy button. Tapping the Install button installs a free app.

4. Tap the notification to see the install status.

5. Tap an app, and then tap Pause Download to pause the download of the app.

6. Tap Cancel Install to cancel the app's installation.

7. When a notification that the app has been installed appears, tap the app's tile on the Start screen to launch the app.

Canceling the Installation of a Purchased App

If you cancel the installation of an app that you purchased, you can install the app later without paying for it again. I show you how in the "Reinstalling Purchased Apps" section of this chapter.

Uninstalling Apps

If you want to free up space on your Surface 2, you can uninstall apps that you no longer want. You can always reinstall the app later without having to pay for it again, and I show you how in the next section.

1. Locate the app's tile on the Start screen, and tap and hold on it to select it.

2. Tap Uninstall to uninstall the app.

3. Tap Uninstall to confirm the uninstall of the app.

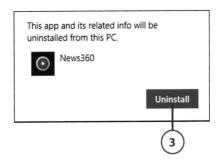

Reinstalling Purchased Apps

Microsoft keeps track of the apps that you purchase, and you can reinstall any apps you've purchased under your Microsoft account.

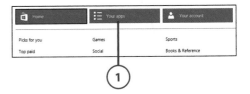

1. From the Windows Store, swipe down from the top of the screen and tap Your Apps.

2. By default, apps not installed on your tablet are displayed. Tap the drop-down and select a different option to see all apps you own or apps that are installed on another PC you own.

3. Tap the Sort drop-down to change the sort order of apps.

4. Swipe down on one or more apps that you want to install to select them, or tap Select All to select all apps.

5. Tap Install to install the selected apps.

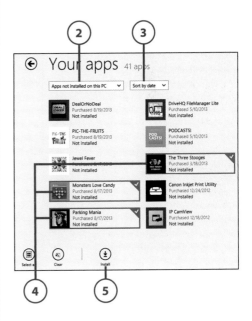

Details While Reinstalling Apps

You can tap on an app's tile to see details of the app before you decide to reinstall it.

It's Not All Good

Removed Apps

Just because you purchased an app doesn't mean you can always reinstall it. I've encountered a few situations where I tried to reinstall an app and was notified that the app was removed and is no longer available.

Updating Apps

By default, the Windows Store automatically updates your apps for you when an update is available. However, if you turn off this feature, a numeric indicator in the upper-right corner of the screen appears whenever one or more apps have an update available. Updates for apps are free, and you should install them when they're available because they often fix bugs and provide added stability.

Manually Checking for Updates

Windows 8.1 RT automatically checks for updates for your apps, but you can also manually check for updates.

1. From the Windows Store, swipe in from the right side of the screen and tap Settings.

2. Tap App Updates.

3. Tap Check for Updates to check for app updates. (I show you how you can install updates for your apps in the next section.)

Sync Licenses

If you're not seeing updates for apps you own, you can tap Sync Licenses and Windows 8.1 RT will ensure that it has up-to-date information for all of your app licenses.

Installing App Updates

There are a few ways you can be notified of app updates. When updates are available, the Windows Store tile displays the number of available updates in the lower-right corner of the tile. The Windows Store app also displays the number of available updates in the upper-right corner of the app interface. Finally, you can manually check for updates. When an update is available, you can install it quickly and easily.

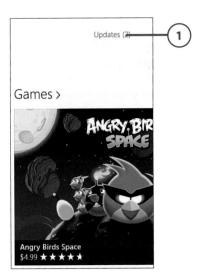

1. From the Windows Store, tap the Updates link in the upper-right corner of the app.

2. Tap Install to install all updates.

3. If you want to install updates only for specific apps, tap to deselect any apps that you do not want to update.

4. The status of update installs is displayed as the updates are downloaded and installed.

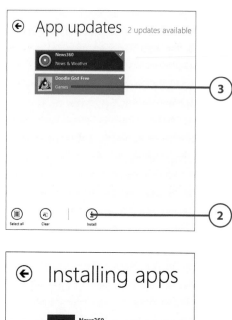

Great Apps for Your Surface 2

Thousands of apps are available in the Windows Store. Here are a few that I find particularly nice for enhancing your Surface 2.

Netflix

If you're a Netflix subscriber, the Netflix app will almost certainly become one of your favorite apps. You can browse the Netflix library, manage your instant queue, and watch TV shows and movies on your Surface 2.

1. Tap a user to change to a different profile.

2. Tap a recently watched title to continue watching it.

3. Tap an item from your instant queue to watch it.

4. Tap Top 10 for You to see recommendations from Netflix.

5. Tap New Releases to see all new releases.

6. Tap Genres to browse the Netflix library by genre.

7. Tap a title to see more details.

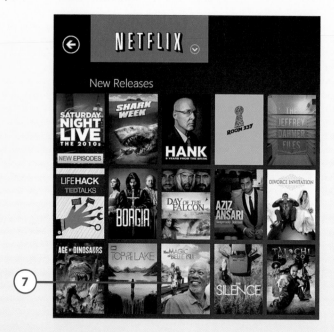

8. Tap Add to My List to add the item to your instant queue.

9. Tap a star to rate the title.

10. Tap a name to see other titles for that actor or director.

11. Tap Play to play the title.

Skype

Skype turns your Surface 2 into a videoconferencing device. You can make both video and audio calls to other Skype users using the camera and microphone on your Surface 2. Skype comes pre-installed on your Surface 2.

1. Tap the phone icon to make phone calls (for a fee) with Skype.

2. Tap one of your contacts to initiate a call with that person. If the person is not a Skype user, you'll have the option of sending a message using the Windows Messenger service.

3. Tap the status icon to change your status when you don't want to show as available for calls.

4. Tap the plus sign to add favorite contacts.

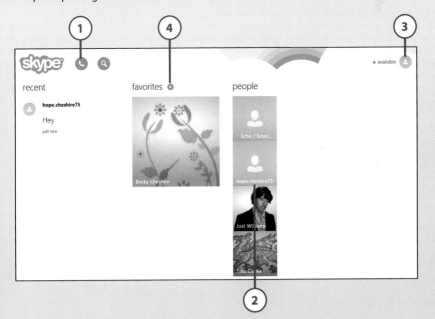

Microsoft Minesweeper

Minesweeper is a classic game that has been reinvented in Windows 8.1.

1. Tap a square.

2. Tap and hold on a square to flag it if you think a mine is there.

3. Continue to tap squares and avoid the mines.

Hyper for YouTube

Plenty of YouTube apps are available in the Windows Store, but Hyper is the best I've found.

1. Tap Search to search for YouTube videos.

2. Tap Watch History to see a history of the videos you've watched.

3. Tap Downloads to see videos you've downloaded from YouTube.

4. Tap a video to watch it.

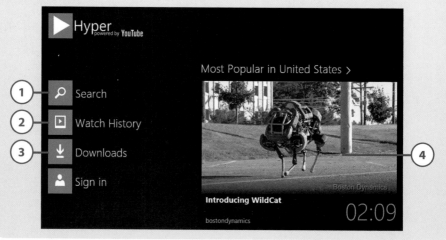

5. While a video is playing, swipe up from the bottom of the screen for more options.

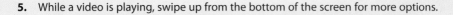

iHeartRadio

iHeartRadio is a streaming music app that makes your favorite music available to you on your Surface 2. You can listen to radio stations all over the country, but you can also create your own station by entering an artist and letting iHeartRadio find music that you might enjoy.

1. Tap a station or artist to listen to music.

2. Tap Create Your Own Kind of Radio to create your own station.

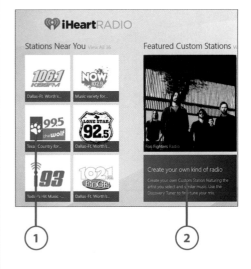

3. Enter an artist, a song name, or another search term.

4. Tap a search result to create your own station.

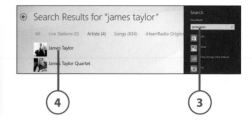

Kindle

The Kindle app makes your Amazon Kindle eBook library available on your Surface 2.

1. Tap Cloud to see books in your library that are stored on Amazon's servers.

2. Tap On Device to see books that are stored on your Surface.

3. Tap Sort By to sort your results.

4. Tap a book to open it for reading.

5. While reading, swipe up from the bottom of the screen to display a menu of options.

6. Tap Library to return to your library.

7. Tap Notes/Marks to display notes and bookmarks you've added to the book.

8. Tap View to change view options such as typeface, size, and background color.

9. Tap Back to go back to the previous location in the book.

10. Tap Go To to navigate to sections of the book or to a particular location number.

11. Tap Sync to manually sync to the furthest page read across your devices.

12. Tap Pin to Start to pin the current book to the Start screen.

13. Drag the slider to quickly move to a part of the book.

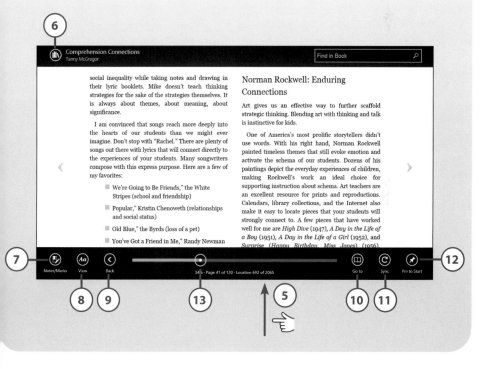

WeatherBug

Windows 8.1 RT comes with a weather app, but WeatherBug is a much better app for weather. You can see weather for your current location and add additional locations.

1. Tap Current to see detailed weather information about current conditions.

2. Tap Today to see an hour-by-hour forecast for today.

3. Tap Forecast for a six-day forecast.

4. Tap Notifications to set up notifications for different types of weather. Notifications appear on your tablet.

5. Tap Alerts to see any active weather bulletins, such as storm warnings.

6. Tap Maps to see weather maps.

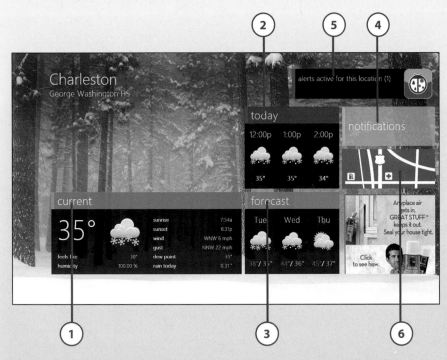

Adding Locations

If you want to add more locations to WeatherBug, swipe down from the top of the screen and tap Locations. You can search by city name or ZIP code.

News360

News360 is a highly customizable news app for your tablet. You can browse news stories using an attractive and functional app that makes the most of the Windows 8.1 RT interface.

1. When you first launch News360, choose the types of news that you want to see.

2. Swipe left all the way and tap Assemble News360 to continue.

3. Swipe left and right to see additional stories.

4. Tap a tile to see the entire story.

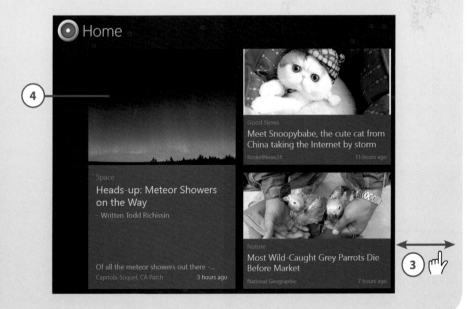

5. Swipe left and right on images to see pictures from various sources.

6. Tap a news source to read more from that source.

7. Swipe up and down to read more of the current article.

8. Tap the browser window to read the article from the original source in Internet Explorer.

9. Tap Back to return to the previous screen.

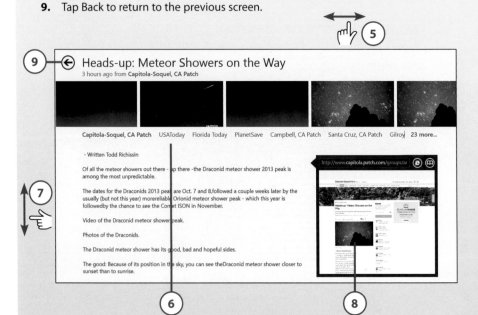

Custom News Sources

If you swipe down from the top of the screen in News360 and tap Add/Edit, you can add other news sources, including custom news sources based on search terms.

eBay

The eBay app makes browsing and buying items on eBay a pleasure. Touch is a great way to peruse eBay, and the eBay app is well-designed and simple to use.

1. Tap a tile to see items or search for items.

2. Tap a daily deal to see details on specials.

3. Tap View to switch between List and Gallery view.

4. Tap Sort to sort items.

5. Tap Condition to filter on condition of items.

6. Tap Price to filter by price.

7. Tap Format to filter on auctions and Buy It Now items.

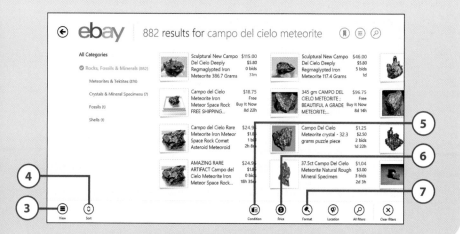

8. Tap Location to filter based on location.

9. Tap All Filters to perform a complex filter on items.

10. Tap a category to see items in that category.

11. Swipe left and right to see additional items.

12. Tap an item for more details.

13. Tap the arrow to see additional pictures.

14. Tap a picture to see a larger image.

15. Tap Place Bid to bid on an item.

16. Tap Watch to watch an item.

17. Slide left to see additional details, such as a description and information on the seller.

18. Tap Back to return to the previous screen.

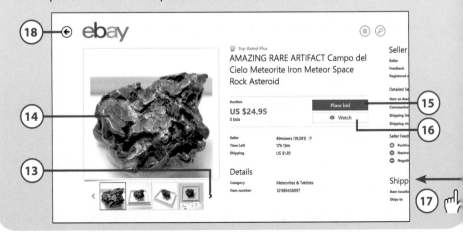

Update your
Surface 2
with Windows
Update.

Refresh your
Surface 2 while
keeping personal
files.

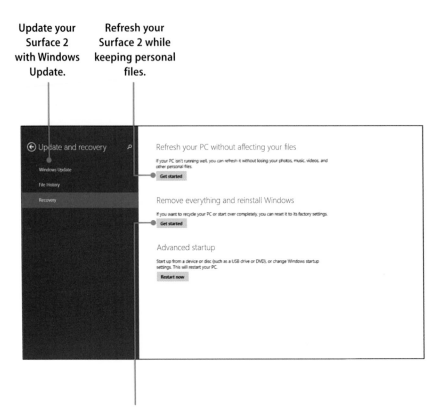

Reset Windows
and remove your
personal files.

Updating and Troubleshooting Windows 8.1 RT

Updating with Windows Update

Windows Update automatically keeps your Surface 2 up to date. By default, updates are downloaded automatically, and many updates install automatically behind the scenes without your even knowing about it. However, if a restart is required to install an update, you'll be notified.

What's in a Name?

Windows Update's name isn't by fluke. Windows Update downloads and installs updates for Windows (and Office 2013) only. Updates for Windows Store apps, including those that came with your Surface 2, are installed through the Windows Store app and not Windows Update. I cover this in Chapter 22, "Enhancing Windows with Apps."

Checking for and Installing Updates Manually

Your Surface 2 checks for updates to Windows every day. However, you can force a manual check for updates if you want to and then choose to manually install any updates that are available.

1. From the Start screen, swipe in from the right and tap the Settings charm.

2. Tap Change PC Settings.

3. Tap Update and Recovery.

4. Tap Windows Update.

5. Tap Check Now.

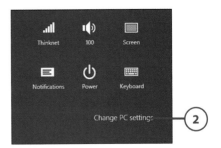

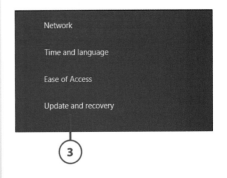

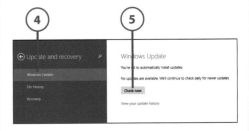

6. Tap View Details to see what updates are available.

7. Tap Install to install updates that are available.

8. Tap Cancel while updates are installing to cancel the updates; otherwise, wait until the updates are complete.

9. If prompted , tap Restart Now to complete the installation of updates. Your computer will be updated and then restarted.

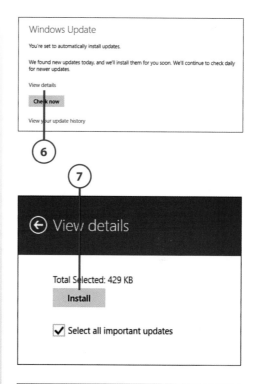

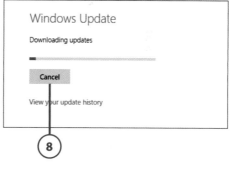

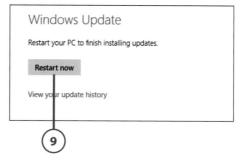

Installing Optional Updates

Windows Update automatically installs important updates. However, some updates (including updates to your Office apps) are optional updates and you'll need to install them manually.

1. From the Start screen, swipe in from the right and tap the Search charm.

2. Enter **windows update**.

3. Tap Windows Update, which takes you to the Windows desktop.

4. Tap Check for Updates to check for optional updates.

5. Tap the link to see details on available updates.

6. Check the updates that you want to install, and tap Install.

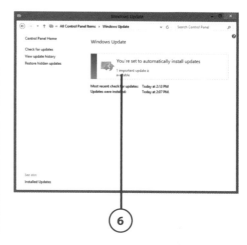

⑥

Troubleshooting Windows 8.1 RT

If you are having trouble with Windows 8.1 RT on your Surface 2, you have a couple of options for troubleshooting. You can refresh and repair your PC, a process that restores all Windows settings while keeping all your personal files. You can also reset your PC, a process whereby Windows 8.1 RT is reinstalled and all your personal files are removed.

Refreshing and Repairing Your PC

If you find that your Surface 2 is having problems and not operating correctly, you often can fix it by refreshing and repairing your PC. When you do so, your personal files are not impacted and remain on the device.

What About Apps?

When you refresh or repair your Surface 2, any apps you've installed remain on the device.

Before you start this process, plug in
your Surface 2 so that it's running on
AC power and not the battery.

1. From the Start screen, swipe in
   from the right side of the screen
   and tap the Settings charm.

2. Tap Change PC Settings.

3. Tap Update and Recovery.

4. Tap Recovery.

5. Tap Get Started under Refresh
   Your PC Without Affecting Your
   Files.

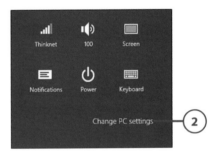

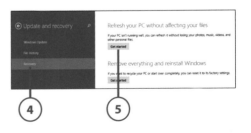

6. Tap Next.

7. Tap Refresh to refresh your PC. Your PC will restart and refresh back to its original settings without affecting your pictures, music, or other personal files.

Refreshing to Defaults

After you run a refresh on your PC, your PC reverts to the settings that existed when you powered it on for the first time. After you refresh, checking for updates and installing any that are available from Windows Update and the Windows Store is a good idea.

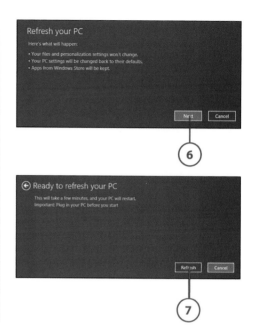

Refresh your PC

Here's what will happen:
- Your files and personalization settings won't change.
- Your PC settings will be changed back to their defaults.
- Apps from Windows Store will be kept.

Next   Cancel

(6)

(←) Ready to refresh your PC

This will take a few minutes, and your PC will restart.
Important: Plug in your PC before you start

Refresh   Cancel

(7)

It's Not All Good

When to Refresh

Your Surface 2 is a reliable PC, and there's a good chance that you will never have to refresh it. However, when it comes to technology, there's always the possibility that things can go wrong. How will you know when you need to refresh? There aren't any specific rules for when to refresh, but if you notice that you are seeing numerous errors, if your Surface 2 restarts on its own, or if you are experiencing slowness when using your Surface 2, refreshing your PC is a good first step. There's a good chance that refreshing will fix any problems you're having.

Resetting Windows

You can reset Windows 8.1 RT completely, restoring your Surface 2 to the state it was in when it was new. This is a good idea if you are giving or selling your Surface 2 to someone else.

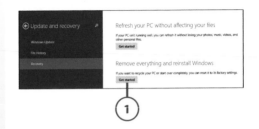

Before you go through this process, make sure that you plug in your Surface 2.

1. From the Update and Recovery screen, tap Get Started under Remove Everything and Reinstall Windows.

2. Tap Next.

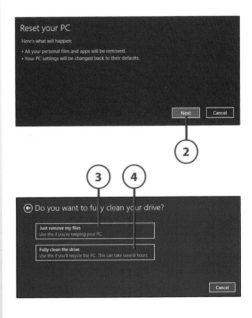

3. To remove your personal files and reset settings while leaving the current Windows 8.1 RT installation intact, tap Just Remove My Files. This is a good choice if you are giving or selling your Surface 2 to someone else.

4. To fully clean the drive and reinstall Windows 8.1 RT, tap Fully Clean the Drive.

Use File History

If you use File History to back up your files, you can safely reinstall Windows and then restore your files. For information on using File History, see Chapter 6, "Backing Up Your Data."

5. Tap Reset to reset your PC.

Troubleshooting Battery Draining on Standby

Your Surface 2 can use what is known as *connected standby* to allow for apps to run and communicate with the Internet while your tablet is in standby mode. If you notice that your battery is draining too quickly while in standby mode, you can determine what app or component is draining your battery.

When to Perform These Steps
You should perform these steps as soon as you sign into your Surface 2 and realize that the battery has drained faster than normal while the tablet was in standby mode. Standby mode is when the Surface 2 is in sleep mode.

1. Swipe up from the Start screen and tap and hold on Command Prompt.

2. Tap Run As Administrator.

UAC Prompt
When you are prompted and asked whether you want to run the Windows Command Processor, tap Yes.

3. Enter **powercfg /sleepstudy** at the command prompt.

4. After you are notified that the report has been saved, type **sleepstudy-report.html** at the command prompt.

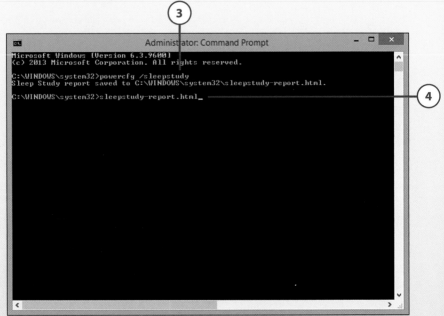

5. Review the Sleep Study report to determine what is draining your battery.

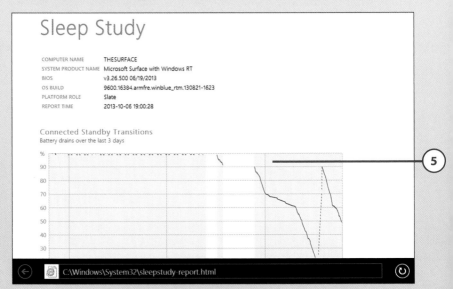

INTERPRETING THE SLEEP STUDY

>>Go Further

The Sleep Study report shows you which components have the most battery usage. However, the component names are likely not going to be directly related to any particular app. Instead, they often refer to some system software that is used to interact with hardware on your Surface 2. The best way to determine what is responsible is to search the Internet for the components you see using the battery. You can then use the information you find to look for updates to the software.

If all else fails, show a computer geek the sleep study and he should be able to get useful information to help troubleshoot your problem.

Index

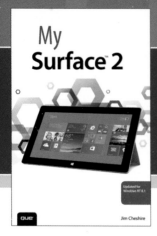

My Surface 2

Updated for Windows RT 8.1

Que | Jim Cheshire

Safari
Books Online

FREE
Online Edition

Your purchase of **My Surface 2** includes access to a free online edition for 45 days through the **Safari Books Online** subscription service. Nearly every Que book is available online through **Safari Books Online**, along with thousands of books and videos from publishers such as Addison-Wesley Professional, Cisco Press, Exam Cram, IBM Press, O'Reilly Media, Prentice Hall, Sams, and VMware Press.

Safari Books Online is a digital library providing searchable, on-demand access to thousands of technology, digital media, and professional development books and videos from leading publishers. With one monthly or yearly subscription price, you get unlimited access to learning tools and information on topics including mobile app and software development, tips and tricks on using your favorite gadgets, networking, project management, graphic design, and much more.

Activate your FREE Online Edition at
informit.com/safarifree

STEP 1: Enter the coupon code: RJOQYYG.

STEP 2: New Safari users, complete the brief registration form.
Safari subscribers, just log in.

If you have difficulty registering on Safari or accessing the online edition,
please e-mail customer-service@safaribooksonline.com

Addison
Wesley

Adobe Press

ALPHA

Cisco Press

FT Press

IBM
Press

Microsoft

New
Riders

O'REILLY

Peachpit
Press

PRENTICE
HALL

que

Redbooks

SAMS

SAS
Publishing

vmware PRESS

WILEY

wrox